CREATING A Connected CLASSROOM

Also by

Marti Smith, OTR/L

The Connected Therapist, Relating Through the Senses

PVC for Rehab

Sensory Healing after Developmental Trauma: The Connected Therapist's Guide to Low-Cost Activities for Working with Children

Handwriting Helpers

Calming Strategies for Autism

Also by Amie Huggins, M.Ed.

Tools for Transformation: Curriculum for schools who want to create relationally based classrooms and school cultures (Available from the non-profit, Raise the Future)

CREATING A Connected CLASSROOM

Connection, Compassion, and Classroom Strategies

Amie Huggins, M.Ed
Marti Smith, OTR/L

For information, contact:
http://www.creativetherapies.com
https://www.amiehugginsconsulting.com
https://www.walendesigns.com/

First Edition

Published by Marti Smith Seminars, Inc.
Interior Design & Formatting by Karen Walen, Walen Designs
Interior Illustrations by Dr. Jamie Tanner
Cover Illustration by Clair Reichert

ISBN: 978-1-7372052-1-0

To my coffee club, you know who you are.....For my girls and my babies...you taught me everything – Amie

To the teachers who shaped me and the teachers who sustain me. My mother, my mentors, my many favorite mates. And to every teacher who has ugly-cried in a supply closet, laughed at something deeply inappropriate, and shown up anyway. This one's for you. - Marti

FORWARD

by Casey Call

"You're not a fixer. You're a possum persuader."

Curious about this statement? I was too. At first it made me smile, after all, fixing problems isn't much fun. But being a possum persuader? That's playful, memorable, and, most importantly, possible (most of the time). That spirit perfectly captures what I love about this book. Marti and Amie have created a book that is not only enjoyable to read but also filled with practical tools that equip us to better support and meet the needs of children in schools.

I first met Marti around 2013 and was immediately struck by her immense knowledge, boundless energy, and practical, sensible approach to supporting children. At the time, the Institute of Child Development at Texas Christian University (now the Karyn Purvis Institute of Child Development) was leading the Travis County Collaborative for Children in Austin, Texas. Marti joined the collaborative to learn about Trust-Based Relational Intervention® (TBRI®), but it didn't take long for us to realize that we had just as much to learn from her.

Marti has a remarkable ability to make complex ideas understandable. She translated neuroscience and sensory processing into language that made sense to those of us who weren't occupational therapists. Even better, she paired that knowledge with solutions that caregivers and professionals could implement immediately. Need a fidget for a child and don't have a budget? Give them a pipe cleaner or place a small strip of Velcro under their desk. Practical, accessible, and effective – that is Marti!

Now, in The Connected Classroom, you have the opportunity to learn from Marti and Aime. Aime's story resonates deeply with me. Her journey, from experiences within her own family to insights in her classroom, is one I deeply admire. Recognizing familiar behaviors in both her own children and her students and allowing that realization to spark a commitment to learn more, is both courageous and inspiring. Her experience of being influenced by TBRI and Dr. Karyn Purvis is one I share. As I read Amie's classroom stories, I found myself transported right back into the classroom.

Before joining the Institute in 2007, I worked in public education as an elementary school teacher and later as a middle and high school counselor. I loved those roles. Yet, with the knowledge I now have, there are many moments I would like to ask for a re-do. I believe I brought warmth, authentic relationships, and predictability to my classroom, but I didn't understand about regulation and sensory needs. I worked hard to keep my classroom orderly and "under control." If I could go back, I would do things very differently.

I would intentionally help students experience dysregulation and teach them how to regulate themselves, I would look for the need beneath the behavior instead of simply addressing the behavior itself. I would proactively meet sensory needs rather than reacting to them. The list goes on and on.

That is why I am so excited for this book.

The Connected Classroom gives educators what I wish I had then, practical understanding paired with strategies that can be tried tomorrow. I especially love the book's format, conversations, key takeaways, reflections, and one thing to try tomorrow. This is a book designed not just to inform, but to transform practice.

Teachers, classrooms, and education are my passion. Having a resource like this feels like a dream come true for me and a tremendous gift for educators everywhere. The timing couldn't be better. This book arrives in our hands like exactly the gift we need.

Thank you, Marti and Amie for your courage in writing this book, for sharing your wisdom and experience, and for inviting us into your conversations. Your work equips educators to see children more clearly and to respond with connection, understanding, and hope.

Now, if you'll excuse me, I'm off to be a safe owl nearby for someone who needs it and perhaps persuade a few possums along the way.

Casey Call, Ph.D., LPC
Associate Director of Education
TCU's Karyn Purvis Institute of Child Development

Table of Contents

PREFACE
A Teacher and A Therapist Together

Organization of the book (the practical stuff)

We wrote this book with teachers in mind, and each chapter follows a similar pattern. We start with information we invite you to learn and consider. Then we share stories and content to bring those ideas to life. At the end of each chapter, you'll find four things:

Let's Get Real: Excerpts from actual conversations between Marti and Amie as we wrote the book. Unfiltered. Occasionally caffeinated.

Takeaways: A good little review session, like good pedagogical teaching does.

Reflection Questions: There if you want them, totally skippable if you don't.

One Thing to Try Tomorrow: Because we believe in action, not just inspiration.

This design is intentional. Like all good teaching, we tell you what we want you to know, teach it, and then invite you to reflect on what you've learned.

We also want to model something important: the difference between structure and rigidity.

In education, we often get sucked into rigidity. We keep things on a tight schedule, everything hyper-organized, hoping that if we control enough of our surroundings, we can control the kids and the chaos. It's an understandable coping mechanism. Logical, even. But here's the thing: it doesn't really work. Not for kids, and not for teachers either.

What we actually need is structure. We'll talk more about this throughout the book, but the short version is this: we want to create a world that is predictable and organized without becoming so rigid that we forget we're human.

This book is structured. It is not, however, rigid. Each section is written as a unit and each chapter is a lesson.

We've written it so you can "choose your own adventure." Stick with us through Part 1 in order. After that? Read what you need, when you need it. Go chronologically. Jump from Chapter 8 to Chapter 11 to Chapter 6. Read it backwards while you sip cold coffee from your appreciation week "# 1 TEACHER" mug that is already fading into "# 1 EACH".

Whatever your heart desires. The structure will hold, but we will never demand rigidity.

Move through it in whatever way fits your personality, your strengths, and your classroom.

We also want to address something that might be uncomfortable, the Claude Clause. We used Claude AI to help with this book. We were very thoughtful and intentional about this. We are not editors; we are educators. We understand the controversy surrounding AI right now. We also recognize the benefit of having a bestie who doesn't mind reading and correcting the same sentence 15 times and helping to merge our individual voices into one. Claude did help us create some of the writing prompts and suggested content. However, we have personally pored over each word countless times ourselves. All artwork was commissioned by an actual human artist, Jamie Tanner. Amie and Marti created the other content in Canva. This book was AI assisted. But it was humbly humanly created. These are truly our stories and our words. Composed with care for you.

Happy adventuring, friends.

Now, let's begin.

Section One

The Foundation

Seeing behavior through the lens of connection and relational neuroscience

CHAPTER 1

We See You

Amie's Origin Story

~ Amie ~

My journey with occupational therapy and the relational approach didn't start in a classroom. My journey started in my own home, with my own kids. I went looking for help and stumbled into an entirely new world. I'll never forget my child's first OT appointment. The therapist had built this elaborate obstacle course. My kid was thrilled. Climbing, crawling, crashing, spinning. Pure joy.

As I watched this OT work her magic, something clicked. I started seeing a gaping hole in my 30 years of teacher in-service education. The same behaviors I was watching us address in OT were showing up in my classroom every single day. But in the classroom, we weren't using anything close to the same strategies. We were using consequences. Redirection. The classic "just sit still and focus" approach that works great for kids who can already sit still and focus, and works terribly for everyone else.

Most teachers barely know their OTs. Because so many school OTs are spread thin and are working more with classroom modifications, old-school behavior plans, and fine motor skills.

(Marti's professional goal is to invite more school based OTs into the relationally-informed work. Hopefully if you read this in later years, you will have access to a great OT to work alongside you in your classroom.)

Once I started connecting the dots between what my child needed in OT and what I was seeing in my students, I began experimenting. What if I responded to that fidgety kid the way the OT responded to mine? What if I offered sensory breaks instead of behavior charts? What if I assumed the behavior in my classroom was communication instead of defiance?

This was the moment everything changed.

It took me a few years to figure it all out. I sought training, including becoming a TBRI® Practitioner. I made mistakes. I tried things that flopped spectacularly. (There was an incident involving a therapy ball and a very unfortunate trajectory. We don't need to get into details.) But once I started truly implementing these strategies? I never looked back.

This approach brought me from the brink of teacher burnout to genuinely loving what I do again. That's not an exaggeration. I was counting down the days to retirement, and now I actually look forward to Mondays. (Most Mondays. Let's not get crazy.)

How I Met Marti

When I'm speaking in trainings, educators are always asking me about sensory stuff, regulation, co-regulation, window of tolerance, felt safety, proprioceptive input, vestibular needs. It can sound like a foreign language. And I kept thinking: I know someone who can explain this without making everyone's eyes glaze over. She's practical, funny, and full of energy.

That someone was Marti, the missing school OT piece for me.

I first saw her at a conference in Utah. She was delivering a keynote on sensory processing and regulation, and within about five minutes, I thought: I like her. She has this gift for making the brain science actually stick. Ten years as a school-based occupational therapist in rural Indiana. She's trained in Dr. Bruce Perry's Neurosequential Model © of Therapeutics. She was a ChildTrauma Academy Fellow. She's a TBRI Practitioner who helped develop the sensory portions of their trainings. She works closely with Robyn Gobbel as a coach in her Baffling Behaviors Training Institute. She basically collected all the infinity stones of trauma-informed care. If that were a thing, she's the type who would even wear the gauntlet.

After her session, I cornered her. (In the most professional way possible.) I told her about my classroom, the changes I'd made, the results I was seeing. She shared my excitement and passion to help kids.

Then I asked her to take an "usie" with me (thanks, Ted Lasso) and asked her to be my friend.

She joked that her friend card was full. I told her mine was too. We agreed to re-assess in four years.

About four *months* later, I bravely sent an email and asked to write this book together. She agreed and quickly added a line to her friend card. I guess our friend cards weren't actually laminated.

I'm the classroom expert. She's the OT sensory and regulation expert. (She prefers "funcle," which apparently stands for "fun uncle," because related service providers are the relative that swoops in, does the cool stuff, and leaves before bedtime tantrums or state-mandated testing.)

Most of the OTs I work with ARE funcles. They help so much but can't be around as much as I want them. Ideally, they would be in my building full time. But since that's often not the case, this book needs her voice. It's written with an OT lens. But in a way we don't have to be an OT to implement in our classrooms. It also gives us a common language when that funcle does show up so they can best help us help our students.

Why This Book, Why Now

I want to honor something before we continue. Five years ago, Marti was already working on a TBRI-for-teachers book with Dr. Casey Call and Callie Lackey. That project went on hold after Callie passed away unexpectedly. Callie was a true champion for children in Florida, and we hope this book honors her legacy.

When I reached out to Marti, she felt like the time was right to reference back to that earlier work and carry it forward.

Readers of her first book, The Connected Therapist, often said it felt like having coffee with an old friend. That's exactly what we want this book to feel like, too.

My story will weave throughout these pages, but here's what I want you to know at the start: I believe this approach is what education has been missing. It's the link between the behaviors we see and the strategies that actually help. It's the reason some teachers seem to have a magic touch while others are drowning. (Spoiler: it's not magic. It's science. And you can learn it.)

We're both practitioners. We use this stuff every day. And it works. Not perfectly. We're not peddling perfection here. But it works enough that I'm not counting down to retirement anymore. For the first time in over twenty years, I'm not just surviving. I'm loving it.

Because when we know better, we do better.

And soon, you're about to know a whole lot better.

I'm so glad you're here. Let's figure this out together.

The Truth About Teaching Today

Let's be honest about where we are.

Teachers are drowning.

According to research by the University of Missouri, after surveying almost 500 teachers, 78% say they have considered leaving since the pandemic. In a meta-analysis of over 70 scholarly articles, researchers found stress affecting more than 60% of teachers.

Sixty percent. More than half of us are operating under levels of stress that would be considered clinical in other professions.

And yet we show up. Every single day.

We smile at the door. We teach the lessons. We hold small support groups in back offices, corners of noisy cafeterias, and the ends of hallways. We grade the papers. We attend the meetings. We drink strong coffee purchased with old gift cards gifted to us half-used from three holidays ago. You know the ones. You end up paying for the gift yourself because there is only $2.63 left on the card.

And yet, we manage behaviors. We contact parents. We differentiate instruction. We write IEPs. We implement IEPs. We track data. We adjust practices.

Repeat until summer. Or burnout. Whichever comes first.

We see you. We know what you're carrying.

This isn't about blame. It's about finding commonality in community. It's about decreasing shame and ditching the toxic negativity. It's about naming what's true so we can actually do something about it.

As Dr. Dan Siegel says, "Name it to tame it".

The Trickle-Down Effect (Or: Why Everything Feels Impossible)

Want to know why teaching feels so impossible? Because you're being squeezed from every direction.

Federal mandates and funding requirements. State expectations, testing protocols, and constantly changing requirements. District mandates that seem to shift with the wind. Administrative demands that can make or break your entire year.

It's a pressure sandwich, and you're the filling.

For most teachers we know, the reality feels like everyone is telling you what to do, but no one is actually helping. There's plenty of lip service about wanting to support teachers but very little action behind it.

So what do teachers do? We've learned to use compliance as resistance.

We listen to the newest program. We figure out how to make it look like we're complying. And then we do whatever we actually know works in our classroom.

We nod in the professional development. We smile in the faculty meeting. We close our doors and, as the actual degreed professionals, teach the way we know these kids need.

But here's the problem: this constant pressure from above, this trickle-down effect of everyone telling us how to do our jobs, is exhausting. It's demoralizing. It makes us feel like our expertise doesn't matter. Like we're just cogs in a machine, easily replaced, constantly evaluated, never quite good enough.

Teachers need to be treated as professionals, not micromanaged like we can't be trusted with a lesson plan.

Until that changes systemically (and we're not holding our breath), we have to find ways to survive within a broken system. That's what this book is about. Not fixing the whole mess. That's above our pay grade, and even Claude AI doesn't have those answers. But we can help you thrive despite the mess.

Your Nervous System Matters (Really, It Does)

Here's something they probably didn't teach you in your teacher training program: your nervous system is just as important as your lesson plans.

Maybe more important.

Let us introduce you to a concept we'll use throughout this book and expand upon as we go: the upstairs brain and the downstairs brain.

The upstairs brain is where the good stuff lives. Thinking. Reasoning. Problem-solving. Creativity. Empathy. Patience. All those things that make you a great teacher on your best days. This is where relational connection mode lives. As we lose access to our upstairs brain, we lose access to connection to ourselves and those around us.

Marti likes to think of the upstairs brain like a loving grandma's guest room. Full of memories, A big cozy quilt and furniture neatly arranged with care and precision. A place you can relax with a nice novel and cup of something warm.

The downstairs brain is survival central. Fight, flight, freeze, or fawn. React first, think later (or never). This is the part that kicks into action when you feel attacked. You stop thinking and start protecting yourself. It is like we have a dimmer switch on the stairs that moves our relational capacities between upstairs connection mode and downstairs protection mode.

If grandma's vibe is upstairs, downstairs is like a sensory room. Things don't always match but they are functional. It's a bit chaotic and there are all kinds of equipment haphazardly placed in an attempt to help the body feel safe and connected. There is a watchdog and a hidden owl we will explore later. Fuse boxes, trampolines, oxygen masks, and fidget spinners.

Here's the thing: when the downstairs brain takes over in moments of extreme stress, the upstairs brain doesn't politely pause. The dimmer switch dysfunctions. It goes completely offline. Lights out. Cord ripped from the wall. Fuse box fried.

Forget the cozy chair and the carefully curated bookshelf. In survival mode, you can't browse. You can't reflect. All you've got is whatever's within reach that helps your body remember it's safe.

Because teaching often involves multiple ways to view things, here is another metaphor. Think about your classroom as having an emotional temperature. Some days it's a cozy upstairs brain room: warm, connected, everyone learning and laughing. Other days it's a dark, shadowy basement brain: cold, chaotic, everyone just fumbling in the dark trying to survive. You're the thermostat for your classroom, not just the thermometer. Your dimmer switch controls the felt-safety of the entire room.

This isn't about adding one more thing to your plate. It's about understanding why some days flow and others flop. Why the same lesson plan that worked beautifully on Monday crashes and burns on Wednesday. Why some kids seem fine one period and fall apart the next.

Nervous systems are running the show. Yours and theirs.

And here's the kicker: you can't meet the needs of someone else's nervous system when you have unmet needs yourself. It's like brushing your teeth while eating Oreos. You can't keep up and it's pretty obvious.

When Your Regulatory System Is Struggling

Let us paint you a picture. See if any of this sounds familiar.

It's Tuesday morning. (Why is it always Tuesday?)

You woke up late because you stayed up too late grading papers. Or doom scrolling. No judgment here. We've all been there, watching videos of people organizing pantries at midnight like alphabetizing your spices is going to fix anything.

You skip breakfast. You hit traffic. You walk in to find your classroom a mess because the janitors didn't clean it yesterday. First period starts in five minutes, and you haven't made copies yet.

A student walks in and immediately starts complaining about the assignment. Another student is popping loud bubbles with chewing gum even though you've asked them not to approximately one hundred times. A third student is wearing a ball cap and acts like it's a personal insult when you remind them of the dress code.

Now check your body.

Your shoulders are climbing toward your ears. Your jaw is clenched so tight you could crack a walnut. Your stomach is in knots. Your hands feel shaky. You snap at a student for something minor and immediately regret it.

Sound familiar?

You're stressed. You are descending the stairs to your downstairs brain.

The regulatory threat assessment structures in your brain have shifted from connection to protection mode. The basement just got cold and dark. You can't see objectively.

And from that dark basement, everything feels like a threat.

The gum chewing isn't just annoying; it's a personal attack. The dress code violation doesn't just require a friendly reminder; it's defiance. The complaint about the assignment isn't just feedback; it's disrespect.

When the lower parts of your brain are running the show, you can't access the parts that help you respond with patience, creativity, or empathy.

You're not teaching. You're reacting from primitive survival instincts.

~ Marti ~

Stress Lives in the Body

Here's something important to understand: trauma and stress don't just live in our minds. They live in our bodies. Our muscles remember. Our nervous systems remember.

The brain takes "snapshots" of impactful situations. It stores sensations together: the smell, the sound, the feeling in your stomach, the way your hands felt. And when something triggers that snapshot, the whole sensory event replays. It feels like it is repeating in the present. Even the sensations that aren't present in the current moment. Often without your conscious permission.

This happens to you. And it happens to your students.

Your attachment patterns, your own childhood experiences, your parenting journey, your teaching experiences: all of it shows up in how you respond in the classroom. Because here's the thing, the brain doesn't like change. It built neural pathways that kept you safe during your earliest life experiences. Even if your circumstances have changed, your body can still respond using old neural networks. Networks that might even be working against you in your current life circumstances. You can't change those networks until you can understand them and make new ones.

Ever wonder why one particular student gets under your skin more than others? Why one behavior triggers you while another barely registers? It's related to attachment styles that we will talk about soon.

We will explore: "Why is this bugging me THIS much? What's getting triggered in ME?"

Naming what's happening in you helps you separate your stuff from the student's stuff. That separation is powerful. It creates space between stimulus and response. And in that space, you climb those dimmer switch stairs to the grandma room and you get to choose how you respond.

The Stress Contagion Cycle

Here's where it gets really interesting (and by interesting, I mean slightly terrifying).

Your stress triggers your students' stress. Their stress triggers more of yours. And suddenly everyone's nervous system is having a conversation nobody planned, like emotional WiFi with everyone connected to your network. It's called neuroception, and we will explore it more in chapter three when we talk about brain science.

Students pick up on teacher stress whether you want them to or not. You can say "I'm fine" all you want, but your body is telling a different story. Your tight shoulders. Your clipped tone. Your hard eyes. It's the Oreo stuck between your teeth that you can't brush out. (I smile when I imagine an inside joke between our readers when someone says, "I'm fine." and the other says, "Your Oreo is showing." Which means; you need some self-care or at least a coffee and a hug.)

Kids who've experienced trauma or adversity? They're especially attuned to this. They learned to read adults for survival. They can sense when something's off before you even know something's off.

Your face, voice, and body are broadcasting constantly. Your students pick up your chaos. But they can also pick up your calm. This book will help you find that calm.

The Oxygen Mask Principle (Brief Version)

You've heard it before: put on your own oxygen mask before assisting others.

It's such a cliche that we want to skip over it. But let's actually sit with what this means for teachers.

Taking care of yourself is NOT selfish.

We'll say it again because teachers need to hear it about forty-two times before it sinks in.

Taking care of yourself is NOT selfish.

Here's the hard truth: if you burn out, if you quit, if you end up too broken to continue, that's not good for kids either.

You staying healthy, connected, and present in your classroom? That's what's best for kids. It's also what's best for you.

You have permission to struggle. You have permission to prioritize your own needs. You have permission to say no to things that drain you. You have permission to protect your time, your energy, your well-being.

Not because you're selfish. Because you're human. And humans need rest, connection, nourishment, and care to function well.

We have an entire chapter dedicated to self-care and survival strategies at the end of this book (Chapter 14). We'll give you practical tools for regulation, strategies that work while you're teaching, and permission to lower expectations when needed.

For now, just know this: your well-being matters. It's not separate from your teaching. It's a foundation of it.

Can we really do better?

To paraphrase Maya Angelou: when we know better, we can do better. Not perfect. Better.

But here's the honest truth: knowing better doesn't guarantee we'll do better every time. Because we're human. And sometimes being human means losing your cool over an ill-timed crude or snarky teenage joke or hint of disrespect.

We only have to be "good enough" caregivers about 30% of the time. Dr. Ed Tronick's research on mother-infant interaction found that even the most attuned caregivers are only in sync with their babies about 30% of the time. The other 70% involves misattunements, miscommunications, and missed signals. And here's what matters: it's the repair of those misses that actually builds resilience. Not the perfection. The repair.

No one likes being corrected, especially us educators. We are seldom wrong. We know things. Important things.

But when you have a relationship grounded in the belief that each person has infinite worth, and that we're truly doing the best we can in any given moment, there's grace for a gentle reminder now and then.

Even when you want to passive-aggressively remind the "corrector" right back about a few things. Practicing a pause and giving more context to our emotions and attachment styles can provide enough felt-safety to keep the upstairs brain online to allow a breath, pause, and reframe the situation for a better interaction. Not every time. But enough.

So yes, we recognize **you won't always do better even when you know better.** Join the club. We have t-shirts. But if you never learn and grow, doing better isn't even an option. Bonnie Badenoch, a therapist and author, says, "We can only work toward an outcome we can imagine". We need to know what the options are. We need others to encourage us to discover those options.

Here's what we want to offer as you move through this book: hold two truths at once. First, past decisions and actions made when "not knowing" in your past doesn't excuse the harm that may have happened. Second, learning new ways offers compassion and a path forward. It matters that you're here now, learning, and working toward repair.

Perfection is the Enemy of Progress

Here's some more permission, because we understand teachers need a lot of it:

You're allowed to not be perfect. You're allowed to still be learning. You're allowed to have hard days. You're allowed to feel overwhelmed. You're allowed to want to quit sometimes.

Thirty years in, and we're still learning. Still messing up. Still having moments where we think, "I could have handled that better."

The difference now? We have a framework. We have tools. We have language for what's happening. We have strategies that work more often than not.

And we have hope.

Not the naive, sunshine-and-rainbows kind of hope. The realistic, grounded kind. The kind that says, "I don't have to be perfect. I just have to keep showing up."

That's what this book offers. Not perfection. Progress. Not fixing everything. Understanding enough to make things better.

We see you. We care about you. We know what you're going through.

We know you're tired. We know you're trying. We know some days you're hanging on by a thread and other days you wonder why you ever thought this was a good career choice.

We've been there. We're still there sometimes. You're not alone in this. And you don't have to figure it all out today.

You're here, learning, trying. That makes you exactly the kind of teacher kids need. Not a perfect teacher. A present one. A growing one. A human one.

Keep reading. We are with you.

Let's Get Real: Why We Wrote This Book

Marti: Can I be honest about something? I'm genuinely excited about this book. And I don't say that about most professional development resources.

Amie: Same. I've sat through so many trainings where someone who hasn't been in a classroom since the 1990s tells me to "build relationships" without giving me a single practical tool. Thanks, super helpful.

Marti: Or the opposite: here's a binder full of behavior charts and token economies that assume kids are vending machines. Insert correct consequence, receive desired behavior.

Amie: (laughing) If only it worked that way.

Marti: Right? So here's what makes me excited about what we're doing. We're not choosing between warm and fuzzy OR rigid and systematic. We're saying: here's the science of why kids do what they do, AND here's what you can actually do about it tomorrow morning with 30 kids and no prep time.

Amie: That's the piece that's been missing for me. I've read the brain books. I've read the behavior books. But I needed someone to connect the dots. To say, "Okay, you understand polyvagal theory now. Great. Here's how that changes what you do when Marcus throws his pencil."

Marti: And we've both lived this. I'm not writing from a research lab. I've been the school-based OT with 190 kids across 18 buildings, running between classrooms with a bag full of fidgets, crafts, and a prayer.

Amie: And I've been the classroom teacher for 30 years, trying everything, burning out, finding my way back. I've been the skeptic in the back of the PD making sarcastic comments. So when I tell you something works, I mean I tested it on actual teenagers who did not want to cooperate.

Marti: We're also not pretending this is easy. Some books make it sound like if you just believe hard enough, every kid will transform by October. That's not real life.

Amie: Real life is messy. Progress is slow. Some days you nail it and some days you snap at a kid before your coffee kicks in. We're writing for THAT teacher. The one who's already tired but still trying.

Marti: We want this to feel like sitting down with two friends who get it. Who've been in the trenches. Who will give you real talk and real tools, not just theory and inspiration.

Amie: Practical, proven, and peppered with enough humor to keep you awake.

Marti: That's the goal. We think this book is different because WE needed this book. And we couldn't find it. So we wrote it.

Amie: For educators like us. For educators like our readers.

Marti: Let's do this together.

Takeaways

1. **You don't have to be perfect. You have to be present.** The Tronick research is clear: 30% "good enough" is actually good enough. You're going to miss cues, lose patience, and have days where your downstairs brain runs the show. That's not failure. That's being human. What matters is the rhythm of rupture, repair, and reconnect. You'll mess up. You'll make it right. And in that cycle, kids learn that relationships can survive conflict. That's a gift you give just by showing up and trying again.
2. **Your nervous system is contagious, so your regulation matters as much as your lesson plans.** You're the thermostat, not the thermometer. When your upstairs brain is online, you create conditions for your students' upstairs brains to come online too.

When you're stuck in survival mode, that stress ripples out like emotional WiFi. This isn't pressure to be calm all the time (impossible). It's permission to prioritize your own regulation as part of the job, not a distraction from it. We'll give you tools for that.

Reflection Questions

1. What brought you to this book right now? What's the student, the class, or the moment that made you think, "I need something different"? Hold that picture in your mind as you read. That's your "why." We'll keep coming back to it.
2. What would change if you believed that "good enough" really is good enough? If you let go of the pressure to get it right every time, what space might that open up? What would you try that you've been too afraid to attempt?

One Thing to Try Tomorrow

Name What's Nagging You

Before you dive into the rest of this book, take a minute to get honest with yourself.

Grab a sticky note (or the back of a receipt, or your hand, we don't judge). Write down:

What feels hard about this? Maybe it's "I don't have time for one more thing." Maybe it's "This sounds soft and my kids need structure." Maybe it's "I've been teaching for 20 years and now you're telling me I've been doing it wrong?" Whatever it is, name it. No one's grading this.

That's it. Acknowledge the resistance. Then challenge yourself to stay curious.

Here's a secret: the teachers who struggle most with this approach are often the ones who end up championing it. Your skepticism isn't a barrier. It's proof you're thinking critically.

Bring your doubts. Bring your "yeah, buts." Just keep reading.

We'll meet you where you are

CHAPTER 2

The Science of Attachment

Let's dig into attachment theory, brain development, and the nervous system. Don't worry, we promise to keep it practical. No jargon without translation. No theory without application.

Here's why it matters: understanding attachment will change how you see every kid who walks through your door. You'll meet two students, Marcus and Juleigh. One feels like a gift. The other feels like a grind. By the end of Chapter 2, you'll understand why. And that understanding? It changes everything.

You might even see yourself a little differently along the way.

Grab your coffee. Let's learn some brain science.

The Kid Who's Harder to Connect With

You probably have an Marcus on your roster.

He's in your third-period class. Bright smile, quick to help, eager to please. When he's struggling with an assignment, he raises his hand politely and asks for help. He notices your new outfits and is sure to compliment them. When you give him feedback, he thanks you and tries again, apologizing for wasting your time. Even on his worst days, he's pleasant to be around. A delight to connect with.

And then there's Juleigh. Juleigh walks in late. No apology. She rolls her eyes when you give instructions. Makes sarcastic comments under her breath just loud enough for you to hear. When you offer help, she says she doesn't need it. Then she fails the assignment. She seems determined to make your life difficult.

Here's the thing: both of these kids are struggling. Both of them need support. But Marcus's struggles feel manageable, even endearing. Juleigh's struggles feel personal. Like a failure. Like a challenge you can't win.

Why?

It's not because Marcus is a "good kid" and Juleigh is a "bad kid." It's not because you're a better teacher for Marcus than you are for Juleigh.

It's attachment.

Marcus's early experiences taught him that adults are fragile. If his needs came across as difficult, the adults around him were overwhelmed. So he learned to people please. He learned to smile just the right way and give just the right compliments in order to gain the favor and attention of the adults in his life.

Juleigh learned something different. Maybe adults in her life got angry when she asked for things. Maybe they ignored her. Maybe they were so inconsistent that she never knew what she'd get. So she learned: "Asking for help isn't safe. Adults can't be trusted. I have to protect myself."

Neither of these kids chose their attachment pattern. It was built into them before they had words, before they could consciously remember, before they had any say in the matter. And now, both kids are doing the best they can with what they learned.

That's what this chapter is about. Understanding attachment won't make Juleigh easy. But it might help you see her differently. And that shift, from judgment to curiosity, from frustration to compassion, changes everything.

What Is Attachment, Anyway?

At its most basic, attachment is the emotional bond between a child and their primary caregiver. It's how humans are wired to survive.

Think about it: a human baby is the most helpless creature on the planet. Can't feed themselves. Can't run from danger. Can't do anything to meet their own needs. They are 100% dependent on adults for survival.

So nature built in a system to make sure those needs get met: attachment.

Babies are biologically programmed to seek closeness with caregivers. They cry when distressed. They coo and smile when content. They track faces. They reach for familiar arms. There's even research showing that infants initially present with more of the father's facial features as a way to encourage connection with dad. We like things that look like us. (Think about those first family gatherings with a newborn, where every relative hunts for genetic markers that match their side. It's practically an Olympic sport. "He has my nose!" "No, that's definitely my dad's nose!" Meanwhile the baby just wants milk and a nap.)

When caregivers respond consistently and lovingly to those cues for connection, the baby learns something fundamental: "When I have a need, someone will meet it. The world is safe. I am worthy of care."

This is called secure attachment. And it's the foundation for healthy development.

But what happens when caregivers can't or don't respond consistently? When babies cry and no one comes? When they're scared and no one comforts them? When they're hungry and have to wait too long? When their cries are met with shouts?

They still attach. Because they have to. Their survival depends on it.

But they attach insecurely. They develop strategies to cope with unpredictable or unresponsive caregiving.

And those strategies? They follow kids into school. Into your classroom. Into their interactions with you.

The Attachment Cycle (How It's Supposed to Work)

Let us walk you through what healthy attachment looks like. We call this the attachment cycle, and it plays out hundreds of times a day in the first years of life, especially the first two months when a baby seems to have exhaustingly constant need.

Step 1: Baby has a need. They're hungry, tired, scared, uncomfortable, or just wanting connection.

Step 2: Baby expresses the need. They cry, fuss, reach out, make eye contact.

Step 3: Caregiver responds. They pick up the baby, feed them, change them, soothe them, engage with them.

Step 4: Need is met. Baby feels satisfied, safe, co-regulated.

Step 5: Trust deepens. Baby learns: "When I have a need and express it, someone responds. I can trust. I am safe. I matter."

This cycle repeats over and over. Need. Expression. Response. Met Need. Trust.

When this cycle happens consistently, children develop secure attachment. They learn that relationships are safe. That they're worthy of care. That the world is generally predictable and responsive. That they can be uncomfortable for brief periods but another human will help them get back to steady ground.

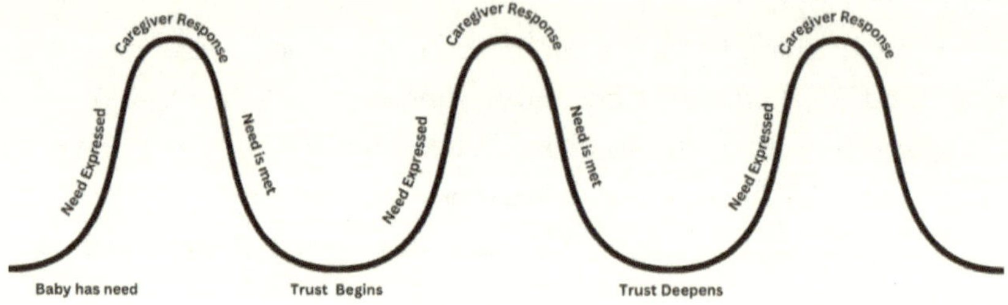

But when this cycle breaks, when needs aren't met, when caregivers are inconsistent, when responses are harsh or absent, children adapt. They develop insecure attachment patterns as survival strategies.

And here's what's wild: these patterns don't just affect childhood. They shape how we navigate relationships for the rest of our lives.

Including how we show up as teachers. How parents show up to IEP meetings. How principals show up to staff meetings. How students show up in our classrooms.

We're all walking around with attachment patterns influencing everything.

Why Attachment Matters in the Classroom

You might be thinking, "Okay, but I'm not a parent. I didn't raise these kids. How does this apply to me?"

Fair question. Here's how.

Your Own Attachment Pattern Influences How You Teach

~ Marti ~

As we begin to talk about attachment, it's helpful to hold a neurological principle. Human brains don't like change. We would rather stay in difficult situations that are familiar than risk change for something better. There are even extreme studies of people who stay in abusive situations because they are predictable. Predictable is coded as safe in the brain, even if the prediction is for harm. It's harm we have survived.

What we call fear is often just unfamiliarity. The brain isn't asking "Is this dangerous?" It's asking, "Do I know what happens next?" Most fears are really "what if" scenarios. Scenarios we haven't seen ourselves survive yet.

Think about this. Firefighters run into burning buildings, practically fear-free, because they have thousands of hours of practice. Their brain can predict what happens in these truly unsafe situations. Because the actual danger is predictable, it isn't coded as fear for these firefighters.

The brain has limited resources and works predominantly on predictive expectations. It takes less energy to use protective patterns from our past than to forge new neural connections where we don't have memories of how things will play out.

If you had to yell for food as a kid, your brain learned that yelling works. Now, even when asking politely would get better results, your brain prefers the known path. Yelling with consequences over the unknown. The pattern that got your needs met then becomes your default now, even when it no longer serves you.

If you had secure attachment growing up, if your needs were mostly met, if your caregivers were mostly responsive, you probably find it easier to be warm and responsive with students. Connection feels natural to you. You have more capacity for chaos and change.

If you had insecure attachment, if your early experiences taught you that relationships are unpredictable or unsafe, you might struggle with boundaries. You might take things personally. You may "keep the peace" to the detriment of your own health. You might feel wounded by student behavior in ways that surprise you. Certain kids might push buttons you didn't even know you had. Chaos and change can feel overwhelming.

We all bring our attachment history into our classrooms.

Here's a sobering statistic: studies show that a higher percentage of people who enter caring professions like counseling, nursing, and education have insecure attachment backgrounds. We're often drawn to help because we know what it's like to need help. That's a noble motivation. But it can be problematic if we haven't examined our own patterns.

The Good News: Earned Secure Attachment

Attachment isn't destiny.

Secure attachment is basically the brain's way of saying, "I've got people, and my people have got me." It's the deep-down knowing that when things get hard, someone will show up. Not perfectly. Not with all the answers. But consistently, warmly, and without making you feel like a burden for needing them in the first place. Kids who develop secure attachment have learned through hundreds of tiny moments that their feelings make sense, their needs matter, and relationships are a safe place to land. It's not about having a flawless childhood (spoiler: those don't exist). It's about having enough experiences of being seen, soothed, and supported that the brain builds a template for trust.

Here's where the hope comes in, and it's the kind of hope worth holding onto: attachment patterns aren't permanent. They're not tattooed on the soul. The same brain that learned "people are unpredictable and I'm on my own" can learn something new when it encounters consistent connection and care. This is what we call earned secure attachment, and it's available to anyone at any age. Every time we offer a child (or an adult, for that matter) the experience of being truly seen and safely held, we're literally rewiring their expectations about relationships. When we know better, we do better, and when we do better consistently, brains change.

So if you're working with kids whose early experiences taught them that the world is scary and people can't be trusted, take heart. You're not trying to erase their history. You're helping them write a new chapter. Connection by connection, calm presence by calm presence, you're proving that people can be safe. And that proof? It sticks. It builds. It becomes the foundation for everything else.

This principle applies to teachers, too. You're not stuck with what you were given.

Students Are Going Through the Attachment Cycle With You

Here's something powerful: your students are going through the attachment cycle with you every single day. They have needs. They express them (sometimes in really frustrating ways). You respond (or don't). Their needs get met (or don't). Trust deepens (or doesn't).

Your response matters. Your consistency matters. Your warmth matters. That consistency provides the predictability the brain needs to re-wire. For some of your students, you might be helping them *imagine* something better. A better response or outcome than they have ever experienced before. A safe adult who shows up, keeps promises, and doesn't disappear when things get hard.

Attachment Helps You Decode Behavior

Let's say you have a student who asks for help with EVERY. SINGLE. STEP. of every assignment. Drives you crazy.

Without understanding attachment, you might think: "This kid is manipulative. Lazy. Attention-seeking. They just want me to do the work for them."

With understanding attachment, you might realize: "This kid learned that the only way to keep adults close is to constantly need help. If they seem capable, adults leave. So they stay helpless to stay connected."

Same behavior. Completely different thought response.

Compassion opens up far more effective responses than frustration ever could.

The Four Attachment Styles (Classroom Edition)

Researchers have identified four main attachment patterns. Here's what each one looks like in your classroom, and what these students need from you.

Secure Attachment

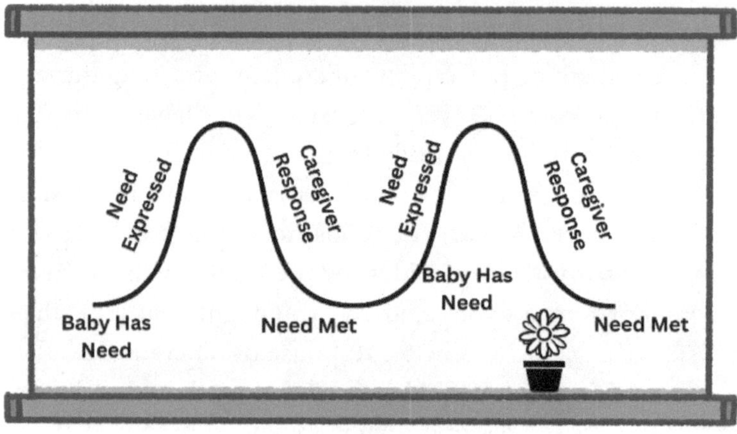

What You See: Comfortable asking for help. Handles correction without falling apart. Bounces back from setbacks. Trusts you.

What They Learned: "Adults are safe. My needs matter. I'm worthy of care." "We can disagree and stay connected."

What They Need: Consistent warmth, clear expectations, encouragement to keep growing.

What It Feels Like for You: Easy. Natural. Rewarding. "A joy to have in class."

These students make you feel like a good teacher because connection flows naturally.

Anxious-Avoidant Attachment

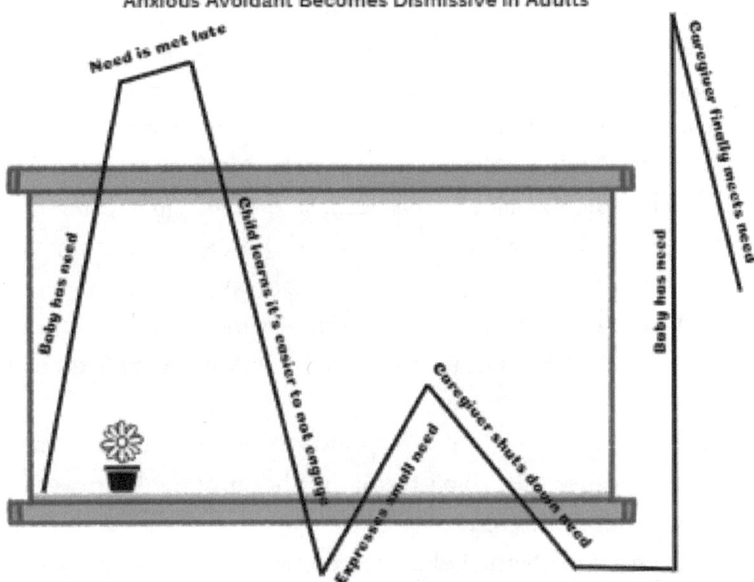

What You See: Independent to the point of isolation. Doesn't ask for help even when struggling. Uncomfortable with praise or attention. "I'm fine" is their favorite phrase.

What They Learned: "Adults aren't available. Emotions make people uncomfortable. I have to take care of myself." "I have to pretend everything is OK at all costs."

What They Need: Consistent presence without pressure. Respect for their space. Patience. Small, predictable connections that don't demand vulnerability.

What It Feels Like for You: Frustrating. Can't break through. Like talking to a wall. You offer help and they refuse it, then fail.

Remember: Eye rolls and sarcasm are armor, not attacks. There's a kid under there who desperately needs connection but doesn't trust it yet. This is Juleigh.

A crucial caveat: Before you decide a child has avoidant attachment, consider neurodivergence.

Autistic students often get mislabeled as avoidant when they're actually just... autistic. Here's what we mean:

An autistic child might not make eye contact. Not because relationships feel unsafe, but because eye contact is genuinely uncomfortable or overwhelming for their nervous system.

An autistic child might not ask for help. Not because they learned adults aren't available, but because they struggle to recognize when they need help, or they can't find the words in the moment, or the social script for "asking" feels impossibly complicated.

An autistic child might seem to prefer being alone. Not because connection is scary, but because social interaction is exhausting and they need solitude to regulate.

An autistic child might not respond to your warmth the way you expect. Not because they don't feel it, but because they express and receive connection differently.

See the pattern? Same behaviors, completely different roots.

If you're looking at a student and thinking "avoidant attachment," pause. Ask yourself: Could this be neurodivergence instead? Could this be both? Could I be misreading their communication style?

The intervention for attachment wounds is different from the support needed for neurodivergent processing. Getting this wrong means we're addressing the wrong thing entirely. And that's frustrating for everyone, especially the kid.

Anxious-Resistant (Anxious-Ambivalent) Attachment

Attachment Cycle

Anxious Ambivalent Becomes Entangled in Adults

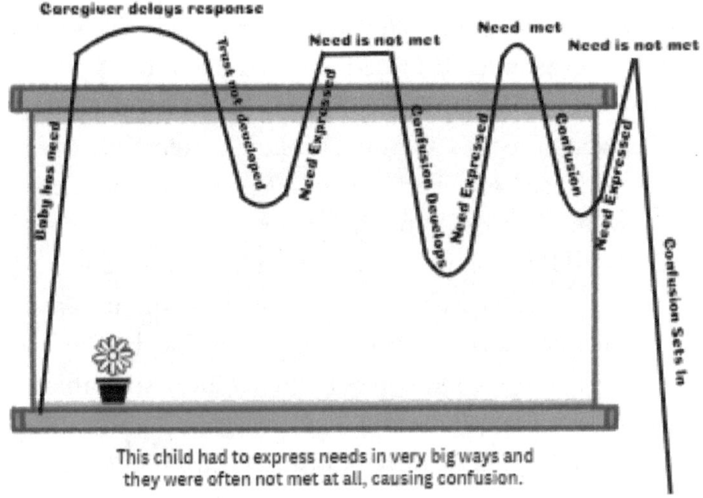

This child had to express needs in very big ways and they were often not met at all, causing confusion.

What You See: Constantly seeking reassurance. Never satisfied no matter how much you give. Clingy. Big reactions to small things. Sometimes angry even when you're trying to help.

What They Learned: "Adults are unpredictable. Sometimes they come, sometimes they don't. I have to fight for attention because it might disappear."

What They Need: Predictability above all. Clear routines. Acknowledgment without feeding the drama. Gentle nudges toward independence with lots of support.

What It Feels Like for You: Exhausting. Never enough. Like filling a bucket with no bottom. You give and give and they just want more.

Remember: They're hungry for PREDICTABLE connection. Their intensity isn't manipulation. It's desperation. They learned that inconsistent attention is better than no attention. This is Marcus. He has simply learned to hide his clinginess with his over vigilant observing and people pleasing.

Another caveat: ADHD can look a lot like anxious attachment, and the overlap gets messy.

Kids with ADHD often experience something called Rejection Sensitive Dysphoria (RSD). It's not an official diagnosis but ask any ADHD adult and they'll nod so hard their head might fall off. RSD means that perceived rejection (even tiny, imagined rejection) feels catastrophic. Devastating. End-of-the-world painful.

So, when your ADHD student seems to need constant reassurance, when they fall apart over minor corrections, when they're hyper-focused on whether you like them... it might not be attachment wounds. It might be their neurology.

Similarly, ADHD brains crave stimulation. Connection is stimulating. So an ADHD child might seek constant interaction not because they learned that attention is unpredictable, but because their brain is hungry for input and you're the most interesting thing in the room. (Take it as a compliment?)

Again: same behaviors, different causes, different supports needed.

This doesn't mean neurodivergent kids can't also have attachment difficulties. They absolutely can. In fact, neurodivergent kids are MORE likely to experience attachment disruptions because their needs are often misunderstood from birth. A colicky baby who's actually sensory-overwhelmed. A toddler whose meltdowns are labeled "bad behavior" instead of recognized as dysregulation. A child whose different communication style leaves them feeling chronically unseen.

Neurodivergence and attachment are frequently tangled together. The goal isn't to pick one explanation and run with it. The goal is to stay curious about all the possibilities.

Disorganized Attachment

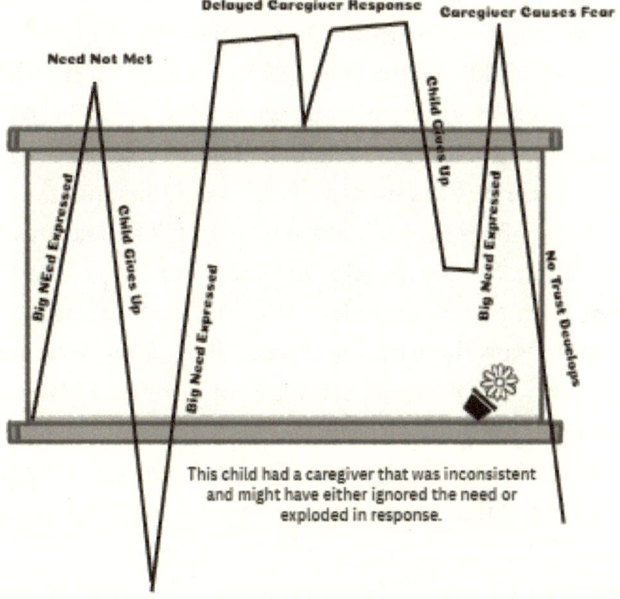

What You See: Contradictory behavior. They seek connection, then push you away. Fearful. Extreme reactions. Freezing or spacing out. Behavior that doesn't make sense.

What They Learned: "Adults are both my source of comfort AND my source of fear. There's no safe strategy. Everything is confusing." "Chaos feels like comfort."

What They Need: Absolute consistency. A calm, regulated presence. Safety above everything. Often professional support beyond what a classroom teacher can provide.

What It Feels Like for You: Walking on eggshells. Unpredictable. The kind of student who keeps you up at night googling "reactive attachment disorder."

Where It Comes From: This pattern develops when the caregiver was BOTH the source of comfort AND the source of fear. The child's nervous system received contradictory messages: "Go toward this person for safety. This person is dangerous." No wonder they're confused.

Permission: This is the most challenging attachment pattern. It's okay to need help with these students. It's okay to ask for support. You are not failing if this feels impossibly hard.

One more consideration: Disorganized attachment can also develop when a child's neurodivergent needs are chronically unmet or punished, even by loving parents who didn't know better.

Imagine being a sensory-sensitive child whose nervous system screams "DANGER!" in environments that adults insist are fine. The lights are too bright. The sounds are too loud. The textures are unbearable. You cry out for help, and the adults who love you tell you to calm down, stop being dramatic, just deal with it.

Your body says the world is unsafe. The people who are supposed to protect you don't seem to notice or care. They might even punish you for your distress.

That's confusing. That's scary. That can create the same "come here/go away" contradictory wiring as more obvious trauma.

This isn't about blaming parents. Most parents of neurodivergent kids are doing their absolute best with limited information and exhausted nervous systems of their own. But it helps explain why some kids from "good homes" still present with disorganized patterns. The mismatch between their needs and their environment was itself traumatic, even if no one meant any harm.

A Note on "Good" Families and Invisible Trauma

Before we go further, let us clear something up.

Sometimes teachers look at a kid's family situation and think, "But they come from a good home. They don't have trauma." And then they dismiss attachment difficulties because there's no obvious abuse or neglect.

Here's the thing: trauma isn't always visible.

Like we just mentioned, trauma happens when a child's nervous system doesn't get safety signals when their senses are signaling danger. That can happen in all kinds of families.

When a parent withdraws during conflict, it can feel like abandonment to the child.

When a parent is overwhelmed by their own anxiety, a child can learn that their needs are "too much."

Modern complications we're only beginning to understand:

- Sensory processing differences that went undiagnosed
- Medical trauma (NICU stays, surgeries, hospitalizations)
- Postpartum depression (parent physically present but emotionally unavailable)
- "Covid babies" who spent critical attachment periods looking at masked faces
- High parental stress from financial struggles, relationship problems, or health issues

You don't need a child's full history to respond with compassion. You just need curiosity.

Culture, Context, and Curiosity

Let's talk more specifically about how culture shapes what we're seeing.

Communication styles vary wildly. In some families, children are expected to speak when spoken to. In others, kids are encouraged to advocate loudly for themselves. A quiet, deferential child isn't necessarily insecure. A loud, assertive child isn't necessarily anxious. They might just be well-adapted to their family's cultural norms.

Parenting practices differ across cultures (and none of them are wrong). Co-sleeping, extended breastfeeding, and "wearing" babies are standard practice in much of the world. In other contexts, early independence is encouraged. Neither approach automatically creates better or worse attachment. What matters is responsiveness, attunement, and consistency within that family's framework.

Family structures vary. Not every child is raised primarily by one or two parents. Grandparents, aunties, older siblings, and community members are primary caregivers in many cultures. A child who has secure attachment with their grandmother but ambivalent attachment with their mother isn't broken. They're navigating a complex relational world, which is actually good preparation for life.

Trauma histories affect whole communities. Let's consider a few community traumas. Indigenous communities affected by boarding schools. Black communities affected by slavery and ongoing systemic racism. Immigrant families navigating displacement and documentation fear. Refugee families carrying war and loss. These experiences don't just affect individuals. They shape entire cultural approaches to trust, authority, and relationships.

When a child from a marginalized community seems distrustful of school authorities, it could be attachment insecurity. Or, it could be a perfectly reasonable adaptation to a world where institutions have historically not been safe for people who look like them.

Probably both. Almost always both.

Your job isn't to diagnose cultural trauma. Your job is to be a safe adult in a potentially unsafe world. To be trustworthy. To be consistent. To be someone who earns trust rather than demanding it.

Intergenerational Trauma

Here's something important to understand: trauma can pass through generations.

Not just through behavior (though that happens too). Through actual biology. Epigenetics research shows that traumatic experiences can change gene expression in ways that get passed down to children and grandchildren.

Descendants of Holocaust survivors show different stress responses than control groups. The effects of slavery and forced relocation are visible in communities generations later. Family patterns of anxiety, depression, and addiction run through bloodlines.

This isn't about making excuses. It's about understanding.

When you look at a struggling student, you're not just seeing that kid. You're seeing generations of survival strategies, coping mechanisms, and adaptive responses to adversity.

But here's the good news: healing also passes through generations.

When you break cycles, when you offer something different, when you help a child experience safe connection, you're not just helping that child. You're potentially changing what they pass forward to their own children someday.

What will we hand forward next? That's a question worth asking.

All Children Have Worth

Let's pause here and say something important.

ALL children have worth. Not just the easy ones. Not just the ones who make us feel like good teachers. Not just the ones who thank us and try hard and follow directions.

All of them.

This is hard. We know it's hard. When a kid is making your life miserable day after day, when they seem determined to sabotage every good thing you try to do, when they hurt other students or destroy property or say things that cut deep, it's hard to remember they have worth.

Dr. Ross Greene, who wrote *Lost at School*, puts it this way: "Kids do well if they can."

Not "kids do well if they want to." If they CAN.

If a kid isn't doing well, something is getting in the way. Our job is to figure out what that something is and address it.

Dr. Bruce Perry (you'll meet him properly in Chapter 3) has done tons of research that informs us that when threat is detected, the survival parts of the brain take over. The thinking parts go offline. Kids in survival mode aren't CHOOSING to be difficult. They're trying to survive.

We face a choice in how we respond:

Judgment: "What's wrong with you?"

Curiosity: "What happened to you?"

The first closes doors. The second opens them.

Here's a perspective shifter that helps me on hard days: "What's harder: being WITH this student for an hour, or BEING this student for their whole day?"

You're Not Their Parent, But You Can Be a Safe Adult

Let us be clear about what's NOT your job:

- Fixing their attachment wounds
- Healing their trauma
- Being everything to everyone
- Replacing their parent
- Making up for years of inconsistent caregiving in a single school year

That's too much. That's not possible. That's a recipe for burnout.

But here's what you CAN do: be a safe adult.

What does that mean?

- Showing up consistently (even when you don't feel like it)
- Following through on what you say (small promises kept build big trust)
- Taking care of your own nervous system (so you can actually be present)
- Really seeing them (not just their behavior, but them)
- Holding boundaries with compassion (structure AND warmth)
- Believing in their worth when they can't believe it themselves

You won't be perfect at this. Nobody is. Consistency doesn't mean perfection. It means showing up, over and over, even imperfectly. Students don't need perfection. They need your presence

The Power of One Caring Adult

Here's something that gives me hope on the hardest days.

Research by Dr. Perry and others has shown that kids who overcome adversity have one thing in common: at least one caring adult who believed in them. One.

Not a team of therapists. Not a perfect family. Just one stable, supportive person who saw them, believed in them, and kept showing up. That could be you.

What does "one caring adult" look like in practice?

- Standing at your door every morning with a genuine greeting
- Noticing when a kid seems "off" and quietly checking in
- Remembering that conversation from yesterday and following up
- Knowing their interests (even if you don't share them)
- Believing in their capability when they've given up on themselves
- Not taking their worst moments as their whole story

The student who feels invisible? You see them. The student who feels stupid? You believe in them. The student who feels unwanted? You make space for them.

It matters more than you know. Even when you can't see the impact. Especially when you can't see the impact.

Repair After Rupture

Okay. Here's the part we need to talk about honestly.

You are going to mess up.

You're going to snap at a student when you're tired. You're going to misread a situation and respond poorly. You're going to let your own downstairs brain take over and say something you regret.

This is not just a possibility. This is a certainty.

Join the club. We meet daily at the donut shop. We've all been there. We'll all be there again.

The question isn't whether you'll rupture relationships. You will. The question is what happens next.

Why Repair Matters

When there's rupture without repair, it confirms what insecurely attached kids already believe: adults can't be trusted. They mess up and they don't care. Relationships are disappointing.

But when there's rupture WITH repair, something powerful happens. The child learns: "Adults mess up, but they come back. They admit when they're wrong. They make it right. Relationships can survive conflict."

For a kid who has never experienced repair, this might be revolutionary. **This might be the most important thing we teach. Inviting them to imagine a safe relationship can exist.**

What Repair Looks Like

It's simpler than you think. It's also harder than you think (because it requires swallowing your pride).

"Hey, I was short with you earlier. That wasn't fair. I'm sorry."

"I got frustrated and my tone was harsh. That wasn't about you. You didn't deserve that."

"I made a mistake. I want to make it right. How can I do that?"

That's it. Name what happened. Take responsibility. Apologize sincerely.

The Strength of Repair

Here's something beautiful: repair doesn't just fix relationships. It actually STRENGTHENS them.

Think about a bone that breaks and heals. The healed spot is often stronger than the original bone.

Relationships work the same way. When we rupture and repair, we build something stronger than if the rupture never happened. Kids learn that relationships can survive hard things. That conflict isn't the end. That people can mess up and still be trustworthy. Rupture isn't failure. Refusing to repair is failure.

What You're Modeling

When you repair with students, you're teaching them:

- Adults can be wrong (revolutionary for some kids)
- Adults can admit it (even more revolutionary)
- Relationships are worth fighting for
- Mistakes aren't the end of the story
- It's safe to be imperfect

You don't have to be perfect to be effective. You just have to be willing to come back, own your mistakes, and try again. That rupture, repair, and resilience cycle helps students learn to trust. A first step in earned attachment.

~ Marti ~

When I first learned about attachment, I thought it was about the kids. It took me longer to realize it was also about me.

Understanding my own attachment patterns changed how I showed up in every relationship, not just with clients or students, but with my own family. I had to confront some hard truths about how my history shaped my responses, my triggers, my blind spots.

This work is personal. And that's what makes it powerful.

If you're feeling uncomfortable right now - if some of this is hitting close to home, that's okay. That discomfort is often the beginning of growth. You don't have to have it all figured out. None of us do. We're all just doing the best we can with what we've learned, and then learning to do a little better.

Our histories are important. They set the outline for our life stories. But we have more chapters to write and we can always make edits to that outline. Grab your red pens, teacher friends. Let's start learning some new ways to edit our biases in relationships.

Let's Get Real: When Attachment Theory Meets Your Actual Students

Amie: Attachment isn't as simple as four neat categories. Kids can show different patterns with different adults, or in different contexts.

Marti: Exactly. And here's what I want educators to know: you don't need to diagnose your students' attachment styles. That's not your job. What you need is to understand that these patterns exist and they influence behavior.

Amie: Yes! It's about shifting your lens. When a kid is being clingy and needy, instead of thinking "This kid is so annoying," you can think "This kid's nervous system is fighting for connection."

Marti: And that changes how you respond. You're not going to suddenly have infinite patience. You're human. But you might set the boundary differently. "I see you need some reassurance right now. I'm going to check in with you in five minutes. Can you work on this until then?" Then set a timer so you don't forget. Let them know you'll show up when you say you will.

Amie: That's meeting the attachment need while also teaching independence. Much better than "Stop bothering me, I just helped you!"

Marti: Which is what I have wanted to say. Many times. Before I knew better.

Amie: We all did. But here's something I want to address: teachers sometimes worry that understanding attachment means letting kids off the hook for bad behavior.

Marti: Oh, I hear that all the time. "So you're saying I should just accept it when a kid is disrespectful because they have attachment issues?"

Amie: No! Understanding attachment helps you respond more effectively, not more permissively. You still hold boundaries. You still teach better behavior. You just do it in a way that doesn't reinforce their core belief that they're unworthy.

Marti: Right. So instead of "You're being disrespectful, go to the office," it might be "That tone isn't okay. Let's try that again. I believe you can do this respectfully."

Amie: You're responding to the behavior while maintaining connection. That's the key.

Marti: And sometimes you're going to mess this up. Sometimes you're going to react poorly. I still do.

Amie: So what do you do after you react poorly?

Marti: I repair. I apologize. "Hey, I was short with you earlier. That wasn't fair. I was stressed about something else and I took it out on you. I'm sorry."

Amie: That's huge. That's showing kids that adults can mess up and make it right. For kids with insecure attachment, that might be a completely new experience.

Marti: It takes the pressure off me to be perfect, too. I can be human, make mistakes, and model how to repair relationships.

Amie: Which might be the most important thing we teach.

Takeaways

1. **Attachment isn't destiny; it's a starting point.** The patterns students bring are survival strategies, not character flaws. Marcus's ease and Juleigh's armor both make sense when you understand what they learned about adults. Those patterns can change with consistent, caring relationships.
2. **You don't have to be their parent to matter.** One caring adult can change a child's entire trajectory. Your consistency, warmth, and belief in them makes a difference, even when you can't see it. Especially when you can't see it.
3. **This work is personal.** Your own attachment history shapes which kids feel easy and which feel hard. The students who push your buttons the most are often the ones who most need what you have to offer. Awareness is power.

Reflection Questions

1. Think about a student who gets under your skin. What might their behavior be communicating about what they learned about adults?
2. What was your own attachment experience growing up? How might that influence which students you connect with easily and which ones challenge you?
3. Who was YOUR "one caring adult"? What did they do that made the difference?
4. How comfortable are you with repair? What gets in the way of apologizing to students when you mess up?

One Thing to Try Tomorrow

Practice Curiosity with One Challenging Kid

Pick one student who frustrates you. Just one. (We all have one. Or twelve.)

Before reacting to their next difficult behavior, pause. Take a breath. Ask yourself: "What might their attachment history be telling them right now? What did they learn about adults that makes this behavior make sense?"

Then try responding from that place.

Script to try: "I'm noticing you seem really frustrated right now. What's hard about this?"

The mindset shift: "This kid is being difficult" becomes "This kid is having difficulty."

See what happens. And remember: understanding doesn't mean excusing. It means responding more effectively.

CHAPTER 3

The Science of Stress and Safety

Amie's Story: How a Burned-Out Teacher Found Her Way Back

~ Amie ~

The year was 2010. I had been teaching for about 15 years. Single, solvent, and spontaneous. I owned all my time and all my money. Life looked like what I thought I wanted it to be.

But I also felt like I was missing something.

That was when I decided to do respite for foster care: taking kids for short stints when they first come into care or when the placement family needs a break. I figured I was really good at building relationships for short periods of time. I could pour into them, then send them out the door knowing at least one adult cared.

When I filled out my paperwork, I said no long-term placements, no adoptions, no one with serious behaviors. (If you know foster care, you're already laughing at my naïve little checklist.)

I got my first call in October of 2010. In June of 2025, fifteen years later, that first placement moved out of my basement. Nothing about what I thought I would do is what I ended up doing.

I brought five foster kids into my home. I adopted three and had guardianship of one. In four years, I went from no kids to four kids and two grandbabies. My life felt like it was spinning, swerving, and spiraling out of control, probably because it was.

I also had no idea how to navigate this world of baffling behaviors I didn't recognize and couldn't handle. Grounding? Didn't work. Punishment? Pointless. I was desperate for help.

Somewhere along the way, I stumbled onto TBRI. I can't pinpoint my first exposure, but this acronym started to change my world. All of a sudden, I was learning why kids acted the way they did. I was learning skills to handle those behaviors. Most importantly, I was learning how to build relationships (connecting) and create safe and sensory-friendly environments (empowering) so these beautiful humans could find success and begin to heal.

As I implemented TBRI at home, I found myself moving some of those skills into my classroom. Don't think it turned to roses and champagne overnight, though. It took me over a decade to articulate what I was doing at home and translate that to my teaching.

By 2019, I was a 20-year teaching veteran. Twenty years! I really thought that by this point in my career, I'd have it all figured out. But that year, like the years before it, had me spinning toward burnout.

I was drowning.

I had a difficult administration, and education no longer felt like my safe place. The joy I'd once felt walking into my classroom had been replaced by dread. I would go through the motions of teaching every day but felt a complete exhaustion that went far beyond anything sleep could fix. I checked out from relating to kids. I stopped caring about curriculum. My goal each day was simple: survive.

On top of school stress, my own family was changing rapidly. My kids were growing up, their needs shifting. Life was moving faster than I could keep up with, and I truly had nothing left to give.

The best part of my workday? The morning meeting of "coffee club," where my teacher besties and I would stand around and complain about everything. Community through toxic negativity. We had no solutions, but we had solidarity, sarcasm, and really mediocre coffee.

When 2020 hit, I knew something had to change. I actually started outlining my own charter school. Can you imagine? Me, starting a school! This school would be led by teachers who understood trauma, embraced TBRI, and we were going to fix the whole flawed, frustrating system.

Spoiler alert: that school didn't happen. The pandemic ate away at whatever hope I had left. So I made a difficult and dismal decision: stay in my classroom and wait for retirement. I would disengage. Do my time. Show up physically but protect myself emotionally. I had become one of those teachers I used to judge, the ones who seemed to have given up. But now I finally understood why they'd checked out. When you have nothing left to give, you stop giving.

I was counting down the years to retirement like a prisoner marking days on a cell wall, with off-brand crayons. You know the ones.

The Training That Changed Everything

In 2023, I became a TBRI Practitioner. I'd already taken the caregiver series for parenting, but this training was different. This was the deep dive.

Honestly? My goal was to find a way out of the classroom. Soak in the academic vibes. Just remember that I was a human being. I had no idea it would become one of the major pivot points of my life.

I sat in that ballroom, enthralled, writing notes so fast I couldn't keep up. I found the explanation for so much in my life. The science of attachment. The impact of trauma. The three principles: Connecting, Empowering, Correcting.

I also found solutions. And friends. And, finally, hope.

Through conversations with colleagues who became friends, we realized: we needed TBRI not just for parents, but for schools. Think about it. When not on break, kids spend more weekday waking hours in school than they do with their families. If relationally-informed care matters at home, it matters in classrooms.

While in that training, I was offered the chance to work for an organization that taught TBRI. My purpose? Figure out how to translate TBRI into the classroom.

Going All In

When I first started implementing relationally-informed practices in my classroom, I did it slowly and steadily, in small chunks. But eventually, I decided to go all in.

It was during a second-semester class with a pretty big number of students who had failed the previous terms. These were 9th graders, and failure to pass impacted graduation. The kids were disengaged, and I was feeling hopeless.

This time, I tried something different. I made sure my lessons had sensory elements. I encouraged play through the curriculum. I tried to greet every kid at the door. I built in choice wherever I could. "You can work at your desk or at the back table. Your choice." "Want to use a pen or pencil?" Small things that gave them some sense of control.

I sent students to the office far less often. I allowed second chances instead of punitive measures. I focused on my own regulation so I could co-regulate with kids when they needed it.

In essence, I changed how I was showing up.

I didn't change the kids. I didn't alter the academic expectations. I changed my approach and my perception.

And here's what happened: by the end of that term, we dropped from over 20 F's to 5 total.

Let me say that again. From 20+ failures to 5.

When administrators asked what changed, the only answer I had was my shift toward more trust, compassion, and curiosity. Everything else stayed the same. Same direct instruction. Same basic assignments. It was my perception and interaction that made the difference.

That's when I realized this shift in mindset is the best answer we have right now. Not a perfect answer. (There are no perfect answers when you're working with humans.) But the best tool we currently have to help both teachers and students.

I've spent the last several years figuring out how to bring relationships and sensory-friendly interventions into classrooms. And the most amazing outcome hasn't been the data or the test scores. It's been the slow rekindling of my love for teaching.

I now greet students with "hello, sunshine." I have rediscovered my joy, and that joy is transferring to my classroom and my students.

Don't kid yourself. The job is still ridiculously difficult. Some days I just want to quit, crawl under my desk, and pretend I'm furniture. I'm not sure teaching will ever be less stressful.

But my ability to cope, connect, and honestly enjoy it has returned.

That's what I want for you. Not perfection. Not an end to the stress. But the ability to cope. To find moments of joy again. To remember why you started teaching in the first place.

This road has had so many ups and downs, but what I have learned is this: **when we put the foundation of our interactions with people in connection and relationship, we won't be disappointed.**

This chapter introduces the framework (TBRI) plus the other great works that brought Amie back.

By the end of this chapter, you'll have:

- A quick tour of the brilliant people who figured this out
- A visual way to understand what's happening in nervous systems (yours and your students')
- Three principles that form the foundation of everything else in this book
- And maybe, just maybe, a little more hope than you had when you started

The science isn't extra credit. It's the foundation.

And now you're ready to build on it. Let's start pouring into that foundation.

The Infinity Stones of Relationally-Informed Care

~ Marti ~

Before we get further into the research, I want to thank and introduce a few of the people whose work changed my life. These aren't ivory tower academics only publishing papers. These are people I have worked with who have influenced my life both personally and professionally. These are practitioners who got their hands dirty, who worked with real kids in real crisis, and who developed strategies that actually work. These are the people we refer to as the infinity stones in the opening.

Dr. Karyn Purvis (1949-2016)

Karyn Purvis is the reason Amie is still teaching.

She co-created Trust-Based Relational Intervention (TBRI) with Dr. David Cross at Texas Christian University, and here's what we love about her: she didn't develop these strategies in a research lab. She developed them in her living room with real kids.

Dr. Purvis cared for children everyone else had given up on. Kids labeled "too damaged" or "too difficult." Kids the system had written off. And then she proved everyone wrong.

Her approach was beautifully simple: work with families, try something, see what works, adjust what doesn't. Street-level problem-solving. Figuring it out because you have to.

It sounds familiar because that's what classroom teachers do every day. We loved her immediately for that.

Dr. Purvis challenged us to see children as kids who've been hurt, not kids who are broken. She believed behavior makes sense when you understand the story behind it. And she showed us that kids can heal with the right support.

She passed away in 2016, but her work lives on in thousands of practitioners, parents, and yes, teachers who are doing things differently because of what she taught us.

Dr. David Cross

If Dr. Purvis was the heart of TBRI, Dr. Cross was the brain. He's a developmental psychologist who brought the academic rigor that made TBRI evidence-based, not just heart-based.

He's the one who got TBRI listed on the California Evidence-Based Clearinghouse for Child Welfare. That matters because it means this isn't just feel-good stuff. It's research-backed, outcome-measured, "show me the data" stuff.

Marti describes him as one of the kindest, most helpful, most humble humans she's ever worked with. At his retirement party, she was not alone in describing him as a father-like figure. His quote that sticks with us: "TBRI is like DNA: it's inert until someone brings it to life." That someone is you. You're the one who brings it to life.

Dr. Bruce Perry

You know how we've shifted from asking "What's wrong with you?" to "What happened to you?" That's Dr. Perry.

He's a psychiatrist and neuroscientist who has spent his career studying how trauma impacts developing brains.

What he discovered changed everything: you can't do cognitive work with a kid whose survival brain is running the show. This isn't a choice. It's biology.

His books, including *The Boy Who Was Raised as a Dog* and *What Happened to You?* (co-authored with Oprah), are essential reading. But his bottom line is simple: "Healing happens in relationships, in rhythm, in repetition."

Marti has been on his team since 2010 when he formed the Neurosequential Network, a vast community committed to researching, educating, and implementing trauma-informed, compassionate, and developmentally based treatment plans. He is the reason Marti left the school system when she answered his call. He is the catalyst of her career arc into relationally-informed advocation.

Robyn Gobbel

Robyn is a trauma therapist and advocate. She and Marti developed a close friendship and shared clients when they both worked in Austin. Marti currently sits on her team as a coach for her immersive program.

Robyn created the owl, watchdog, and possum framework that we'll explore soon, and she has a gift for explaining brain science in ways that are relatable.

Her book, *Raising Kids with Big, Baffling Behaviors*, and her podcast, *The Baffling Behavior Show*, are Marti's go-to resources. She founded a professional on-line immersion program and The Club. It is the best on-line resource available for caregivers who love kids with big, baffling behaviors.

Robyn's mantra: "Regulated, Connected [humans] who feel safe and know what to do behave well." Write that down. Put it on a sticky note. It will save you on hard days.

Tracy Stackhouse, MA, OTR/L

Tracy is the co-founder of Developmental FX and a go-to guru for understanding sensory, affective, and motor processing. Her free *Spirited Conversations* podcast is packed with practical wisdom. Find her at developmentalfx.org. Marti has taken her SpIRiT Model and S.T.E.P.P.S.I. courses and is a loyal listener of her podcasts. Tracy also consulted with Marti's second book, *Sensory Healing Through Developmental Trauma.*

Amy Lewis, MS OTR/L

Amy is an OT friend of Marti's who has spent hours with her thinking about anatomy and regulatory responses of the nervous system. As another champion for children, Amy coauthored Powerfully You with another OT, Heather Spann. Powerfully you is a self-regulation curriculum, that emphasizes a lens of compassion, connection, and the value of individual differences. The curriculum brings together concepts of interoceptive awareness, sensorimotor tools, relationship-based approaches, and self-compassion practices in kid friendly ways. It's great for classrooms. Powerfullyyou.org is where you can lear more.

Kelly Mahler, OTD, OTR/L

Kelly's award-winning *Interoception Curriculum* helps people understand what's happening inside their bodies, because you can't regulate what you can't feel. Tons of free resources at kelly-mahler.com. Marti has taken her course and uses many of her worksheets and quick content with caregivers.

Cara Koscinski, OTD, OTR/L

Cara is the author of *Interoception: How I Feel, Sensing My World from the Inside Out*, a practical, research-backed guide to understanding why kids (and grown-ups) struggle to read what their own bodies are telling them. As a parent to children with autism and sensory processing disorder herself, Cara brings both professional precision and personal passion to her work, which is exactly the kind of combination we love. Find her and her fabulous resources at CaraKoscinski.com.

Dr. Stephen Porges

Dr. Porges gave us the owner's manual for the nervous system. He created Polyvagal Theory, which explains why we have three different states (not just "fight or flight" but also "shut down" and "safe and social"). He also gave us the concept of "neuroception," which is your body's below-the-radar detection system for safety and danger.

His key insight for teachers: "Your presence matters. Your tone matters. Your face matters. Felt safety is a biological necessity for learning."

A Note on Going Deeper

This list barely scratches the surface. Each of these researchers has a lifetime of work behind them, and there are dozens of other brilliant thinkers we could have included.

If this field captures your interest (and we hope it does), keep reading. Keep learning. Follow these researchers on social media. Listen to their podcasts. Attend their trainings if you can.

The more you understand about how brains and nervous systems work, the more effective you'll be in your classroom. And the more compassionate you'll be with yourself when things get hard.

Here are a few more names worth exploring:

- **Dr. Bessel van der Kolk**: Author of *The Body Keeps the Score*, essential reading on trauma and the body.
- **Dr. Ross Greene**: Author of *Lost at School* and *The Explosive Child*, creator of Collaborative and Proactive Solutions.
- **Dr. Mona Delahooke**: Author of *Beyond Behaviors*, focused on understanding behavior through a neurodevelopmental lens.

- **Dr. Nadine Burke Harris**: Former Surgeon General of California, author of *The Deepest Well*, focused on ACEs (Adverse Childhood Experiences).

The field is full of brilliant, compassionate thinkers who are all working toward the same goal: helping kids heal, helping adults understand, and creating a world where relationships come first.

Welcome to the conversation.

Quick Reference: Books to Start With

If you're feeling overwhelmed by all these recommendations, here's where to start:

For understanding trauma and the brain:

- *What Happened to You?* by Dr. Bruce Perry and Oprah Winfrey
- *Sensory Healing from Developmental* Trauma by Marti Smith

For practical strategies with kids:

- *Raising Kids with Big, Baffling Behaviors* by Robyn Gobbel
- *The Whole-Brain Child* by Dr. Dan Siegel and Tina Payne Bryson
- *The Connected Therapist* by Marti Smith

For understanding your own nervous system:

- *Anchored* by Deb Dana

For the foundational TBRI® approach:

- *The Connected Child* by Dr. Karyn Purvis, Dr. David Cross, and Wendy Lyons Sunshine

For deeper academic understanding:

- *The Boy Who Was Raised as a Dog* by Dr. Bruce Perry

Start with one. See where it takes you. And remember: you don't have to read everything to make a difference. We are grateful that you picked up our book. Sometimes one book, one concept, one shift in perspective is enough to change how you show up for kids.

That's all it takes. One teacher. One relationship. One moment of connection.

The Science Behind "I Just Knew Something Was Wrong"

You've felt it before. You walk into a room and immediately sense tension, even though nobody has said a word. Or you meet someone new and your gut says "nope" before your brain can explain why. Or maybe your brain says, "yup" and you quickly add them to your friend card.

That's not intuition. That's not magic. That's your nervous system doing exactly what it evolved to do: scanning for safety and danger faster than your conscious mind can process.

Dr. Stephen Porges calls this neuroception. It's your body's below-the-radar detection system, constantly reading cues from the environment and from other people to answer one critical question: Am I safe here?

This happens without your permission. Without your awareness. And it happens to your students all day long.

Understanding how this works changes everything about how we teach.

Arousal Continuum and State Dependent Functioning if They Were Our Animal Friends

This is where a deeper dive would be great. Because this is pretty complex stuff and there are some excellent videos, graphics, and books by the actual authors that explain this better than a little chapter section.

Maybe take a pause here and go read "*What Happened to You? Conversations on Trauma, Resilience, and Healing*" by Dr. Perry and Oprah. Then grab "*Raising Kids with Big Baffling Behaviors*" by Robyn Gobbel. They would be great pre-requisite texts for this chapter.

To summarize inadequately: Dr. Perry informs us that our state of being is dependent upon what affordances are available to the different parts of our brain based on our level of perceived stress vs. safety. As the threat increases and safety decreases, the brain moves "resources" to the lower parts of the brain that will match the reaction time and physical needs for that moment. It's really just an academic, more encompassing, and more accurate, way to talk about the upstairs/downstairs brain.

Robyn then matches these states with adorable befriendable animals that give great metaphorical representation of what this looks like in behavior form. Dr. Porges adds the neurological explanation of what parts of the nervous system engage strongest, indicating which of Robyn's owl, watchdog, or possum will be in charge. (Robyn matches her animals with the arousal continuum states. We simplified in this text by adjusting the sizing of our animal friends.)

If we feel like we are safe, our owl is in charge. If we feel threatened and our brain decides hiding is better, the possum gets incrementally bigger with the level of threat. If we feel like getting active is the better option for safety, our watchdog will begin to grow to match the level of threat.

Sometimes, when we are only a little stressed or scared, we can still access the middle parts of our brain. We are on the staircase, so to say. At these moments, the owl and watchdog/possum might play together. Because the brain is complex. Structures don't really just unplug or turn on or off. They are on that dimmer switch. They dial up or dial down instead.

We aren't asking you to fully understand these concepts from this little blurb. Simply let them percolate as we dive a little deeper into the polyvagal theory and TBRI. These concepts will weave within them and hopefully you will feel comfortable with them by the end of this chapter. If this feels like too much, welcome to the buffet. Maybe this tastes like Kale. There are plenty of other sweet treats here if you decide not to put this green science-y stuff on your plate.

Polyvagal Theory in Plain English

Safe and Social (Ventral Vagal State) Robyn's owl is in charge

This is the penthouse suite of nervous system living. When your nervous system detects safety, you have access to your "social engagement system." You can think clearly, connect with others, be curious, learn new things, and regulate your emotions.

This is where we want students to spend most of their time. This is where learning lives in your owl brain.

What it looks like: Relaxed face, easy eye contact, responsive to others, able to listen and process, flexible thinking, sense of humor intact. (If a kid laughs at your terrible teacher jokes, they're probably in ventral vagal owl state.)

Imagine a wise owl sitting on top of a stack of books. He's the biggest in the room and wisely in charge of your control panel and actions/behavior at this moment. Maybe a tiny watchdog or possum is by his side. Content. But ready to assist if needed.

Fight or Flight (Sympathetic Activation) Robyn's watchdog is in charge

When your nervous system detects a threat and it mobilizes for action. The watchdog takes the control panel. Heart rate increases. Muscles tense. Stress hormones flood the system. The body prepares to fight the threat or flee from it. This is incredibly useful if you're being chased by a bear. It's not useful for learning long division. Or fractions. Or honestly any math that requires sitting still and visually tracking something.

What it looks like in other modes: Restlessness, fidgeting, aggression, defiance, hypervigilance, scanning the room, difficulty sitting still, explosive reactions. "Fight" behaviors (yelling, hitting, arguing) or "flight" behaviors (running away, hiding, avoidance).

Imagine a dog moving from being playful, whining for attention to full on barking and biting. Sometimes that watchdog is chasing the owl away. The energy from your nervous system is moving from the upstairs owl brain into more active protective downstairs energy of a watchdog.

Shutdown (Dorsal Vagal State) Robyn's possum state

When the nervous system decides the threat is too big to fight or escape, it goes into energy conservation mode. The body essentially plays possum.

What it looks like: Zoned out, flat affect, "checked out," excessive compliance, difficulty speaking, slowed responses, appearing "lazy" or "unmotivated," dissociation, numbness. This is the kid staring at the wall who looks like they're planning to grow roots.

Imagine a little shy possum that grows bigger as it takes over the brain control panel. As the threat increases, it can fall over and play dead. Maybe the owl is trying to do CPR. Probably not. The stink of a possum usually sends the owl flying away.

Who's in Charge Isn't a Choice

Here's what's crucial to understand: students don't choose which brain state they're in. They have no choice in who is in charge.

When a child's nervous system detects threat (and remember, this detection happens below conscious awareness), they don't decide to become defiant or shut down. Their bodies respond automatically. The "downstairs brain" takes over, and the "upstairs brain" goes offline. They move from connection to protection.

This is why punishing a child in fight-or-flight mode rarely works. They don't have access to the cognition required for consequences. Wise owls know "whooo" is talking. But possums and watchdogs don't understand your verbal words.

You're trying to reason with a nervous system that has temporarily lost access to reason. It's like yelling directions at someone who doesn't speak your language and also happens to be fumbling around in the dark cold basement.

This is also why the quiet, compliant child who never causes problems might actually be struggling the most. Shutdown can look like "good behavior" when it's actually a stress response. And people-pleasing (like Marcus) can mask anxiety rather than signal felt-safety. These are the kids we miss.

The Arousal Continuum: Where Polyvagal Meets the Classroom

Let's connect Dr. Porges's polyvagal theory to Dr. Perry's arousal continuum with a hint of Robyn Gobbel's animal friends.

This chart shows our visual representation of the overlap between Gobbel, Perry and Porges. In short, this shows a continuum from dissociation (possum) towards arousal (watchdog). We have overlayed a window of tolerance to illustrate the optimal learning states as a person moves through this graphic.

The sweet spot for learning is the middle of this continuum. Not too revved up. Not too shut down. Alert enough to engage, calm enough to think.

This is what Dr. Dan Siegel calls the "window of tolerance." Inside that window, we can handle stress, process information, and connect with others. Outside that window, we're either climbing the walls or collapsed on the floor. (Some days, we're both before lunch.)

State	Fear/Terror	Alarm	Alert	Calm	Alert	Alarm	Fear/Terror
Brain Region Active	Brainstem *survival brain*	Midbrain *reactive brain*	Limbic *emotional brain*	Cortex *thinking brain*	Limbic *emotional brain*	Midbrain *reactive brain*	Brainstem *survival brain*
Cognitive State	Dissociation, shutdown	Robotic compliance	Concrete thinking, emotional thinking	Abstract thinking, reflection, creativity	Concrete thinking, emotional reactions	Fight, flight	Reflexive, attacking
Student Behavior	Unresponsive, blank stare, zoned out	Running away, hiding	Restless, distracted	Engaged, curious, able to problem-solve, collaborative	Argumentative, "attention seeking"	Defiant, aggressive	Rocking, running, thrashing
Learning Capacity	**None** Focus on safety	**Almost None** Focus on meeting sensory and safety needs	**Limited** Can learn with support Connect	**Maximum** Ready to learn new concepts	**Reduced** Can learn with support	**Declining Rapidly** Focus on meeting sensory and safety needs	**None** Focus on safety Ensure physical
Teacher Response	Ensure physical safety, quiet presence, rhythmic/repetitive activities	Stay calm, reduce demands, use few words, offer movement or sensory input	emotionally, validate feelings, offer choices, simplify tasks Brain breaks, check-	Teach, challenge, discuss, encourage higher-order thinking	Connect emotionally, validate feelings, offer choices, simplify tasks	Stay calm, reduce demands, use few words, offer movement or sensory input Calm corner,	safety, quiet presence, rhythmic/repetitive activities
Helpful Strategies	Soft blanket, dimmed lights, quiet space	Calm corner, breathing exercises, fidgets, walk breaks	ins, visual supports, predictable routines Fawn	Projects, debates, group work, creative expression	Brain breaks, check-ins, visual supports, predictable routines	breathing exercises, fidgets, walk breaks	Rocking, humming, mirroring Sympathetic
Nervous System	Dorsal Vagal Dissociation	Freeze		Ventral Vagal Social	Flock	Flee	Arousal
Animal							
What it looks like	Checked out	Zoned out, flat, checked out	Slow to respond, disengaged, sluggish	Alert, engaged, curious, connected	Restless, agitated	Reactive, escalating.	Explosive, aggressive, fleeing

Figure by the authors, synthesizing Dr. Bruce Perry's Arousal Continuum, Robyn Gobbel's creature companions (Owl/Watchdog/Possum), and Dr. Stephen Porges's Polyvagal Theory. See Appendix D for recommended reading from these researchers.

Everyone has a different window. Some people have wide windows and can handle a lot of stimulation before they tip over the edge. Others have narrow windows and move into survival mode at the slightest provocation.

Our job is to help students stay inside their window, or get back inside when they've fallen out. We will add some graphics to these windows in the next chapter to help clarify this concept.

Neuroception: The Unconscious Safety Scanner

Remember, all the animals inside our brain control our bodies and behaviors through neuroception. Here's where it gets really important for educators: neuroception reads people more than it reads situations.

Your nervous system isn't primarily asking "Is this classroom safe?" It's asking "Is this person safe?"

And it answers that question by reading nonverbal cues. Specifically:

Facial expressions. Is this face showing warmth or threat? Softness or hardness? Interest or irritation?

Tone of voice. Is this voice melodic and warm, or flat and cold, or sharp and loud? (High-pitched, fast voices signal danger. Low, slow voices signal safety.)

Body language. Is this person's posture open or closed? Relaxed or tense? Moving toward me or away? (We will talk more about body language later.)

Eye contact. Is this person looking at me with warmth, or with judgment, or not at all?

This is happening constantly. Below awareness. In milliseconds.

When your student's nervous system scans you and detects cues of safety (warm face, calm voice, relaxed posture, kind eyes), it sends an "all clear" signal. The social engagement system can stay online. The owl takes control of the brain and learning can happen.

When your student's nervous system scans you and detects cues of threat (tense jaw, sharp voice, rigid posture, cold eyes), it sounds the alarm. The watchdog and possum move towards the brain controls. Fight-or-flight or shutdown begins.

You are a walking, talking cue of safety or threat.

This is why your regulation matters so much. Not because you need to be perfect (please, nobody is perfect, and we've got the therapy bills to prove it), but because your nervous system is literally communicating with your students' nervous systems all day long. Your calm can be contagious. So can your stress.

Interoception: The Missing Piece

There's one more concept that ties all of this together: interoception. Interoception is your body's ability to sense what's happening inside itself. Hunger. Thirst. Temperature. Heart rate. Muscle tension. The need to use the bathroom. Emotions (which are, at their core, body sensations). Think of it as your internal GPS. It tells you where you are on the arousal continuum.

When interoception is working well, you notice early warning signs. "My shoulders are tight. My stomach feels funny. I'm getting irritated. I need a break." You can catch yourself before you tip out of your window of tolerance. *Powerfully You* curriculum would state that your body battery is full. Cara Koscinski has another good resource on this.

When interoception is underdeveloped or disrupted (which is common in kids who've experienced trauma or chronic stress), those internal signals are harder to read. If there was chaos all around them and their caregiver insisted they were "fine", they don't have words for the hard feelings. They may also not want to feel "fine" anymore if "fine" feels so terrible. Emotions become very complicated.

The body might be screaming "DANGER!" but the child has no idea why they suddenly punched someone. (Honestly, they're as surprised as you are.)

This is why "use your words to tell me how you feel" doesn't work for many kids. They literally can't access the information. Their interoceptive system isn't giving them clear data. It's like asking them to read a book that's written in invisible ink. They simply can't see it on their own pages. Even when they know words in other books.

Teaching body awareness matters. When we help kids notice what's happening in their bodies ("Your hands are in fists. Your jaw looks tight. I'm wondering if your body is telling you something"), we're building interoceptive awareness. We're helping them read their own internal cues so they can eventually regulate themselves.

The Big Picture

Polyvagal theory gives us a map. The arousal continuum shows us the territory. Neuroception explains why kids respond to us before they respond to our words. Interoception reveals why some kids can't "use their words" and what we can do about it.

All of these concepts point to the same truth: **felt safety is a body experience, not just a mind experience.**

We can't talk students into feeling safe. We have to help their nervous systems experience safety through our presence, our tone, our face, our consistency, and our care.

This is the science behind everything else in this book. Connection strategies work because they send cues of safety. Sensory supports work because they help regulate the nervous system. Behavior interventions work (or don't) based on whether the child's thinking brain is online.

When we understand how the nervous system works, we stop taking behavior personally and start getting curious. We stop demanding compliance and start offering co-regulation. We stop punishing stress responses and start creating conditions for safety. Conditions for repair, restoration, reflection, and learning.

And that changes everything.

Quick Reference: Neuro Cheat Sheet

Concept	Plain English	Classroom Application
Neuroception	Your body's unconscious safety scanner	Students are reading your face, voice, and body all day. Your nonverbal cues matter more than your words.
Calm/Alert (Safe & Social) Robyn's owl	Thinking brain online	This is where learning happens. Our goal is to help students access this state.
Arousal (Fight/Flight) Robyn's watchdog activation	Mobilized for action	Looks like aggression, defiance, hyperactivity, or fleeing. Not a choice. Needs co-regulation, not consequences.
Dissociation (Shutdown) Robyn's possum De-activation	Conservation mode	Looks like compliance, zoning out, "laziness." Actually a stress response. Needs gentle activation and connection.
Window of Tolerance	The zone where we can learn and connect	Every student's window is different. Our job is to help students stay inside or get back in.
Interoception	Noticing what's happening inside your body	Many kids can't read their internal signals. Teaching body awareness builds this skill.
Co-regulation	Your calm nervous system helping someone else settle	Your regulation is contagious. Find your calm before you try to share it.

The Three Principles of TBRI®: Connecting, Empowering, Correcting

TBRI® (Trust Based Relational Intervention) was developed by Dr. Karyn Purvis and Dr. David Cross at TCU, originally for children who experienced trauma, abuse, or neglect. Dr. Perry would say these children experienced early childhood adversity. Robyn Gobbel would say they have big baffling behaviors.

Here's the thing: all humans have nervous systems. All humans need to feel safe. All humans do better when the other humans around them understand how brains actually work. TBRI was created for everyone.

The framework has three principles:

TBRI Principle	What It Means	What We'll Call It
Connecting	Building trust through relationship	Building Relationships
Empowering	Meeting physical and sensory needs so body can settle	Creating Safe and Sensory-Friendly Environments
Correcting	Responding to behavior in ways that teach rather than punish	Responding to Behaviors in Ways That Actually Work

Let us briefly explain what each TBRI principle means before we talk about how they work together.

Building Relationships (Connecting): Felt Safety First

Building relationships is about creating felt safety. Not just actual safety (though that matters too), but safety a child can feel in their body. Before we can teach, before we can influence behavior, before we can do anything else, a child needs to know: "This adult is safe. This place is safe. I'm okay here."

Remember the upstairs brain and downstairs brain from Chapter 1? A child whose downstairs brain is running the show can't access the parts of their brain where learning happens. Building a safe relationship is what "connects" their upstairs brain to come back online.

A stressed, terrified child can't learn social theories. They're too busy surviving.

And here's something worth pausing on: felt safety looks different for different people. For a neurotypical child from a stable home, felt safety might come from a warm smile and predictable routines. Pretty straightforward.

For an autistic child, felt safety might require dimmer lights, fewer unexpected sounds, and knowing exactly what's happening next. The smile helps, but only if their sensory system isn't screaming "DANGER!" from the fluorescent lights buzzing overhead.

For a child from a culture where authority figures have historically been unsafe (think: communities with complicated relationships to police, schools, or government systems), felt safety with YOU specifically might take much longer to build. It's not personal. It's protective. Their nervous system learned that people in positions of power can't always be trusted. You'll need to earn that trust through consistent, trustworthy behavior over time.

For a child who's been in the foster system, felt safety might mean knowing you'll still be there tomorrow. And the day after. And the day after that. Permanence matters when you've experienced too much impermanence.

The point? "Safe" isn't one-size-fits-all. We have to learn what safety feels like for each individual child, not just assume our version of safety translates to theirs.

Creating Safe and Sensory-Friendly Environments (Empowering): Giving Back What Trauma Takes

Trauma steals a child's sense of control. Things happened to them that they couldn't stop, couldn't predict, couldn't escape. Their brain learned: "Remember these sensations. Protect the body at all costs if we start to feel them again."

This is why some kids seem so controlling. They're not trying to take over your classroom. They're trying to predict what's going to happen so they can protect themselves. It looks like control, but it's really a desperate search for safety.

Empowering means giving back appropriate control. Offering choices within structure. Meeting sensory and physical needs so the body can settle. Helping kids feel capable instead of helpless.

This is NOT about letting kids run wild. Trust us, we've tried that as fresh new educators full of energy and optimism. Zero stars. Do not recommend. There may have been glitter involved. It's still in the carpet. It will outlive us all.

Creating safe and sensory-friendly environments says: "You're not powerless. You have some say in what happens here. And I'll teach you the skills you need to make good choices."

Creating safe and sensory-friendly environments is also recognizing our different sensory needs. Recognizing our different neurotypes. Recognizing how our past and attachment styles influence what we need to feel safe and connected. Then meeting those needs without shame, punishment, or judgment. It means there's no perfect "sensory diet" that's universal for all people. We must ask questions and seek to understand the world's sensations through the eyes of people different from us. Less cookie cutter, more curiosity.

Responding to Behaviors (Correcting): Discipline That Connects, Not Isolates

This is the principle people question most. How do you influence behavior while maintaining connection?

The key is responding in ways that teach rather than punish. Responding to behaviors while keeping the relationship intact. Reframing the child's beliefs about themselves from "I'm bad" to "I made a mistake and I can try again."

Traditional correction often severs connection. Time outs that isolate. Consequences that shame. Punishments that confirm what the child already believed: "I'm not worth caring about."

Relationally responding to behaviors does the opposite. It holds the boundary while holding the relationship. It says "I see you made a mistake AND I still believe in you." That's revolutionary. Especially for kids who've learned the opposite.

And here's the optimism: respected people mirror respect. When we fill someone else's cup, they can then pour into others.

We'll dive deep into what this looks like practically in its own chapter later. For now, just know: correction without connection rarely produces lasting change. We can't teach manners when our needs aren't met.

You might hear other names for these same ideas. Dr. Perry talks about "Regulate, Relate, Reason." Trauma-informed circles talk about "bottom-up approaches."

Marti's personal favorite: "Needs-es before pleases."

Say it out loud. It's catchy. It rhymes. And it's true.

This Isn't a Checklist (It's a Dance)

Here's something critical to understand before we go any further: these three principles are NOT a linear process.

You don't complete Step One: Build Relationship, then move on to Step Two: Create Environment, then finally arrive at Step Three: Influence Behavior.

That's not how it works. That's not how kids work. That's not how nervous systems work.

In reality, you're doing all three at once, adjusting the balance moment to moment based on what the situation needs. Like a DJ at homecoming. You are dialing between all three for that perfect dance vibe.

You're building relationship AS you influence behavior. You're meeting sensory and safety needs WHILE you connect. You're meeting needs IN THE MIDDLE OF setting limits.

Let us show you what this looks like:

The Redirect with Warmth: You're physically redirecting a student back to their seat, but your voice carries warmth instead of irritation. Building relationship and behavioral influence happening simultaneously.

The Wiggly Kid Strategy: You're letting a wiggly kid sit next to you during circle time, maybe even letting their foot rest against your leg so they don't launch themselves across the room. Meeting sensory needs and building relationship, woven together.

The Peppermint Solution: You're handing a student a piece of gum to keep their mouth busy so they stop interrupting your lesson. Sensory support serving behavioral influence while maintaining your relationship.

The Calm Firm Voice: You're using a low voice to give a clear boundary. You're meeting needs (yours and theirs), you're building a relationship (the tone says "I'm still for you"), and you're responding to behavior (the limit is clear). All in one sentence.

That's what relationally informed teaching looks like. You're reading the room, reading the child, reading your own nervous system, and blending meeting safety and sensory needs, building relationships, and influencing behavior in real time.

Some moments need more relationship building. Some moments need more sensory support. Some moments need clear behavioral influence. Most moments need all three in varying proportions.

Let's Get Real: When You're Not Sure Which Animal You're Dealing With

Amie: Okay, I love these animals. Owls, watchdogs, possums. Adorable. Very helpful metaphors. But here's my problem: in real life, kids don't come with labels. Nobody walks in wearing a "Hello, I'm a Watchdog Today" name tag.

Marti: That would make our jobs significantly easier.

Amie: Right? So how do I actually tell the difference? Because sometimes a kid looks calm and I'm thinking "great, there's my owl," but you're telling me they might actually be a people pleasing possum?

Marti: Welcome to the trickiest part of this whole framework. Owls and possums can look almost identical from the outside. Both are quiet. Both are compliant. Both are sitting in their seats not causing problems.

Amie: So how do I know which one I've got?

Marti: Look for signs of life. An owl is engaged. They're tracking you with their eyes, maybe nodding, responding when you ask questions. There's a warmth there, a presence. A possum is... vacant. The lights are on but nobody's home. They might be staring at you, but they're staring through you. Flat affect. Minimal response. They're not calm. They're dissociating.

Amie: What about the watchdog? That one seems easier to spot.

Marti: Usually, yes. Watchdogs are loud. They're the fight-or-flight kids. Arguing, pacing, can't sit still, maybe getting aggressive. Their nervous system is screaming "DANGER" and they're ready to fight back or bolt. But here's the twist: some watchdogs don't bark. Some pace quietly. Some just vibrate with tension while staying perfectly silent.

Amie: So I could have a quiet watchdog AND a quiet possum AND a quiet owl, all sitting in the same row, all looking "fine"?

Marti: Welcome to teaching! It's basically a video game where all the animals are shape shifters.

Amie: (laughing) Great. This is very reassuring.

Marti: Here's what helps: watch the body. Owls have relaxed shoulders, open posture, easy breathing. Watchdogs have tension. Clenched jaw, tight shoulders, restless legs, shallow breathing. They're coiled. Possums have almost NO tension. They're floppy. Slumped. Like someone let all the air out.

Amie: Coiled versus collapsed.

Marti: Exactly. Watchdog is all wound up with nowhere to go. Possum has given up entirely.

Amie: And what if I genuinely can't tell? What if I'm staring at a kid and I have no idea which animal I've got?

Marti: Start with connection. A soft voice, a gentle check-in, proximity without pressure. If they're an owl, great, you've just reinforced safety. If they're a watchdog, your calm might help them settle. If they're a possum, your warmth might help them peek out. Connection is rarely the wrong move.

Amie: So when in doubt, be a calm and connected owl yourself and see what happens.

Marti: Now you've got it. Your safety invites their safety. Be the owl you wish to see in the world.

Amie: That belongs on a motivational poster. With a very wise, very adorable owl.

Marti: Robyn Gobbel has some great graphics about this already. Let's hit the next chapter to see some of the adorable animals we created in Canva.

Takeaways

1. **TBRI wasn't built in a lab; it was built in living rooms.** Dr. Purvis and Dr. Cross developed these strategies with real kids solving real problems. That's why they work and why they translate from foster homes to classrooms.
2. **Compliance Can Be a Costume.** That quiet kid who never causes trouble? They might be in dorsal vagal shutdown, not peaceful engagement. Shutdown looks like "good behavior" but it's actually a stress response. The possum isn't calm. The possum is playing dead. These are the kids we miss, and missing them matters.
3. **It's a Braid, Not a Staircase.** connecting, empowering, correcting aren't steps you complete in order. They're strands you weave together constantly. You're building relationship AS you redirect behavior. You're meeting sensory needs WHILE you connect. Less linear checklist, more live jazz.

Reflection Questions

1. Which of the three principles (Building Relationships, Creating Safe Environments, Responding to Behaviors) feels most natural to you? Most challenging? Why?
2. The Possum Parade: Think about your quiet, compliant students. The ones who never cause problems. Could any of them actually be in shutdown mode rather than genuinely engaged? What would help you tell the difference between peaceful participation and playing possum?
3. The Invisible Ink Problem: The chapter describes interoception like "reading a book written in invisible ink." Think of a student who seems genuinely surprised by their own behavior. Could they be struggling to read their internal signals? What might help them notice their body's early warning signs?
4. Your Broadcasting Body: The chapter says you're a "walking, talking cue of safety or threat." When you're stressed, what does your body broadcast? (Tight jaw? Clipped tone? The dreaded Teacher Glare of Doom?) How might your students be reading those signals?

One Thing to Try Tomorrow

Feel Before You Speak

Before you speak to a student who's escalating (or shutting down), take three seconds to adjust your broadcast:

- **Face:** Soften it. Unclench that jaw. Maybe even let your eyebrows relax from their "I've asked you seventeen times" position.
- **Voice:** Drop it lower and slower. High and fast signals danger. Low and slow signals safety.
- **Posture:** Open up. Uncross those arms. Relax those shoulders from their vacation near your ears.

Then speak.

Three seconds of body awareness can change the entire interaction. Your nervous system is contagious. Make sure you're spreading the good stuff.

CHAPTER 4

From Science to Strategy

~ Marti ~

I need to confess something: I love shortcuts and novel ways to imagine possibilities.

Possibilities where you look at a complicated problem, squint at it sideways, and think, "There has to be an easier way to explain this."

It's an occupational therapy thing. We spend our careers breaking down tasks into smaller pieces, finding workarounds, and hunting for that one tweak that makes the impossible suddenly possible. I love seeing someone's face light up when something finally clicks. That's the good stuff. That's why I do this work.

So when I started learning about attachment theory, polyvagal theory, arousal continuums, windows of tolerance, and seventeen other frameworks with intimidating names, my OT brain immediately started looking for patterns. Where do these theories overlap? What do they all agree on? And how can I explain this to a teacher who has forty-five seconds between classes and zero bandwidth for jargon?

Turns out, all these brilliant researchers were circling the same basic truths. This chapter connects them. Consider it your cheat sheet for seeing the need behind the behavior. Maybe even a "window" into the why.

This first graphic is my attempt to introduce the window of tolerance with the arousal continuum, and attachment concepts. With a touch of adorable animal cuteness.

A Window into the World of Attachment & Adorable Animals

How attachment influences arousal continuum animal tendencies.

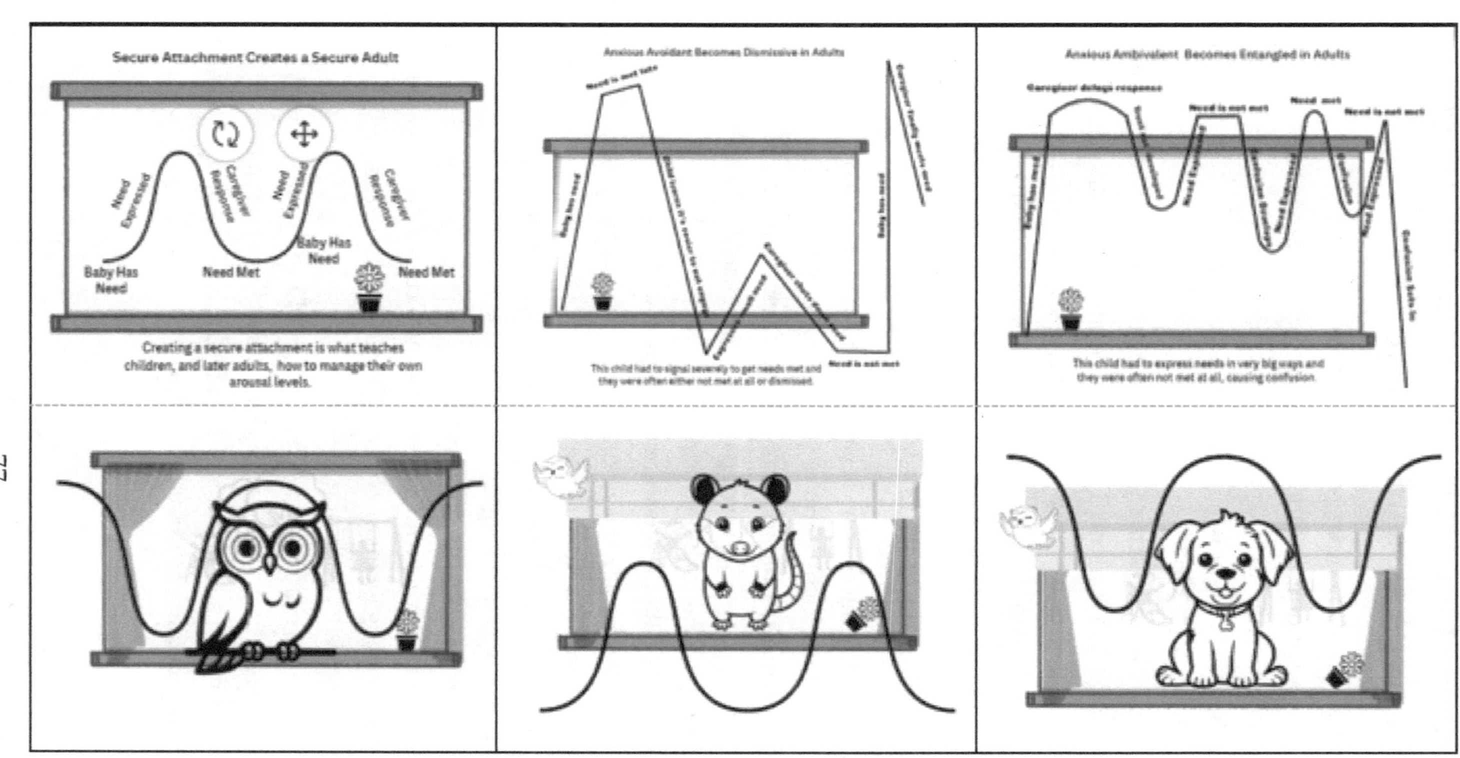

The Impact of the Infinity Stones on The Window of Tolerance: A Visual Framework

Marti thinks in pictures, so we will present this concept visually.

Imagine a window. Not a fancy window with wireless shades or fancy window treatments. Just a regular window in your classroom. The kind that lets in light when it's open and leaves you fumbling in the dark when it's closed.

That window represents your capacity to handle what's coming at you in any given moment. The word "moment" is important. Dr. Perry's work informs us this window changes with each new sensation. Humans have many sensations. Some of your students have LOTs of big sensations.

When the Window Is Wide Open

When your window is wide open, you feel connected. Present. Maybe even a little joyful. You're fully engaged with what's happening while also able to think ahead. Your students ask questions and you answer them patiently. A kid spills something and you handle it without losing your cool. Principal Navy walks in and you think, "Great, they'll see something good."

Dr. Perry would say this is a state of calm emerging into alert. Attachment theory says you are secure. You can express a need and trust it can be met with ease, without being outside of your window.

In Robyn Gobbel's language, your **owl** is in charge. Wise, watchful, ready to learn and connect.

In polyvagal terms, your **ventral vagal pathway** is activated. That's the social engagement system. The part that allows for connection, curiosity, and calm.

This is where learning lives. For you AND for your students.

What does it look like? Relaxed face. Easy eye contact. Responsive to what's happening. Flexible thinking. Humor intact.

"If you can laugh at the fart jokes, you're probably in this state."

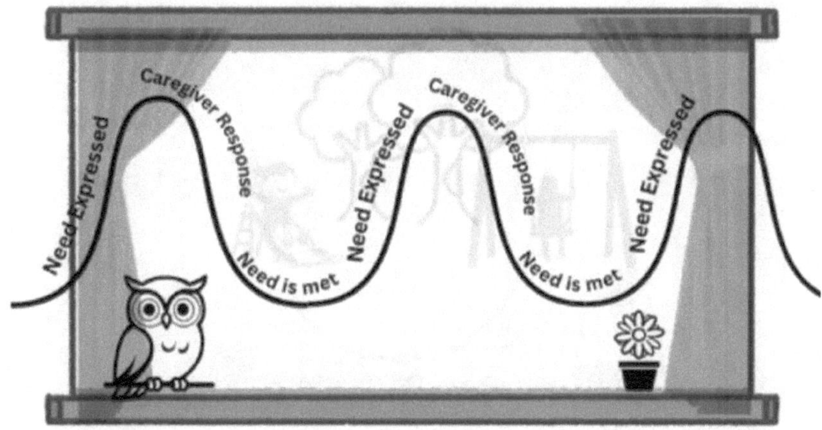

In the graphic, we have overlayed the window of tolerance with the secure attachment illustration. This illustrates that when a person has secure attachment. They have practice being upset and then a caregiver co-regulating them back into optimal arousal levels that help keep their nice big window open.

When the Stress Is Bumping the Edges of the Window

When your stress response is bumping the edges of the window, the same situations that would normally be fine now feel harder. You're managing, but just barely. The stress feels a little bigger.

Maybe you're running late. Distracted by something at home. Didn't sleep well. Skipped breakfast. Your window isn't closed, but you don't have much margin.

The metaphor I love: "Driving with a full gas tank versus driving on fumes. Same car, same road. One has margin for detours."

This state can also illustrate energy going UP (restlessness, need for movement) or energy going DOWN (need for rest, quiet). Both are normal. Both are manageable. But you're closer to the edge than you'd like to be.

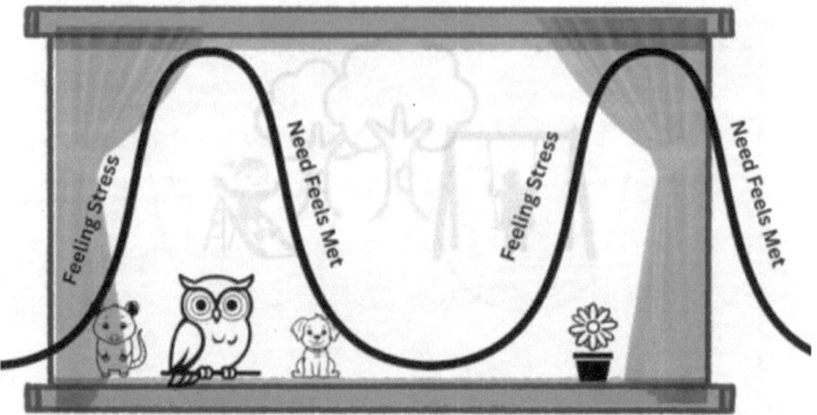

This could also represent play and rest. When Robyn's owl and watchdog hop up on our window sill to say "what's up?" or "let's chill." Maybe the upward energy is from a short movement break you do as a class and the downward energy is settling into silent reading time. You're still within your window of tolerance, but it won't take much more to push you out of it. Your owl is still bigger and in charge. But your watchdog and possum are starting to engage.

When we are Outside Our Window of Tolerance

This window represents when situations are more stressful than we have affordance for. Instead of just being thirsty, you have a migraine. They're doing construction on the playground and the noise is distracting you from your classroom. Principal Navy is knocking on your door because it's an unexpected fire drill.

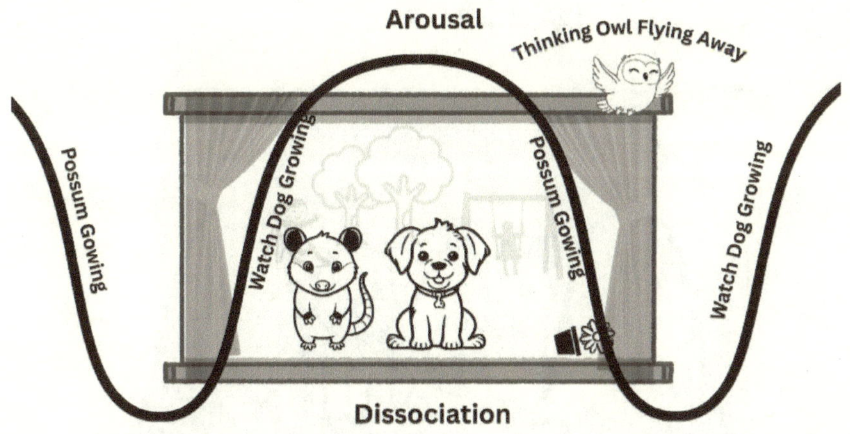

When the stressors become bigger, we can start to get outside of our window of tolerance, and our owl begins to fly away. This is being human. We're no longer our "best selves." We may be thinking short term. What do I need to do now? instead of What will I do later? We may flinch when a noise startles us when we wouldn't flinch without the migraine.

Every teacher knows this feeling. It's 2:47 PM on a Friday before a long weekend, someone spilled glue in the art corner, the copier jammed on your worksheets, and a parent just sent their third email of the day. Your owl has officially left the building.

The animal that steps up depends on how your brain predicts the outcomes based on your past experiences. If the copier jams all the time and you know the right open/slam sequence, your watchdog will engage and frustratingly fix the problem. If you feel helpless, your owl will engage and those copies just moved online or got cut from the lesson plan.

What Narrows the Window?

When our things happening in our "background" give us less affordance or capacity for stress, our window gets smaller. It starts to close in on us. The same stress that wouldn't bother us on a *good day* is too much for *this day*.

Things can shrink that window down to almost nothing from moment to moment:

- **Trauma history:** Past experiences that taught the nervous system the world isn't safe
- **Anxious, avoidant, or dismissive attachment styles:** these impact our ability to trust and predict the ebb and flow of relationships
- **Chronic stress:** Ongoing pressure at home, at school, in relationships
- **Lack of sleep:** The brain literally can't regulate well when exhausted
- **Hunger:** Low blood sugar makes everyone's window smaller
- **Sensory overwhelm**: Too much noise, light, movement, or stimulation
- **Sensory ambiguity:** not enough noise, light, movement, or stimulation for the nervous system to diagnose threat level
- **Relational disconnection:** Feeling alone, unseen, or unsupported

- **Unpredictability:** Not knowing what's coming next

It is also worth noting here that adults should have bigger windows as a base. Because more of their frontal cortex has been developed as they age. When the adult's window begins to narrow, their window gets smaller and they may behave as if they are younger. And when a child's window is wide open, it is still not as wide as an adults should be in the same conditions. This is another reason the teacher needs to keep their window open. Remember, you are the thermostat. Your window needs to be open let more warm fresh spring air in to help co-regulate your classroom.

A few more window-shrinkers that deserve specific attention:

Code-switching exhaustion. Students who navigate between different cultural contexts (home language vs. school language, home communication style vs. "professional" communication, cultural identity vs. dominant culture expectations) are doing invisible labor all day. That labor costs energy. Energy that then isn't available for learning, self-regulation, or resilience.

Masking. Neurodivergent students (especially autistic students and those with ADHD) often "mask" their natural ways of being to fit in. They suppress stimming. They force eye contact that feels uncomfortable. They try to follow unwritten social rules that don't come naturally. Masking is exhausting. By the end of the school day, these students may have nothing left. Their window has been slowly shrinking all day while they worked to appear "normal."

Microaggressions. Small, repeated slights based on race, ethnicity, gender, disability, or other identities add up. Each one is a tiny stress. But they accumulate. A student who experiences multiple microaggressions throughout the day has a narrower window by afternoon than a student who didn't have to navigate any of that.

Unrecognized needs. When a child has sensory needs, learning differences, or other support requirements that haven't been identified or accommodated, they're constantly working harder than their peers just to stay afloat. Undiagnosed ADHD? Narrow window. Unrecognized auditory processing differences? Narrow window. Sensory sensitivities no one has noticed? You guessed it.

The point isn't to feel overwhelmed by all the possible window-narrowers. The point is to stay curious. When a student's window seems surprisingly small, there might be factors you can't see. Respond with compassion rather than frustration.

For students with adversity in their backgrounds, windows are often chronically smaller. Their owl might be seasonal at best. Like a bird that migrates south for the winter, except this winter has lasted their whole life.

Here's something important: you can't always know which of these factors are affecting a particular student on a particular day. You don't get a morning report that says "Noah didn't sleep last night, hadn't eaten breakfast, and his parents were fighting again."

All you get is the behavior. The shutdown. The outburst. The refusal.

But when you understand that something is narrowing their window, you can respond differently. Instead of demanding they widen it through sheer willpower (which doesn't work), you can help create conditions that allow it to open naturally.

Dampening the Stress

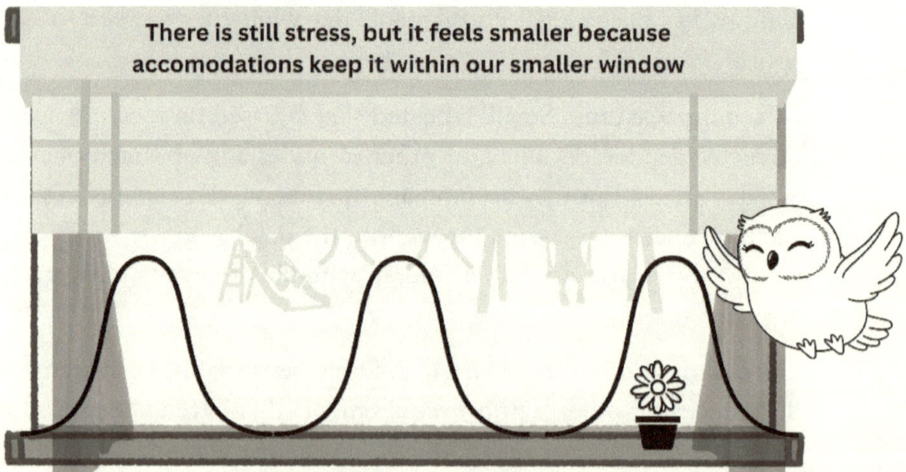

When we have a smaller window of tolerance, we have to lower the stress that we can control. I could opt for glue sticks instead of the spillable bottles. We can play our favorite classical music in the background during the lesson. We can wear our Loop ear buds to dampen the pep rally noise. When we adapt for our own sensory needs, we can still stay within our window with the same stimulus. Because we've dampened the stressors.

IEP accommodations are provided for students so that the demand matches their smaller windows for specific school related tasks. Same for sensory supports.

The key here is that our brain is given predictability. When we can expect stressful things and "control" them by predicting how they'll play out, it dials down the stress response. Sensory support and predictability is practically a superpower in the classroom.

When the Window Is Slammed Shut, Boarded up, or Broken

Sometimes the stressor is more than we can tolerate. Too many straws on the camels back or something really big and scary happens. Our protective responses engage the fight/flight/terror systems. The window slams shut. Now we're in trouble territory.

Situations feel more stressful than you have capacity for.

This can look like movement going UP (watchdog):

- Restlessness and agitation
- Aggression or sharp reactions
- Defiance or "fight" energy
- Heart racing, muscles tense
- Words coming out before you think them through

In Robyn's language, the **watchdog** (fight/flight) has so much energy he has busted the window.

Or the window can look like movement going DOWN (possum):

- Zoned out, flat affect
- "Checked out" and not really present
- Excessive compliance (yes to everything, engaged with nothing)
- Moving slowly, speaking quietly
- Just trying to get through

In Robyn's language, the **possum** (shutdown) wants to be left alone so much he is nailing the boards to the outside. The **owl** has flown away.

Here's the critical understanding and it is worth repeating often because we are asking you to make such a big paradigm shift: **Students don't choose which state they're in.** This detection happens below conscious awareness. Their nervous system makes the call before their thinking brain even knows what's happening.

"Survival isn't the same as learning. And it definitely isn't the same as connection."

Something else that is important to remember from Chapter 1 is that "stress lives in the body". If we don't allow our body to collapse or explode in these times of perceived intense stress, we hold that tension. Our cortical levels remain high. Our metabolism gets stuck. Our muscles get so tight we start having joint pain.

A way that Marti likes to re-phrase this is: "Sometimes, our watchdog needs to really bark and our possum needs that nap". That's biology. It's being human. We shouldn't be calm robots our entire lives.

If you feel like a watchdog, cue up the angry girl music in your car and scream your way home. Or, in the classroom, invite your students to literally "shake it off". Wiggle your body in a rhythmic and jumpy way. Or, let out a really big audible sigh if you are feeling like a possum. There is an entire therapy called somatic healing that we will talk more about in the self-care chapter at the end of this book. For now, cue up the Taylor Swift or a boring midterm paper that will make you yawn. Express the stress. Release the hound and pamper the possum.

Opening the Window Back Up

An important thing to consider as we look at the window of tolerance is how the window can adjust. When our window feels like it is closing down, we can do things to open it before the stressors appear. We can have a plan beforehand (adding predictability again). We can bring in a buddy. We can drink caffeine, go for a walk, or eat something sour to help us open up the window to allow more stress before it tips us out.

Relationships and meeting our sensory needs are great ways to open that window. I like to imagine a good friend being another owl who flies in and helps to open my window when life gets difficult. Sometimes all it takes is a colleague popping their head in to say, "Hey, you doing okay?" "I'll help you make those copies on the band hall printer" and suddenly our window widens.

Window-openers worth noting:

Representation and belonging. When students see themselves reflected in curriculum, classroom materials, and the adults around them, their nervous systems receive a subtle but powerful safety signal: "You belong here." This matters for students of color, LGBTQ+ students, students with IEPs, and anyone who might otherwise feel like an outsider. Belonging opens windows.

Permission to be yourself. For neurodivergent students, knowing they can stim, move, fidget, or use accommodations without judgment is hugely regulating. The energy they'd spend masking gets freed up for actual learning. Acceptance opens windows.Cultural affirmation. When a student's home culture, language, and family practices are honored rather than corrected, their window widens. When they're told (implicitly or explicitly) that the way they do things at home is "wrong," their window narrows. Affirmation opens. Correction closes.

Authentic connection. Not performative "I see you" statements, but genuine interest in who each student actually is. What do they care about? What makes them laugh? What's hard for them? What's their story? Curiosity that's real, not required, opens windows like nothing else.

Meeting sensory and physical needs: Food, water, movement, quiet space, fidgets. Bodies that feel settled help brains that feel settled.

Having some control or choice: Even small choices reduce the desperate grabbing for control. "Would you like to sit here or there?" "Do you want to start with this problem or that one?"

Routine and rhythm: Predictable patterns throughout the day that the nervous system can rely on.

Predictability: When we know what's coming, the nervous system relaxes. Visual schedules, consistent routines, warnings before transitions. These aren't "soft" accommodations. They're neurobiological interventions.

> ***"Predictability is practically a superpower in the classroom."***

When students can predict what's coming, their nervous systems settle. When YOU can regulate yourself (even imperfectly), you model what regulation looks like. When the environment sends safety signals instead of threat signals, everyone's windows stay open a little longer.

Connection with a safe person: One safe and connected adult can help a student settle. This is co-regulation. Your calm nervous system sending signals to their nervous system that safety is possible.

"A good friend is like another owl who flies in and helps open my window when life gets difficult."

Sometimes all it takes is a colleague popping their head in to say, "Hey, you doing okay?" and suddenly your window widens just a bit. **Connection works fast when it's genuine.**

What opens YOUR window?

What Polyvagal Means for Your Classroom

So what does all this science actually mean for your teaching?

1. Your nonverbal cues matter more than your words.

You don't have to be calm all the time (impossible, and also suspicious). We need to simply build awareness of our own nervous system state.

2. Behavior tells you where a student is. It tells you what animal is in charge.

Instead of asking "Why is this kid being so difficult?", ask "Where is this nervous system right now?"

A child in fight-or-flight needs different support than a child in shutdown. A child in the optimal zone can handle instruction that would overwhelm a child who's already at the edge of their window. We have support content in this chapter to help identify these behaviors.

3. "Good behavior" isn't always good.

The quiet, compliant child might be in dorsal vagal shutdown. They're not thriving. They're surviving. Watch for flat affect, checked-out eyes, and over-compliance. These kids need connection and safety just as much as (maybe more than) the kids who are acting out.

4. You can't think your way out of a stress response.

Telling a dysregulated child to "calm down" or "make better choices" is like telling someone having a panic attack to "just relax." The thinking brain is offline. You have to reach the nervous system first.

This means:

Calm your voice (low and slow)

Soften your face

Lower your body (get on their level)

Offer co-regulation (your calm presence)

Reduce demands until they're back in their window

5. Help kids build interoceptive awareness.

Notice body cues out loud. "I see your leg is bouncing. What's your body telling you?"

Teach the vocabulary of body sensations. "When I'm stressed, my shoulders get tight. Where do you feel stress in your body?"

Create opportunities for body check-ins. "Before we start, let's all notice: Are we hungry? Tired? Wiggly? What does our body need right now?"

6. Design your environment to send cues of safety.

Remember, neuroception is scanning everything. Not just you, but the whole space.

Harsh lighting, loud noises, chaotic visuals, and unpredictable routines all send "threat" signals to the nervous system. Warm lighting, predictable structures, calm spaces, and consistent routines all send "safety" signals. Your classroom setup is a form of communication. (More on this in Section Two.)

Common Questions (and Honest Answers)

"Isn't this just making excuses for bad behavior?"

No. Understanding why behavior happens doesn't mean accepting all behavior. We still hold boundaries. We still have expectations. We still respond to behaviors. We just do it in a way that maintains connection and actually produces lasting change.

Think of it this way: understanding that a child has a fever doesn't mean we accept the fever. But it does change how we respond. We don't punish them for being sick. We address the underlying cause.

Behavior is the fever. The nervous system state is the illness. We treat both.

"I don't have time to think about windows and owls when I'm just trying to get through the day."

Fair. And honestly, you won't think about it consciously most of the time. The goal isn't to have a running mental commentary on every student's nervous system state. The goal is to shift your default lens from "Why is this kid doing this TO me?" to "What's happening underneath this behavior?"

That shift, once it becomes a habit, doesn't take extra time. It just changes how you respond.

"What about the rest of the class? I can't focus on one dysregulated kid while 27 others wait."

True. And this is where environment design (Chapter 9) and prevention strategies become essential. When your classroom is set up to meet sensory needs, when predictability is built into your routines, when relationships are strong, you have fewer crisis moments. The work you do proactively reduces the reactive work later.

Also: sometimes your response to one dysregulated kid IS your lesson for the other 27. They're watching how you treat people in hard moments. They're learning what adults do when things get difficult.

"This sounds like a lot of extra work."

Initially, yes. Learning any new framework takes energy. But here's what we've found: the traditional approach (consequences, punishment, control) takes MORE energy over time. You're constantly fighting fires. Constantly battling behaviors that keep coming back.

The relational approach takes more energy upfront but less over time. Prevention is less exhausting than intervention. Connection is less draining than conflict.

Sneaky Regulation Strategies That are Grounded in Polyvagal Theory

Before we move on, let's get practical about something Amie mentioned: regulating yourself when you can't actually stop teaching.

You can't pause your lesson to do a yoga pose every time you feel your nervous system heading south. You've got 28 pairs of eyes on you and curriculum to cover. Here are some strategies that work while you're teaching:

Cold Water Shift: Keep a water bottle at your desk. When you feel yourself escalating, take a drink. The temperature shift is grounding. Especially a cold liquid through a straw.

Pocket Peace: Keep something textured in your pocket. A smooth stone, a piece of velcro, a worry coin. When stress rises, touch it. The tactile input anchors you.

Feet Into Floor: Press your feet into the ground. Really press. This activates your body and sends signals of stability to your brain. Works whether you're standing or sitting.

Strategic Gum: Chewing signals safety to the nervous system. It's rhythmic and activates the jaw muscles. Keep a pack in your desk. Mint gum is even more impactful.

The Teacher Stretch: "I'm going to walk around and check on everyone's progress." What you're actually doing: taking five deep breaths while you walk. Touching the cold window. Adjusting your nervous system under the guise of classroom management. Strategic strolling. A classic.

Mantra Magic: Pick a phrase you repeat to yourself when things get hard. "I can handle this." "This is not an emergency." "30 minutes until lunch." "They're not doing this TO me." Let it be your internal mantra.

None of these will transform a terrible day into a great one. But they might help you stay in your window long enough to help your students stay in theirs.

A Note on Neurodivergent Regulation

If you're neurodivergent yourself (and statistically, many teachers are), some of these strategies might not work for you. That's okay. Regulation is personal.

Some neurodivergent people find that stimming is their best regulation tool. If you can discreetly stim while teaching (bouncing a leg, clicking a pen, rubbing fabric between your fingers), do it. Your students probably won't notice, and your nervous system will thank you. Or, maybe they *do* notice and you have given them non-verbal permission to be their authentic self too.

Some people need MORE input to regulate, not less. If deep pressure helps you (tight clothing, a weighted vest, compression sleeves), wear what works. If intense flavors help (sour candy, strong mints, spicy gum), keep them handy.

Some people regulate through movement. If you're someone who thinks better while pacing, build walking into your teaching style. Circle the room. Use a standing desk. Take the long way to the copy machine.

The strategies that work for neurotypical nervous systems aren't universal. Experiment. Figure out what YOUR nervous system needs. Then give yourself permission to meet those needs, even while teaching.

When Kids Tell You the Hard Stuff: Handling Disclosures

Before we go further, let's clear up some misconceptions.

Having a relationally-focused classroom is not therapy. You're still a teacher, not a therapist. This is a both/and. We want you to hold that boundary. Don't be a therapist.

And. When you become the safe person and you build relationships, you will get what we lovingly call disclosures. Those moments when kids tell you the hardest things in their lives. Someone is hurting them. They want to hurt themselves or others. Things at home are super rough. These are the conversations that make your stomach drop and your heart race.

These moments are terrifying for teachers. Why? Because in all honesty, we are not trained to handle them. We don't really know what to say or do. And frankly, it is well beyond our skill set and licensing.

The good news: you don't have to be a trained therapist to handle a disclosure well. You just need to know a few key things. Here's our practical playbook for these powerful (and sometimes panic-inducing) moments.

The Disclosure Dos and Don'ts

1. **Policy is your protection.** Whenever a student tells you something that should be reported to authorities, Rule Number One is always follow policy. This protects you AND kids. Your school, state, and district have policies in place. Know them. Follow them. Print them out and tape them inside your desk drawer if you need to. When a disclosure happens, you will not be thinking clearly, so having the steps written down somewhere will help keep your owl online.

2. **Keep your response simple and supportive.** When a child tells you something, your only response should be something like, "Thank you so much for telling me. That had to be really hard." Or a variation that fits your personality. That's it. You're not solving anything in this moment. You're simply honoring their courage and letting them know they did the right thing by telling you.

3. **Find your people.** From there, you report to whoever your policy requires. Some states say the teacher calls CPS directly. Some say you notify administration first. Others require you to go through counselors. It doesn't matter necessarily who you report to, as long as policy is followed. The key is knowing your reporting pathway before you need it.

4. **Don't ask questions.** Seriously. Resist every urge. We don't get to ask the questions, and honestly, you don't want to ask the questions. Here's why this matters: if any disclosure goes to law enforcement and they need that disclosure to build a case, your well-meaning questions could actually complicate things. If you've asked leading questions or gathered details, it could make things more difficult if criminal charges end up being filed. Let the trained investigators do the investigating.

5. **Fix your face.** While the student is disclosing, do your best to keep your expression calm and open. Sometimes it's difficult not to get emotional, but do your best to hold it together until you can get them to someone trained to handle this. These kids

already carry enough stress and shame. They don't need to carry yours as well. Your job in that moment is to be a steady, safe presence. Fall apart later. (And you might. That's okay.)

6. **Report quickly.** When kids get to a natural break in the conversation, report to whoever your policy requires. Our rule of thumb: report immediately. If that isn't possible, do it as quickly as possible. Don't wait until lunch. Don't wait until after school. Don't wait until you've had time to "process." The sooner you report, the sooner professionals can step in to help.

7. **This is an inevitable part of relationship building.** When you develop genuine connections with students, disclosures will happen. Here is the permission slip we want to hand you: you are not responsible for treating this or even addressing it. Your only job is to create a safe space for these kids to learn in order to maximize learning and connection. You don't need the details. You don't need the treatment plan. You don't need to be part of the therapy team. You need to be their teacher who made them feel safe enough to speak.

8. **Take care of yourself.** For some teachers, hearing disclosures can create secondary trauma of their own. It could trigger something that happened to you or near you. It could pull every heartstring you have for these kids. We can honestly tell you that between us, we've had our own therapists for decades. Not always the same ones. But just like our kids need help handling some of this stuff, so do we. When we get to the self-care section, we'll give you lots of ideas. Until then, let it percolate: what is your strategy when this happens?

The Bottom Line

When a child chooses you as the person to tell, it's both an honor and a heavy responsibility. You've earned their trust. That matters. But your job isn't to fix what's broken. Your job is to receive what they share with compassion, connect them to the right people, and continue being the safe, steady presence they need in your classroom. That's enough. You are enough.

What Else a Relationally-Focused Classroom Is Not

It's not permissive. This isn't about letting kids do whatever they want. It's about high structure with high nurture. Clear expectations, consistent boundaries, and warm relationships all working together. Structure without rigidity. Boundaries without brutality.

It's not magic. Sorry to burst that bubble. Some kids will respond quickly. Others will take months or years. Some days you'll nail it. Other days you'll want to crawl under your desk and cry. We've been there. Sometimes with the snack box. And chocolate. Definitely chocolate. Possibly also those emergency cheese crackers you hid in your filing cabinet.

It's not one-size-fits-all. The principles are universal, but the application has to be individualized. What works for one kid might not work for another. That's why we stay curious, flexible, and willing to adjust.

It definitely needs to fit your personality. If you try to apply elements that make you super uncomfortable, you won't be successful. You have the skills and the education to take what works for you and leave the rest. We get it and we support it. Use what works. Toss what doesn't.

What a relationally-focused classroom IS: a research-based, brain-aligned, relationship-focused framework that helps us show up for kids in a way that actually supports their development and healing.

That's honestly enough.

A brief conversation on "sexualized behavior"

Whenever we talk about sensory needs and disclosures, there's a watchdog in the room. A big one. The kind of watchdog that makes your possum suddenly find your shoelaces fascinating. That watchdog is children who exhibit behaviors that adults perceive as sexual in nature.

Let's just name it: this topic makes us squirm. It gets dicey from a parental perspective because we never know what's happening at home or in the child's life. It feels scary, sticky, and decidedly not fun. And yet, we have never met a teacher who hasn't had to navigate some version of this. Not one. So let's talk about it together.

Curiosity Is Completely Normal

Children are born curious. Spectacularly, sometimes inconveniently curious. This natural curiosity leads them to touch things and interact with others in ways that can look sexual but are really just developmental exploration. Kids are trying to figure out where their body is in space, learning how different sensations feel. This exploration naturally leads to touching all parts of their bodies. And here's the part that trips us up: touch can bring about a powerful emotional response. Children often find comfort and calming through touching parts of their bodies. It doesn't mean it's sexual. It means their nervous system found something that works.

Context Changes Everything

We also need to recognize that social expectations around touch and physical affection vary widely across cultures. What feels inappropriate in one context may be completely normal in another. Some families and communities are physically affectionate in ways that differ from mainstream American norms. Before we assign meaning to a behavior, we need to consider whether we're viewing it through a culturally limited lens.

Similarly, autistic children often struggle to understand unwritten social rules, including which behaviors are considered private. They may not pick up on the subtle cues that neurotypical children absorb naturally. This isn't defiance or deviance. It's a genuine gap in understanding social expectations. These kids need explicit teaching, not shame.

When Survival Strategies Look Sexual

Some children who have experienced sexual abuse learned that sexual behaviors are a way to get basic needs met: food, attention, affection from caregivers. These children aren't trying to be sexual. They genuinely don't understand other ways to meet these needs. What looks alarming to us is, for them, a survival strategy learned when they were too young to have any other options. This is a teaching moment, not a shaming moment.

Your Role: Safety, Not Sleuthing

As a teacher, it isn't your place to diagnose, assume, or interpret these behaviors. Your job is singular and sacred: create safety. Once safety is established without shame, follow your district policy and procedure.

What does this look like practically? If a child is touching their genitals when upset, can they have a piece of minky fabric or something silky to hold instead? If they're rocking or grinding on furniture, can we offer a rocking chair or flexible seating that provides similar sensory input? We're not ignoring the behavior. We're redirecting the need.

If you see concerning behaviors, do not create shame by calling attention to the situation. No gasping. No public corrections. Quietly move toward the child and offer a gentle redirect. If another child is involved, calmly separate them. Report to the appropriate people in your building and then return to normalizing your classroom.

The Bottom Line

You are a human doing the best you can. So are they. Give them the same grace you're asking for yourself. Sexualized behaviors very rarely indicate predatory intent. Trust your instincts, use your village, and continue working toward felt safety and connection. Respond with grace, compassion, and curiosity. These kids need someone who sees them as whole people, not problems to solve.

The Cost of a New Approach

We need to name something that might be stirring in you right now.

When we learn these new techniques, sometimes it brings up guilt from our past. Because we start to realize how many kids whose true selves we never saw. How many times have we labeled a behavior as "defiant" instead of asking, "What does this child need?" How many opportunities we missed to be a healing presence instead of just another adult doling out consequences.

That regret still haunts us sometimes.

If you're feeling that right now, you're not alone. We've been there. We still go there sometimes, if we're honest.

But here's what we've learned: we can't change the past. We can't go back and redo every interaction with every child who needed us to show up differently.

But we can start today. Right now. With the next kid who walks through our door.

Remember what Maya Angelou said? When we know better, we do better. You didn't know then what you know now. And the fact that you're here, reading this and learning says something about the kind of teacher you are, and the kind of teacher you're becoming.

We can offer you a framework built on hope. On the belief that children can heal. On the conviction that we can be part of that healing, even in small ways, even in our ordinary classrooms.

Let's Get Real: Windows, Wildlife, and Your Wednesday

Amie: When you first explained the window of tolerance with all the owls and watchdogs and possums, I was like, "This is adorable. I love it. But also... I have 28 kids and a fire drill in twenty minutes."

Marti: That's the most teacher response ever.

Amie: My brain went straight to "Cool, but when do I have time to think about windows when I'm trying to survive the day?"

Marti: Here's the thing: the window of tolerance isn't just about understanding your students. It's about understanding YOU. If your window is slammed shut because you're running on coffee and cortisol, you can't help a kid regulate. You can barely regulate yourself.

Amie: That's fair. I definitely know what it feels like when my owl has left the building.

Marti: What are your signs?

Amie: My voice gets tight. I start speed-talking. I get snappy. I say things like "I shouldn't HAVE to tell you this AGAIN." And immediately I think, "Welp, that wasn't my owl talking." Full-on watchdog. Barking at teenagers. Which, spoiler alert, does not improve their behavior.

Marti: So what do you do now when you notice it?

Amie: Try something small. Sip of water. Touch something cold. Three breaths. Doesn't always work, but sometimes it's enough to call the owl back to the windowsill.

Marti: That's literally the science in action. You're giving yourself predictability, a tiny bit of control, dampening the stress enough to stay in your window.

Amie: What surprised me most was that the kids noticed. When I started regulating myself better, they started regulating better too.

Marti: Nervous systems really are contagious. Your felt-safety, or lack of it, spreads. When your window is open, you're inviting their windows to open too.

Amie: What about the kid whose window is basically boarded shut? The kid who comes in Monday morning with that look in their eyes?

Marti: The possum with the hammer.

Amie: Exactly. What do you do with that kid?

Marti: You can't pry a boarded window open. You just can't. What you CAN do is be a safe owl nearby. Stay calm, stay present. Don't demand eye contact, answers, or compliance. Just... exist near them. With warmth. Without pressure.

Amie: That feels really passive. Like, shouldn't I be DOING something?

Marti: Presence IS doing something. For a kid whose nervous system learned that adults are unpredictable or dangerous, your calm consistency is revolutionary. You're not fixing them. You're giving their possum a reason to peek out.

Amie: That's hard. Because I want to help. I want to DO.

Marti: Sometimes the most powerful thing we do is nothing dramatic. We just show up. Predictably. Calmly. Over and over again. Remember, predictability is practically a superpower.

Amie: Okay. But here's my real question. How do I do any of this without stopping my lesson every five minutes?

Marti: You don't have to stop. You just shift the lens. Instead of asking "Why is Marcus throwing pencils AGAIN?" you ask "Marcus's nervous system is outside his window right now. What can I do to help him get back inside?"

Amie: And the answer is...?

Marti: It depends. Sometimes it's "give him space and a stress ball." Sometimes it's "move closer and offer connection." Watchdog kids often need more connection and co-regulation. Possum kids need safety signals and time. Both need you to stay in YOUR window long enough to figure it out.

Amie: So it's really about the reframe. Not diagnosing every kid, but just... noticing that behavior makes sense when we understand the nervous system driving it.

Marti: Exactly. You don't have to perfectly identify watchdog versus possum. You just have to recognize that something's happening beneath the surface and respond to that, not just the behavior you see.

Amie: The shift from "What is WRONG with this kid?" to "What is this nervous system telling me?"

Marti: That shift changes everything. It changed us. Let's help our readers feel that shift next.

Takeaways

1. **You Can't Willpower a Window Open.** Telling a dysregulated kid to "calm down" or "make better choices" is like telling someone mid-panic-attack to "just relax." The thinking brain has left the building. You can't demand that a student widen their window through sheer force of will. What you CAN do is create conditions that let it open naturally: predictability, sensory support, connection, and choices. Stop pulling on the window. Start oiling the hinges.
2. **Predictability Is a Practically Perfect Superpower.** When the nervous system knows what's coming, it settles. Visual schedules, consistent routines, and warnings before transitions aren't "soft" accommodations for sensitive students. They're neurobiological interventions that keep everyone's owl on the windowsill. Predictability prevents possums. Structure soothes the watchdog. Boring routines are secretly brilliant brain science.
3. **Prevention Beats Punishment (and It's Less Exhausting).** The traditional approach of consequences, control, and compliance takes MORE energy over time. You're constantly fighting fires that keep reigniting. The relational approach costs more upfront but pays dividends later. When your classroom is designed for safety, when predictability is baked into your routines, when relationships are strong, you spend less time in crisis mode. Connection is

less draining than conflict. And your emergency cheese crackers last longer.

4. **You're Not a Fixer. You're a Possum Persuader.** Your job isn't to pry kids out of shutdown or wrestle them out of fight mode. It's to be safe and consistent enough that their nervous system starts to believe the coast might actually be clear. You're not performing CPR on the possum. You're just... sitting nearby. Being predictable. Proving that not all humans are threats. Eventually, the possum peeks.

Reflection Questions

1. Think about a currently struggling student. How might understanding their behavior through a window of tolerance lens change how you respond?
2. When do you notice YOUR owl flying away during the school day? What are your early warning signs?
3. What's one small thing you could try to help your own window stay open a bit longer?

One Thing to Try Tomorrow

Window Watch: Check Yourself Before You Wreck Yourself

Before your first class, take 30 seconds to check your own window.

- Wide open? Great. Notice what that feels like. Bookmark it in your body so you can find it again.
- Bumping the edges? Acknowledge it. Take three breaths. You're still in the game.
- Narrowing fast? Do one small thing: cold water on your wrists, feet pressed firmly into the floor, a quick text to a supportive colleague.

You can't widen a student's window if yours is slammed shut. Your regulation comes first. Not because you're selfish, but because you're contagious. Thirty seconds. One check-in. Start there.

Chapter 5
How Learning Works

So we've walked through all these windows. We've met the owl, the watchdog, and the possum. We've talked about what it looks like when our window narrows, when it widens, when it slams shut entirely. We addressed some uncomfortable topics.

If you're anything like us, you might be thinking: *Okay, cool science. But what does this actually look like on a random Wednesday when Joe helped James tape his legs together and Destiny is crying in the corner and you haven't peed since 7:15 AM?*

Fair question. This chapter takes you inside the brain. You'll watch neurons dance, learn why some connections take months to form, and discover why the kid with his hood up might be learning more than the kid taking perfect notes. Let's get into it.

The Dancing Neurons (How Learning Actually Happens)

Here's something wild: in recent years, with new brain imaging technology, we can actually watch learning happen. We can see

neurons connecting in real time. It's amazing. Marti sees oxygen and neurotransmitters and so many things to be excited about.

Amie sees… a dance. Like a gym full of middle schoolers.

Seriously. When you watch these scans, you literally see two little neurons moving and jumping, much like the kids in our classrooms and gym floors, honestly. They're active, bouncing around, full of energy.

After a period of time, they start sending out little arms called dendrites, searching for something to connect to. They dance and search, dance and search, and eventually, when they find another neuron, they create a connection between the two.

This is a neural pathway. This is learning.

Use It, Lose It, or Hold On to It

We also have something called neural pruning. It's the literal "use it or lose it."

We are born with incredibly vast capacity. But if we aren't given the right developmental stimulus during our critical windows, those skills become harder to acquire. There are two seasons of serious neural pruning: toddlerhood and the teenage years. This is one of many reasons the tweenager and teenager can't access their owls. Their brains are too busy running around with garden shears, making life more efficient.

Neural pruning clears the path for new things. It opens the dance floor. It helps keep our pathways efficient. Dancing at a crowded house party makes it really hard to find that perfect partner. Keeping all of our neurons would make it more difficult to form the most efficient connections.

We can easily see this pruning with an example of learning a foreign language. In our toddler and preschool years, the area of the brain that processes language is a prime dance floor. So many dancers looking to hold hands. Like the chicken dance at a 90s wedding.

But if the new language song never comes on, the dancers go back to their sad little round reception tables and we never become bilingual. We don't develop language we don't hear. It's not impossible to learn it as an adult, but definitely more difficult. We don't have as many neurons to dance with after they get pruned in our younger years.

This is important to remember as we think about what skills our students may have missed due to adverse experiences. What if they didn't learn that food would always be available? Or that love was unconditional? What if they never learned how to pour from a cup or turn pages of a library book gently? Those early development skill-ready neurons can get pruned before kids ever arrive in your classroom.

But pruning works both ways. Just as unused pathways get cleared away, heavily used pathways get reinforced and protected. Survival skills like constant vigilance, self-sufficiency, or distrust can become so practiced that they're nearly impossible to prune later. The brain doesn't clear the dance floor when those dancers are performing every single day.

The brain is adaptive to what it experiences. If it experiences frequent chaos, those little dancing neurons choreograph a dance that looks pretty chaotic. Like a neural mosh pit. And once you've learned to mosh, a waltz feels impossibly slow.

The Lightbulb Moment

When Amie teaches, she imagines her students' brains doing a dance. It's exciting to imagine connections being made in real time. They don't get it yet. They're trying. They keep trying. The neurons are dancing, reaching, searching...

And then eventually, the light clicks on. The connection is made. The aha is the neuron music for dancing.

If you're in a classroom, you know this exact moment. The lightbulb. The "Ohhhhh!" The sudden shift from confusion to clarity. Maybe it's the first time they solve that tricky equation. Maybe it's the moment they finally pull off the hoodie and contribute to the class discussion. This is what we live for as educators. We strive for this every single day.

But here's what we need to remember: the dance time varies. Some neurons connect quickly. Other neurons take weeks, months, even years of dancing before they find their partner.

We can't force neurons to connect before they're ready. We can only create conditions that support the learning dance: repetition, multiple entry points, low stress, high engagement. New choreography, new neural pathways.

Neural Pathways: Working With What They Bring

Students don't come to us with blank brains. They come with connections already made based on attachment styles and early life events. They arrive with names already on their dance cards.

Some of those neural pathways are helpful for school:

"When I don't understand something, I ask for help."

"Practice helps me get better."

"Mistakes are part of learning."

Some of those pathways are... less helpful:

"Adults get angry when I ask questions."

"I'm bad at math and always will be."

"If I don't understand something immediately, I'm stupid."

Why "Just Try!" Doesn't Work

Here's the hard truth: building new pathways, especially ones that contradict existing beliefs, is really hard work. It takes time. Repetition. Patience. Relationship.

Think about changing a habit in your own life. Maybe you're trying to drink more water, or go to bed earlier, or stop checking your phone first thing in the morning.

How's that going? Hard, right? Because you're fighting against well-established neural pathways.

Now imagine you're a kid who's spent years building the pathway "I can't do this" every time they encounter something challenging. And then a teacher says, "Yes you can! Just try!"

That's not enough. One statement doesn't override years of repetition. You have to help them build a new pathway: "This is hard AND I can do hard things. With support. With practice. With time."

You're not just teaching content. You're helping rebuild neural architecture. That's why relationships matter so much. A kid is more likely to risk building a new pathway, to try, to struggle, to persist, when they trust the adult guiding them.

And here's where it gets practical: we can use sensory experiences to help rewire those patterns. Neurons that fire together wire together, which means we can intentionally pair new, positive experiences with old, stuck beliefs. It's like helping a kid switch dance partners. They've been dancing with "I can't" for years, and that partner has two left feet. We step in, offer our hand, and show them a new routine. They learn the steps because they're dancing with us first. Success with support becomes the new pathway. Then, eventually, they can dance on their own.

The Brain Under Stress (Why Learning Shuts Down)

When a student is under stress (imagine the owl flying away):

Verbal instructions become harder to process. You can tell a stressed kid what to do, but they're less able to take it in and follow through.

Working memory decreases. They can't hold as much information in their head at once.

Emotional regulation suffers. Little things feel big. Frustration tolerance drops.

Learning new content becomes nearly impossible. Their brain is focused on survival, not on a lesson about photosynthesis or fractions.

The Simple Addition Problem

Let's make this concrete.

Think about explaining two plus two. You know it's four. You could do this in your sleep.

Now, what happens when you're trying to explain that same equation? A child in front of you has a bloody nose. Another kid across the room is throwing something. Administration is at your door. And you're supposed to be teaching 2 + 2?

How well does that go?

Even though you know the answer, even though you could explain the process in your sleep, in that moment you struggle. You're having a hard time accessing your upstairs brain.

Same brain. Same task. Very different results.

That's what's happening to our kids when they're trying to work while stuck in their downstairs brain. This is why students who "know the material" bomb tests. This is why a kid can do math perfectly in a calm one-on-one setting and completely freeze during timed multiplication drills.

The information is in there. They just can't access it when their nervous system is screaming "DANGER!" Their owl has flown away and it took all that memory and information with it.

DeShawn's Story: When "Won't" Is Really "Can't"

~ Amie ~

DeShawn was a brilliant seventh grader. I mean genuinely, remarkably smart. He could verbally explain complex historical concepts, make connections between events that I hadn't even considered, and debate with the insight of someone twice his age.

But he couldn't write a paragraph.

Every time I assigned written work, he'd shut down. Put his head on his desk. Refuse to start. I thought he was being defiant. Lazy. Choosing not to do the work because he didn't feel like it.

So I did what teachers do. I pushed harder. I gave consequences. I called home. I kept him after class for "motivational" talks that were really just me expressing my frustration in a polite voice.

Nothing worked. If anything, he shut down more.

It wasn't until I sat with him one-on-one and actually watched him try to write that I understood. His hand cramped after two sentences. His letters were uneven and labored. The physical act of writing was so demanding that by the time he got words on paper, he'd lost track of his thoughts.

DeShawn didn't have a motivation problem. He had a fine motor problem that no one had identified because he was so verbally gifted. His creative problem-solving had masked his challenges until the workload became so much he couldn't hide it anymore.

Once I gave him the option to type, or to record his answers verbally, everything changed. His grades went up. His attitude shifted. He started participating again.

All that time I thought his neurons weren't dancing. They were. They just couldn't get to the dance floor through the door I'd set up.

I had to build him a different entrance.

Now, whenever I have a student who "won't" do something, I try to ask myself: is this a "won't" or a "can't"? Is there a barrier I'm not seeing? Is there another door?

Won't vs. Can't: The Identical Twins

"Won't" and "can't" are like identical twins wearing the same outfit. From the outside, you cannot tell them apart.

Same behavior: refusal, shutdown, defiance.

Completely different cause.

And here's what makes it even trickier: sometimes the kid doesn't even know which one it is. They just know it feels hard, or impossible, or like too much. They don't have the language to say, "Excuse me, I believe I may have an undiagnosed fine motor delay that's interfering with my ability to transfer my verbal intelligence to written form."

They just put their head down and refuse to start. Their nervous system codes the task as unachievable and the possum takes control.

Which looks like defiance.

Which gets treated like defiance.

Which makes them feel frustrated and misunderstood.

Which makes them shut down more.

Which confirms our belief that they're being defiant. Which might invite the watchdog to the party.

It's a terrible cycle.

How to Break the Cycle

Here's a clue: if a behavior is persistent across contexts and resistant to typical interventions, pay attention. If you've tried consequences and they don't work, if you've tried motivation and it doesn't work, if you've tried relationship-building and the kid still can't do the thing...

Then maybe it's actually a "can't."

Get curious instead of frustrated.

Common "Can'ts" Mistaken for "Won'ts"

Fine Motor Challenges: Writing is incredibly complex from a motor planning standpoint. Hold the pencil, apply the right pressure, form letters in the right sequence, stay on the line, space appropriately... all while thinking about what you want to say. For some kids, the physical act of writing takes so much bandwidth there's nothing left for actual content. They're not lazy. They're exhausted.

Sensory Overwhelm: Some kids are so stressed by fluorescent lights, background noise, scratchy tags, or strong smells that they literally cannot focus on learning. Their brain is working overtime just to filter all that input. There's no capacity left for long division.

Movement Needs: The kid who can't stop moving, who's constantly fidgeting, tapping, getting out of their seat? That movement isn't disruptive on purpose. It's their nervous system trying to regulate itself. When we tell that kid to sit still, we're basically asking them to stop regulating. So we make it worse. With the best intentions, we make it worse!

Accommodating for the Can'ts

Here's how we think about accommodations:

If a kid needed glasses to see the board, would you refuse to let them wear glasses because it's an "unfair advantage" over kids with 20/20 vision?

Of course not. That would be absurd.

Accommodations are just glasses for different kinds of brains. They give kids access to learning they couldn't otherwise reach. It's not about making things easier. It's about making things possible.

What You Can Do

It's not your job to diagnose. But you CAN get curious.

Instead of "Why won't this kid try?" ask "What if they can't do it the way I'm asking? What might be getting in the way?"

Then experiment. Offer a different door.

Can they type instead of write?

Stand instead of sit?

Listen to instructions instead of read them?

Show what they know through drawing, talking, or building?

If you offer a different door and suddenly the kid can do the thing, you've found a clue.

That's not lowering expectations. Your matching the expectation to the student's capacity. That's providing access.

The Care Garden

Sometimes the can't is really just a *can't right now.* They don't have the capacity in that moment when they might have earlier or might again later.

Think of a student's capacity to "can" as a garden. A garden full of their capacity to care about doing the thing they "can" do. Imagine a care garden.

The soil: Their history, attachment, previous experiences.

The seeds: The content you're teaching.

The water and sun: Your relationship, the classroom environment.

The weeds: Stress, trauma, unmet needs.

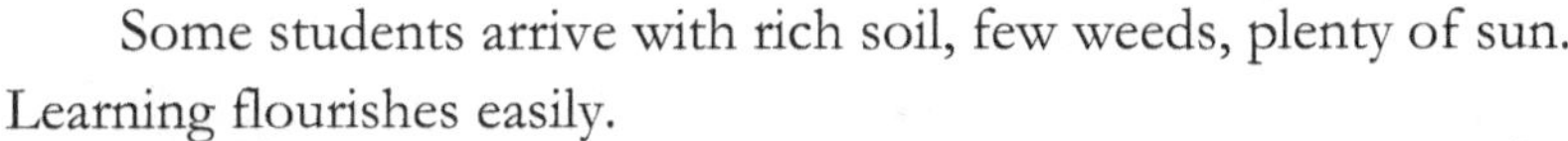

Some students arrive with rich soil, few weeds, plenty of sun. Learning flourishes easily.

Others arrive with rocky soil, invasive weeds, storm clouds overhead. Same seeds. Very different growing conditions.

Here's the thing: we only have so much energy, so much capacity. Each stressor harvests something from our care garden. Running late? That takes a care. Quickly yanked right out of our garden.

Coffee spilled? Another care washes away. Worried about whether mom and dad are fighting? A whole handful of cares, plucked right out.

By the time some students take that test, their care garden is empty. There are no cares left to give. It isn't about ability. It's about capacity.

When someone appears to not care anymore, we can wonder if their garden is undernourished or if their cares are being over-harvested.

What You Can Do to Grow More Cares

You can't control what soil students arrived with. But you CAN:

Pull some weeds (reduce stress)

Provide water (relationship)

Create sunshine (safe environment)

Be patient while things grow

Teachers also have care gardens. All humans do.

When we have no cares left to give, we can help tend each other's gardens.

When you offer to cover recess so a colleague can make a call, you're planting another care for each of you. When you give a compliment, you fertilize the cares we have.

When you validate a student's struggle, that care doesn't get harvested. It can be used for something else. Maybe even that next test.

Let's Get Real: When the System Doesn't Support This

Amie: Okay, but here's the teacher reality check. Even if I identify that a kid needs something different, I can't always provide it. I don't have a laptop for every student. I can't let one kid stand while everyone else sits without chaos ensuing. The system isn't set up for this.

Marti: You're absolutely right. And I don't want to pretend this is easy or that it all falls on teachers to figure out. Sometimes the barrier is systemic, not individual. Sometimes the best you can do is name what you're seeing and advocate for the resources the kid needs.

Here's what I want teachers to take away: you don't have to have all the answers. You don't have to diagnose or fix or solve everything. You just have to stay curious. When something isn't working, ask "what if?" instead of "why won't they?" That shift in thinking opens up possibilities.

Amie: And it's kinder to the kid.

Marti: And to you! Because there's nothing more exhausting than battling a behavior that was never about defiance in the first place. Once you stop fighting the wrong fight, everything gets easier.

Amie: Even if you don't find the solution right away?

Marti: Even then. Because at least you're looking in the right direction. And sometimes, just having an adult who believes "maybe there's something else going on here" is enough to keep a kid from giving up on themselves entirely. Preventing the possum from taking permanent residence.

Amie: That's the real goal, isn't it? Not perfection. Just... not giving up.

Marti: On them or on ourselves. If wondering "is this a can't?" doesn't solve the problem, fine. You've lost nothing. But if it opens a door that changes everything for a kid? That's worth the wondering.

Amie: Worth the wondering. I like that.

Marti: Feel free to steal it.

Amie: Already planning to.

Takeaways

1. **Learning is a dance, not a download.** Neurons need time to connect. We can create conditions that support learning, but we can't force it on our timeline. Patience isn't just kind; it's neurologically necessary. DeShawn was learning the whole time. We just couldn't see it.
2. **Students come with pathways already built.** Some help learning. Some hinder it. Our job isn't just to teach content; it's to help students build new neural pathways that serve them better. That takes repetition, trust, and time. One "you can do it!" doesn't override years of "I can't."
3. **"Won't" and "can't" look exactly the same.** The refusing student might have a barrier no one identified. DeShawn's fine motor challenges looked like defiance until someone got curious. Before labeling behavior as defiance, ask: is there a door I'm not seeing?

Reflection Questions

1. Think about a student who seems "checked out" or disengaged. What might be happening in their brain that you can't see? What connections might they be making that they haven't shown you yet?
2. What neural pathways did YOU build as a student that still affect you today? (For example: "I'm not a math person" or "Asking for help means I'm weak.")
3. Consider a struggling student. Could there be a barrier like DeShawn's that you haven't identified? What "different door" could you offer?

One Thing to Try Tomorrow

Pause Before Pouncing

When a student isn't performing the way you expect, pause before assuming they don't care.

Ask yourself:

"What if their neurons are dancing and I just can't see it yet?"
"What if there's a barrier I'm missing?"

Find ONE way to offer a different entry point:

Verbal response instead of written
Drawing instead of explanation
Conversation instead of quiz

See what happens when you build a different door. Sometimes the kid isn't refusing to come in. They just can't find the handle.

CHAPTER 6

Why They Can't (Yet)

Biology Before Blame: Why Fighting Development Never Works

~ Amie ~

I watched a kindergarten teacher cry in her car after school one day.

"I don't know what I'm doing wrong," she told me. "They can't sit still. They can't focus. They're constantly moving, touching things, getting out of their seats. I feel like I'm failing them."

She wasn't failing them. She was being asked to expect things that five-year-old bodies and brains aren't built to do.

Asking a kindergartner to sit still for two hours is like asking a puppy to practice meditation. Technically possible? Sure. Probable? You'd have better odds winning the lottery while being struck by lightning.

When we understand what's developmentally realistic, and what isn't, we stop blaming ourselves (and our students) for fighting biology. We start creating conditions where learning can actually happen.

Let's talk about what's actually realistic at different ages and stages.

Developmentally Appropriate Expectations (Or: Why Kindergartners Can't Sit Still)

Young Children (PreK-2nd Grade)

Their hands are still developing. Fine motor skills are hard. Holding a pencil "correctly" for extended periods can be painful. The small muscles of their hands haven't developed enough to support the writing utensil. Often, they have to push really hard to stabilize the crayon. If you must do fine motor tasks, investigate loop or spring-loaded scissors and short fat crayons that will set them up for success instead of bad habits.

Their attention spans are short. Five to ten minutes of focused work is realistic. Two hours? That's not learning. That's torture.

They learn through play and movement. Sitting still isn't just hard. It's counterproductive to how their brains work. The sensory motor cortex is what's most easily influenced during this time. There is a flash mob of dancing neurons in that motor part of the brain. Allow them to move frequently between stations. Incorporate movement into circle times.

They're egocentric (developmentally normal). They're not being selfish. They literally can't fully perspective-take yet. Frame requests so that they see the benefit. Instead of "That hurts Amelia," try "If you hit Amelia, she might not want to share her crayons with you."

Upper Elementary (3rd-5th Grade)

They're starting to think more abstractly, but still need concrete examples. You can talk about learning from mistakes on a math test, but then identify specific examples. You can teach the American Revolution and taxation without representation, but help them understand it with a simulation involving M&Ms and taxes.

Peer relationships are becoming crucial. Social dynamics impact learning. A fight with a friend group can make it difficult for a student to focus in class. If they feel like they're "stupid," they may stop engaging or become the class clown. Take five minutes at recess to hear their perspective.

They're developing more self-management skills but aren't masters yet. We still have to do most of their executive functioning for them. They can choose the order of three paragraphs, but you set the structure and timeline. We can't just say "study for the test." We have to teach them HOW. Let's make flash cards. Can we create a funny rhyme? PEMDAS, anyone?

They can handle more complexity but still need scaffolding. Growing independence. Declaring independence. But they can't sign it yet.

Middle School (6th-8th Grade)

Their brains are under massive construction. Literally. Neural pruning and myelination are happening at rapid rates. It's a competitive dance squad for those neurons and the cuts are brutal. There's no JV neuron squad in middle school.

We can also think of it like a complete home remodel. The upstairs is being totally reconstructed. New floors, new walls, so much new. It's a huge mess and benefits from someone joining alongside to help clean up so the construction can continue. That cleanup can look like simply listening and helping them see that this reconstruction is normal for their age, and the result will be beautiful.

Identity exploration is in full swing. Many kids try on new identities here. They try on new nicknames and horrible haircuts. It helps to view these as paint colors that will change over time. They aren't usually permanent, but they make a big impact on the room's vibe in the moment. When we embrace a wide range of colors on their palettes, we help them explore what sticks as they make more permanent design changes to their upstairs brain.

Emotions feel HUGE because emotional processing is developing faster than emotional management. Not to mention that the experiences of puberty, crushes, changing bodies, and navigating new relationships are still novel. The first breakup feels like the end of the world because they've never experienced this! By the time you're in your twenties and have broken up with a significant other multiple times, it isn't as devastating because you have the experience to know you can survive.

Social status matters intensely. This isn't shallow. It's biological. Dr. David Yeager, a prominent developmental psychologist, has research that shows that status and respect are driving forces in adolescent behavior. He says that for adolescents, status is as important as play is for young children. Let that sink in. When they make questionable decisions to impress their friends, they aren't just being foolish. They're participating in developmentally appropriate behavior.

Sleep patterns shift. They want to go to bed later and wake up later. There's a reason your 10th graders are sleeping through 1st period but engaging by 2nd. Their circadian rhythms are shifting. They biologically get their second wind at 10 p.m., just as we're winding down. Teen parents know the exhaustion of the late night couch drama dump.

High School (9th-12th Grade)

The frontal cortex (judgment, planning, impulse control) isn't fully developed until the mid-20s. This is why the same teenager who can discuss geopolitics like an adult can also turn to friends and say "Let's jump off this ledge" without any thought of consequences. When asked why, they say "I don't know, it just looked like fun." So we need to clearly state cautions and safety rules. Repeatedly. Like their lives depend on it. Because they do.

They can handle complex abstract thinking but still benefit from concrete applications. Teaching opportunity cost in economics? You can explain the principle all day. But it clicks when you ask: "You have $20. You can buy the video game or go to the movies with your friends. If you choose the game, what did you give up?" Suddenly the abstract becomes tangible.

They need autonomy and belonging simultaneously. They want to be treated as emerging adults. They push for independence while still needing support. They respond poorly to being treated like children. They respond well to being given appropriate responsibility.

Visual Summary: Developmental Expectations by Age

Age Group	What's Developing	What's Realistic	What Helps
PreK-2nd	Fine motor, attention, perspective-taking, basic self-management	5-10 min focused work; learning through play/movement; egocentric thinking	Movement breaks, hands-on activities, short tasks, patience with motor skills
3rd-5th	Abstract thinking (emerging), self-management, peer awareness	Needs concrete examples; social dynamics impact learning; growing self-control	Scaffolded complexity, attention to social dynamics, peer collaboration
6th-8th	Emotional processing, abstract thinking, identity, sleep shifts	BIG emotions; intense social focus; struggles with long-term planning	Honor peer relationships, provide emotional vocabulary, visual schedules, flexibility
9th-12th	Frontal cortex (judgment, planning), identity, autonomy	Can handle complexity but needs concrete application; wants independence	Multiple reminders, choice within structure, respect for emerging autonomy

Critical Note: These are typical developmental expectations. Students who have experienced trauma may be operating at a different developmental level than their chronological age suggests. Meet them where they ARE, not where they "should" be.

The Three Ages: A Framework for Understanding

Here's a framework that changed how we see students who've experienced adversity.

Every student is navigating THREE ages at once:

Chronological age: How old they actually are in years since birth.

Developmental age: Where their skills actually are. Imagine a 10-year-old who isn't able to pick out clothes independently, tolerate being told to wait five minutes, or pour from a milk jug without spilling.

Experiential age: The weight of what they've lived through. They may have experiences similar to a 30-year-old. They might be keenly aware of how meat is always on sale on the first of the month or know when adults are under the influence of something. They might have awareness of complex relational dynamics and feel a deep sense of responsibility for younger siblings.

How This Shows Up

Jorge is 13 (chronological age). He's in seventh grade. But when it comes to managing frustration and conflict, he operates more like a 6- or 7-year-old (developmental age). Why? Because during the years when most kids are learning those skills, Jorge was learning to survive an unpredictable home environment. His energy went to hypervigilance, not emotional development.

And yet, Jorge has also lived through things no 13-year-old should know about: eviction, food insecurity, witnessing violence (experiential age closer to 30). He carries wisdom and wariness beyond his years.

So when Jorge blows up over a minor classroom conflict, he's not being dramatic. He's responding with the skills of a 6-year-old to a situation that his experiential knowledge tells him could be dangerous.

He's not broken. He's adaptive. And he needs us to meet him where he actually is.

Why This Matters

This is why kids who have experienced significant trauma can act so mature one minute and then like a toddler the next. They're not being manipulative. They're living in multiple developmental realities at once.

When we only see chronological age, we expect things they can't deliver. When we see all three ages, we can meet them where they actually ARE. That's not lowering expectations. That's being realistic about where to start.

What Trauma Does to Development

When a child experiences trauma during a critical window of development, the neural pathways that should be forming during that window may not develop typically. Or they develop in ways that prioritize survival over skill-building.

A toddler who should be developing language might instead be developing hypervigilance. A preschooler who should be learning impulse control might be learning to freeze or flee. A first grader who should be building academic foundations might be scanning for threats.

This doesn't mean these kids can't learn those skills later. They absolutely can. But it means we might need to go back and build foundations that typically developing kids already have in place.

What May Be Missing:

Emotional regulation skills
Executive function
Frustration tolerance

How to ask for help

How to recover from setbacks

How to trust adults

The key reframe: These aren't character flaws when they're missing. We have to teach them, not just expect them.

Beyond "Typical": When the Map Doesn't Match the Territory

Everything we've covered so far about development is true. And it's incomplete.

Here's the thing: developmental charts and arousal continuums and attachment patterns were largely created by studying specific populations. White, Western, middle-class, neurotypical populations, to be precise. The research has expanded since then (thank goodness), but the mental models many of us carry around are still based on a pretty narrow slice of humanity.

So before we move into the practical strategies in Section Two, we need to talk about two massive variables that change everything: neurodivergence and culture.

This isn't a detour. This is a main road. It's getting some fresh pavement.

Neurodivergent Nervous Systems: Different Wiring, Not Deficient Wiring

A neurodivergent brain isn't a broken neurotypical brain. It's a different kind of brain entirely. And when we keep trying to apply neurotypical expectations to neurodivergent kids, we set everyone up for failure and frustration.

Let me tell you about Danielle.

Danielle was seven, diagnosed with ADHD, and her teacher was at her wit's end. "She won't sit still. She won't stop talking. She won't focus for more than thirty seconds." She wasn't wrong about the behaviors. But she was wrong about the "won't."

Danielle *couldn't* sit still the way she was asking. Her nervous system required movement to feel safe. The stillness she was demanding was actually *engaging her stress response.* Every time she told her to stop fidgeting, she was asking her to abandon the very strategy keeping her engaged.

When we shifted the question from "How do I make Danielle act like the other kids?" to "What does Danielle's nervous system actually need?" everything changed. A wobble cushion on her chair. Permission to stand at her desk. A fidget tool in her pocket. Movement breaks built into transitions.

Was she suddenly still and silent? Nope. But she felt safe. Kids can learn when they aren't fighting against their biology.

The Neurodivergent Difference

Here's a quick (and very incomplete) tour of how neurodivergence affects the nervous system concepts we've been discussing:

ADHD:

- The arousal continuum looks different. These kids often need more stimulation to reach optimal arousal, not less.
- Their window of tolerance may be narrower in some contexts and surprisingly wide in others.
- Time blindness is real. "Five more minutes" doesn't compute the way it does for neurotypical brains.
- Movement and fidgeting aren't signs of willful disobedience. They're often signs of attempted obedience.

Autism:

- Sensory processing differences are the rule, not the exception. What feels neutral to you might feel like an assault to them (or might barely register at all).

- Social neuroception works differently. The cues neurotypical people read automatically may be genuinely invisible or confusing.
- Transitions are harder. Period. Build in more buffer time than you think you need, then double it.
- Stimming (repetitive movements or sounds) is a form of self-regulation, not defiance. Taking away a stim without providing an alternative is like confiscating someone's wheelchair and telling them to just run faster.

Sensory Processing Differences (with or without other diagnoses):

- The sensory chapters coming up in Section Two? Multiply their importance by ten for these kids.
- "Unexpected" sensory needs are actually quite predictable once you learn the individual child.
- Dialed up and down sensation registration coexist in the same child (seeking proprioceptive input while avoiding auditory input, for example).

Learning Disabilities:

- The gap between intellectual ability and performance creates its own stress response.
- Years of "try harder" messaging may have taught these kids that effort is pointless.
- Their nervous systems may be primed for shame because they've experienced so much failure.

The Practical Pivot

Here's what this means for you in the classroom:

Instead of asking "Why won't this child...?" try asking "What does this particular nervous system need?"

Instead of seeing accommodations as special treatment, see them as access. A child who needs to stand up to focus isn't getting an unfair advantage. They're getting what they need to reach the same starting line.

Instead of teaching to the middle and hoping outliers adapt, recognize that the "outliers" might be a quarter of your class. Or more. And please, please, please: stop using "neurotypical" as the measuring stick for success. When we define regulated, connected, and successful based on one kind of brain, we guarantee that many kids will feel like failures no matter how hard they try.

What This Looks Like in Real Life

Traditional Expectation	Neurodivergent Reality	Regulation-Focused Response
Sit still to show you're paying attention	Movement may BE the attention strategy	Offer movement options that don't disrupt others
Make eye contact when I'm talking to you	Eye contact can be overwhelming or culturally complex	Offer connection without requiring eye contact
Stop making that noise/movement	Stimming is self-regulation	Identify less disruptive stims rather than eliminating
Just focus	Executive function differences make "just focusing" nearly impossible	Reduce distractions, chunk tasks, provide external structure
Use your words	Verbal processing may be slower or work differently	Offer alternatives (writing, pointing, drawing, waiting)
Calm down	Their "calm" may look different than yours	Learn THEIR felt-safety baseline, not your assumption

Culture Shapes Everything (Yes, Everything)

Now let's talk about the other massive variable we often miss: culture.

A teacher once told Marti, confidently, that one of her students had "attachment issues." The evidence? "She never looks at me when I talk to her. She always looks down."

Marti asked a few questions. Turned out this child's family had recently immigrated from a country where children looking adults in the eye was considered deeply disrespectful. This child wasn't avoidant. She was being exactly what her family had taught her to be: respectful.

That teacher, with the best of intentions, was pathologizing politeness. This happens more than we want to admit.

The Danger of the Default

Here's the uncomfortable truth: most of us carry around a mental model of "normal" child development and "healthy" behavior that's based on dominant cultural norms. When children from different cultural backgrounds don't match our model, we often (unconsciously) label them as problems.

Consider how culture shapes:

Eye contact: In many Western contexts, eye contact signals engagement and respect. In many other cultures, direct eye contact with authority figures signals disrespect or challenge. A child avoiding your gaze might be showing you the deepest respect they know how to show.

Physical proximity and touch: Personal space bubbles vary dramatically across cultures. What feels appropriately warm to one family might feel invasive or cold to another.

Volume and expressiveness: Some cultures value quiet reserve. Others value enthusiastic expression. A "loud" child might be a perfectly regulated child whose baseline volume is just... louder.

Emotional expression: Stoicism is valued in some cultures; emotional expressiveness in others. A child who seems "shut down" might actually be demonstrating the emotional control their family has carefully taught them.

Collectivism vs. individualism: Many classroom strategies assume individual achievement matters most. But children from collectivist cultures may feel deeply uncomfortable being singled out (even for praise) or may prioritize group harmony over individual performance.

Conflict and correction: How families handle discipline, disagreement, and correction varies wildly. A child who won't "advocate for themselves" might come from a culture where children speaking up to adults is unthinkable.

Food and feeding: Connection through food looks different everywhere. Sharing food, refusing food, how food is offered and received... all of it carries cultural meaning we might miss.

The Problem With "Best Practices"

Here's something that's hard to hear: many of our "best practices" in education and child development were developed by and for dominant culture. When we apply them universally, without cultural humility, we risk:

- Misdiagnosing cultural differences as developmental delays
- Creating shame for children (and families) who don't fit our expectations
- Missing genuine concerns because we've dismissed everything as "cultural"
- Demanding that children choose between succeeding at school and honoring their family's values

The answer isn't to throw out everything we know. It's to hold our knowledge with humility and curiosity.

Curiosity Over Assumptions

The single most important shift you can make? Replace assumptions with questions.

Instead of deciding what a child's behavior means, get curious. Ask families. Ask the child (when appropriate). Ask colleagues who share the child's cultural background. Ask yourself what you might be missing.

Some questions to consider:

What does "respect" look like in this child's home?
How does this family express love and connection?
What are the expectations around emotional expression?
How is eye contact understood?
What role do children play in family decision-making?
How is conflict handled? Correction given?
What does "success" mean to this family?

You won't always get answers. But the act of asking keeps you humble and open. And that humility is what allows you to actually see the child in front of you, rather than the child you expected to see.

A Word About Intersectionality

Of course, nothing exists in isolation. A child might be neurodivergent AND from a non-dominant culture AND dealing with trauma AND living in poverty. These factors don't just add up; they interact in complex ways.

A Black boy with ADHD faces different challenges than a white girl with ADHD, because of how race and gender shape the way adults perceive behavior. A Latina child from an immigrant family might have anxiety about disclosure that affects everything in her school life. A child whose family has experienced generational trauma may have nervous system patterns that look different from the attachment research based on different populations.

We can't know everything about every intersection. But we can stay humble, stay curious, and keep asking: "What am I missing?"

Practical Implications

1. Recognize What's Developmental, Not Defiant

Before getting frustrated, ask: "Is this age-appropriate? Is this trauma-impact? Or is this actually defiance? Is this a nervous system difference I'm not accounting for? Is there a cultural mismatch I'm missing? Am I asking for something that feels impossible or wrong to this child?"

2. Use the Three Ages Framework

When behavior doesn't match chronological age, consider developmental and experiential ages.

"What age is this behavior coming from?"

"What does that age need from me right now?"

3. Let Go of Some Academic Expectations When Needed

On days when a kid is clearly in survival mode, academic expectations may need to flex. Remember the "can't vs. won't" concept from the previous chapter and the cortical function capacity we learned about with the arousal continuum. In that moment, when their owl has flown out of the window of tolerance, they literally CAN'T access higher-order thinking.

This isn't about lowering standards permanently. It's about meeting them where they are TODAY. The hope is if we can keep them in their window of tolerance today, they will have a wider window and more cares in their garden tomorrow.

4. Audit your assumptions.

What's your mental picture of a "regulated child"? A "connected child"? A "successful student"? Where did that picture come from? Who does it include, and who might it leave out?

5. Learn about your students' backgrounds.

Not in a check-the-box way, but genuinely. Family conferences, home visits (where possible), conversations with community members, and your own research can all help. Partner with families. They know their child best. They know their culture best. Position yourself as a learner, not an expert. (More on this in Chapter 13.)

6. Build flexibility into your strategies.

The techniques in Section Two are powerful, but they're not scripts. They're starting points. You'll need to adapt based on the actual nervous systems and cultural contexts you're working with.

7. Forgive yourself for getting it wrong.

You will. We all do. The goal isn't perfect cultural competence or neurodiversity expertise. The goal is staying curious, staying humble, and being willing to course-correct when we learn better.

8. Find Safety Before Expectation

First we help them feel safe. THEN we educate.

Not either/or. Sequence matters.

"I focus on helping them feel safe first. Sometimes that means a break. Sometimes it's a walk. Sometimes it's just sitting with them quietly until their nervous system settles. And THEN we return to the learning."

9. You Don't Need Their History

You can't always know what a kid has been through. You don't need trauma details to respond with compassion.

Just assume that any kid who's struggling behaviorally might be struggling developmentally too. Respond to the need, not the behavior.

This Works for ALL Kids

Here's something important: when we adjust our expectations to be more developmentally and culturally appropriate, even our "easy" kids benefit.

Because we're all humans with nervous systems. We all have limits to our capacity. We all do better when expectations match what we're actually capable of at the moment.

Fair isn't Fifty-Fifty

"Fair is giving each kid what they need to be successful."

That looks different for different kids.

This comes up constantly when we talk about accommodations for neurodivergent kids or culturally responsive adjustments. We want to offer a reframe. Fairness isn't about sameness. Fairness is about everyone getting what they need to succeed.

Think about it this way: if three kids need to see over a fence, and one is tall enough, one needs a small step stool, and one needs a ladder... is it "fair" to give them all the same size stool? Technically equal, sure. But the tall kid doesn't need it, and the short kid still can't see. Real fairness is giving each kid what THEY need to see over that fence.

The same applies here. A child who needs movement to feel safe in their body isn't getting an unfair advantage with a wobble cushion. They're getting access. A child whose culture values different eye contact norms isn't getting special treatment when you don't require them to look at you. They're getting respect.

And here's the bonus: when we build flexibility into our classrooms for the kids who need it most, we usually make things better for everyone. More movement options help all kids. More sensory-friendly environments help all kids. More cultural humility makes the whole classroom safer.

This isn't about creating different rules for different kids. It's about recognizing that one-size-fits-all never actually fit all in the first place.

Let's Get Real: Meeting Kids Where They Are

Amie: The "meet them where they are" thing sounds great until you have 30 kids at 30 different places and a curriculum to cover.

Marti: Nobody's asking you to create 30 individual lesson plans. You're looking for patterns. Which kids need more movement? Which need more visual support? Which need you to lower your voice instead of raise it?

Amie: So it's more like categories of need rather than individual prescriptions?

Marti: Exactly. And here's the thing: the accommodations that help struggling kids usually help everyone. More visuals, more movement, more predictability? Every brain benefits.

Amie: Universal design for regulation.

Marti: Basically, yes. You're not adding 30 more things. You're adding a few things that serve most of your students.

Amie: One more thing. I had to let go of "fair means equal." Fair is giving each kid what they need to be successful. That looks different for different kids.

Marti: And some days you get this right. Some days you still lose patience and expect a kid to just "get it together." Then you catch yourself. Repair if needed. Try again tomorrow.

Amie: That's the thing. I'm catching myself faster now. And I'm repairing when I mess up.

Marti: That's all any of us can do. Keep showing up. Keep learning. Not perfectly. But consistently.

Amie: Can we talk about the fear around this stuff? Because I think a lot of teachers are terrified of saying or doing the wrong thing.

Marti: Absolutely. The fear of messing up actually stops people from engaging at all. Which is worse than making mistakes.

Amie: Right. So what do you tell someone who's thinking, "I don't know enough about autism to work with autistic kids" or "I don't understand this family's culture and I'm scared I'll offend them"?

Marti: I tell them: you don't have to be an expert to be helpful. You have to be humble and curious. The kids and families will teach you if you let them. Your job isn't to know everything. Your job is to keep asking, keep learning, keep adjusting.

Amie: And what about when you DO mess up? Because it happens.

Marti: You apologize. Genuinely. You ask what would work better. And you try again. Kids are remarkably forgiving when they sense that you actually care and you're actually trying. It's the adults who pretend they never make mistakes that lose trust.

Amie: I've definitely had moments where I realized, mid-conversation, that I'd assumed something totally wrong about a family's values. It's uncomfortable.

Marti: It's supposed to be uncomfortable! Discomfort is often the sign that we're growing. The alternative is staying comfortable in our assumptions while kids suffer from being misunderstood. I'll take uncomfortable.

Amie: So the message is: you don't need to be perfect. You need to be present, humble, and willing to learn.

Marti: That's it. Start there. Then choose your own adventure as we introduce sections two, three, and four.

Takeaways

1. **Development isn't optional.** When we expect kids to do things their brains aren't ready for, we set everyone up for frustration. Knowing what's developmentally appropriate helps us stop fighting biology and start working with it.

2. **Trauma changes what roads got built.** Kids who've experienced trauma may be navigating three different "ages" at once. They're not being difficult. They're doing the best they can with the neural architecture they have. Sometimes we need to go back and build foundations so new roads have a place to land.
3. **Meeting kids where they are isn't lowering standards.** It's being realistic about where to start. You can still have high expectations while acknowledging that different kids need different starting points and different supports to get there.

Reflection Questions

1. Think about a student who consistently struggles in your classroom. How might their developmental age differ from their chronological age? What about their experiential age?
2. Where might your current expectations be fighting biology? What adjustments could you make?
3. How comfortable are you with "fair doesn't mean equal"? What would it look like to give different supports based on actual needs?
4. What's one developmental reality you've been pushing against that you could stop fighting?

One Thing to Try Tomorrow

Add Access, Not Work

Add one visual support to a lesson you're already teaching.

- If you usually just explain verbally, add a diagram.
- If you usually just show a diagram, add movement (act it out, walk through it, gesture it).
- If you usually just assign reading, add a graphic organizer.

One lesson. One visual. Notice who engages differently. You're not adding work to your plate. You're adding access to theirs.

Section One Closing: From Knowing to Doing

You made it.

You just absorbed a LOT of brain science. Polyvagal theory. Attachment styles. Windows of tolerance. Owls and watchdogs and possums. Upstairs brains and downstairs brains. Roads that got built and roads that didn't. Chronological ages and developmental ages and experiential ages.

If your head is spinning a little, that's normal. If you're thinking "This is fascinating but what do I actually DO with all of this on Monday morning?"... perfect. That's exactly where we want you.

Before we dive in, one more reminder: you don't have to master all of this at once.

You're going to mess up. We still mess up. Thirty years in, and we're still learning. Still having moments where we think, "I definitely could have handled that better." Still occasionally snapping at a kid for stealing from my supply closet and immediately regretting it.

The goal isn't to become a different teacher. It's to become a more informed version of the teacher you already are. To have a framework when things get hard. To understand what's happening underneath the behavior so you can respond instead of just react.

You've done the heavy lifting of understanding. Now let's put it to work. Section Two starts with one simple truth: relationships are the foundation of everything else. Connection comes first. Not because it's the easiest (sometimes it's the hardest), but because nothing else works without it.

Ready?

Let's go build some relationships.

SECTION TWO

Putting it Into Practice

Knowing isn't the same as doing. This section is where we do.

We're shifting gears. The next four chapters are packed with practical strategies you can use tomorrow morning. Real tools for real classrooms. We'll start with connection, because nothing else works without it. Then we'll move through body language, sensory-friendly environments, and responding to those behaviors.

The foundation is laid. Time to drive. Let's go off-road and get some mud on these new tires.

Chapter 7

Connecting in the Classroom

From Understanding to Action: How Connection Through Building Relationships Creates Felt Safety

In Section One, we learned that felt safety (the internal sense that "I'm okay here") is the prerequisite for learning. But here's the question we haven't answered yet: How do we actually create felt safety? Through connection by building relationships.

The skills in this chapter are the practical "how" for building that felt safety we've been talking about. Remember: felt safety isn't something we can give through words alone. It's something students feel in their bodies when they're around adults who are consistent, warm, and genuinely glad to see them. This is the foundation of theory becoming practice.

Connection Is THE Strategy

Let's be absolutely clear about something: connection isn't a warm-up activity before the "real" teaching happens. Connection IS the strategy. It's the thing that makes everything else in this book work.

Without connection:

- Sensory supports feel clinical instead of caring
- Behavior interventions feel punishing instead of guiding
- "Try again" sounds like criticism instead of invitation
- Your calm presence doesn't calm anyone

With connection:

- A fidget basket says "I see you and I made space for your needs"
- A redirect feels like guidance from someone who's on your side
- "Let's try that again" sounds like belief in their ability to do better
- Your regulated nervous system actually helps regulate theirs

This is why we're spending an entire chapter on connection skills before we talk about sensory environments or responding to behaviors. You need this foundation first. The strategies in the next two chapters only work when they're built on relationship.

Connection is the sunshine for the care garden. Everything else we plant needs that warm light to grow.

The Kid Who Just Needed to Be Seen

~ Amie ~

Wes walked into my classroom like he was looking for a reason to leave. Slouched shoulders. Hood up. Headphones in, even though he knew the rules.

He was sixteen. Technically a junior, though his credits told a different story.

He'd been like this for weeks. Sarcastic comments muttered just loud enough to hear. Strategic sleeping (always positioned so I couldn't quite tell if his eyes were closed). One day he just stood up mid-lesson, said "this is pointless," and walked out. Another day he sat in the back corner and drew on his desk for an entire period, making eye contact with me exactly zero times.

I'd tried consequences. I'd tried the classic teacher tactic of pretending I couldn't hear the sarcasm. I'd called home, which I learned later only made things worse because there wasn't really a stable "home" to call. Nothing was working.

Then I found out what was actually going on. His mom had lost her job three months ago. They'd been couch-surfing with relatives ever since, sleeping on sofas and sharing suitcases. His dad had basically bounced from the picture years back. Wes was working nights at a gas station to help with groceries while trying to stay awake through third period.

And here I was, trying to get him interested in the Protestant Reformation.

That's when I changed my approach. I stopped trying to fix his behavior and started trying to see him.

Every time I spotted Wes slouching down the hallway, I made a point to acknowledge him. Every. Single. Time. Even when I was rushing between classes. Even when he'd just done something that made me want to assign detention until graduation.

"Hey, Wes. How's it going?"

No lectures. No "we need to talk about yesterday." Just presence.

At first he'd grunt. Or nod. Or pretend his headphones were too loud to hear me (they weren't connected to anything, I'd noticed).

I started paying attention to what made him perk up. He always had earbuds in but rarely had them playing music. He drew constantly in the margins of every handout. He sat up straighter during any class discussion about music or art history. So I found my angle.

"I saw you drawing earlier. You any good?"

Shrug.

"I'm looking for someone to sketch some visuals for our unit project. No pressure. Just figured you might have some skill I could steal."

He wasn't interested. But he looked at me differently after that. Like maybe I wasn't completely insufferable.

The next week, I noticed his sketchbook had a detailed drawing of a cathedral. Gothic architecture. Flying buttresses and everything.

"That's seriously good," I said. "You know that's literally what we're studying right now, right? Medieval church architecture?"

Another shrug. But this time with the ghost of a smirk.

"Wes. Did you accidentally learn something in my class?"

"Don't tell anyone," he said. His first full sentence to me in weeks.

A month in, the behaviors hadn't disappeared. Let's be honest about that. This isn't an instant fix. He still slept sometimes. Still muttered sarcastic stuff. Still walked out when things got overwhelming.

But the frequency was fading. The severity was softening. We were starting to handle the day together instead of against each other.

When he needed to step out, he'd catch my eye first. A silent signal. I'd nod. He'd come back.

Here's what I learned: Wes didn't need another consequence. He needed to know that at least one adult in his life saw him as more than his worst moments. He needed connection.

The thing about connected relationships is that they take time to build. And they require specific skills. Connection will not change behavior overnight. What it will do is bring more lasting change. Something that might benefit Wes past his time within the walls of the school. Something that will stay with him in his twenties. Maybe even something that shapes how he shows up for his own kids someday. As strange as it sounds, simply greeting someone intentionally could be a catalyst for generational change.

Reality check: if Wes is sleeping on a different couch every week and working nights to keep food on the table, the Protestant Reformation doesn't matter. Not really. Not right now. He's surviving, not studying. But knowing he has worth? Knowing someone actually sees him? That matters no matter where he lays his head to sleep next week.

A wise colleague always says: "What we're doing now is not working, so why don't we try something new?" Either way, we're going to have to deal with the behaviors. Why not deal with them in a way that will at least make it a little easier for us?

Building connected relationships is that way.

But what does that actually look like in a school setting?

Connection in the Real World of Teaching

Connection in a classroom looks different than connection in parenting. And that's not just okay. That's necessary.

You have 30 students. Or 150 across multiple periods. You have them for 50 minutes a day, for a year, or sometimes just a semester. You're also managing curriculum, assessments, behavior, paperwork, meetings, and your own life.

You're not their parent. You're not their therapist. You're their teacher. But you can be a consistent, safe, caring adult in their life. That matters enormously.

Where Amie teaches, class sizes are very large. Some classes have over 40 students. Asking teachers to connect individually with each student feels overwhelming and impossible. We get it. When someone tells you "just build relationships," and you're drowning in grading and your own stress, it feels like one more impossible thing being added to your plate.

But relational connection isn't one more thing. It's the thing that makes all the other things possible. Our response to every child throwing big behaviors is to ask: What is happening with connection? Are they feeling seen? Safe? Valued? Do they trust me?

We know we need to teach content. We know we need to prepare for end-of-level assessments. We know there's pressure from every direction. We also know if a student doesn't feel connected and safe, no learning will occur anyway.

You can have the most brilliant lesson plan in the world. You can have state-of-the-art technology. You can have perfect classroom management. But if students don't feel safe with you, their thinking brain is offline. And offline brains don't learn.

The most effective method we have for getting test scores up is building connection so kids can access learning.

It's not one more thing. It's the foundation for everything else.

Connection Looks Different for Different Kids (And That's the Point)

Here's something we want to say clearly: the connection strategies in this chapter are starting points, not scripts.

A child with autism might find your enthusiastic door greeting overwhelming rather than welcoming. A student from a culture where children don't initiate conversation with adults might freeze when you ask "How was your weekend?" The kid with ADHD might need you to connect through movement and activity, not eye contact and stillness.

This doesn't mean connection doesn't work for these kids. It means connection needs to be customized.

For neurodivergent students, consider:

- Some kids connect better through parallel activity (doing something side by side) than face-to-face conversation
- Predictability IS connection for many neurodivergent kids. Your consistent routine says "I see you" louder than any greeting
- Sensory-friendly connection matters. A fist bump might work better than a high-five if the sound is overwhelming. A quiet nod might land better than an enthusiastic "Good morning!"
- Special interests are connection gold. That kid who won't stop talking about trains? All aboard! That's not a problem to redirect. That's a ticket to relationship.

For students from different cultural backgrounds, consider:

- "Connection" itself is culturally defined. What feels warm in one culture might feel invasive in another.
- Some families teach children that adults initiate, children respond. Waiting for a student to start a conversation might mean waiting forever (and that's not defiance, it's respect).
- Physical proximity norms vary. Standing "too close" or "too far" is relative.

The bottom line: Pay attention to what each student responds to. When your usual connection strategy isn't landing, get curious instead of frustrated. The goal isn't to connect YOUR way. It's to connect THEIR way.

Connection Skills for Teachers

Here are specific, practical skills we can start using tomorrow. These work even with large class sizes. Even when we're exhausted. Even when we don't like the kid very much.

The 10-Second Kid in a 3-Second World

We have so many children who take a little longer to process what is going on around them or what they are being asked to do. We call them "10-second kids."

Unfortunately, so many of our requests are expected to be complied within 3 seconds.

Try this right now: Sit and count to ten very slowly and quietly in your head. Sit in the silence. Feel how long that 10 seconds can be.

It's long, right? Especially in a busy classroom where you have 30 other things happening.

But there are many times in the classroom where we can sit and count to 10 in our head in order to give more kids a chance to process.

"Everyone, please take out your math books."

[Count to 10 in my head]

"If you need help finding it, raise your hand."

[Count to 10 in my head]

Then we start the lesson.

This creates more safety and connection because kids know they will get the time they need in the classroom. They're not constantly behind, constantly panicking, constantly feeling like failures because they can't keep up.

10-second kids deserve a 10-second world. Even if it feels painfully slow to us.

We also need to acknowledge that we have 3-second kids in a 3-second world. When we talk about this with teachers, we hear quite often how if they wait that long it may help the 10-second kid but the classroom loses control. This is where we'd say: practice. Make a game of learning to wait 10 seconds. Give kids permission to stretch, or make a silly face while they wait the 10 seconds.

Many 10-second kids are neurodivergent. Processing differences, attention differences, and executive function differences all contribute to needing more time.

You don't need a diagnosis to give a kid more time. You don't need to know WHY they process slowly to accommodate the reality that they do. Some kids are 10-second kids because of ADHD. Some because of auditory processing differences. Some because of anxiety. Some because English is their second language and they're translating in their head. Some because their home culture values thoughtful pauses before speaking. The reason doesn't change the response: slow down. Wait. Create space.

So much of education feels secretive. We wait 10 seconds, but no one knows why. We let the kids walk around my room, but no one knows why. We are firm believers in being honest with kids. If we have a class that has 10-second and 2-second kids, let's honestly address it. "Some kids need more time to get their book out. Some kids need less. What can we do in the classroom when we are done but we are waiting?" Let the kids problem solve this. Often, they know what they need; they're just begging for someone to let them do it!

The Power of Play (Yes, Even in High School)

Stuart Brown from the National Institute for Play says, "Play disarms fear."

Read that again. Play. Disarms. Fear.

If we want students to feel safe, to take risks, to engage, we need play. "But I teach high school!" We hear you. We teach high school too. And we still use play.

Here's why play matters so much: The National Institute for Play has found that play is essential for learning, emotional intelligence, problem-solving, and social skills at ALL ages. When kids play, they're practicing negotiation and cooperation, building creative thinking skills, experiencing low-stakes failure and recovery, developing emotional regulation, and strengthening relationships.

When brains are in play mode, they're in a state that's optimal for learning. Curious. Engaged. Open. When brains are in survival mode (stressed, scared, defending), learning can't happen.

So if we want our students to learn, we need to create conditions where they feel safe enough to play. To experiment. To take risks. To be wrong without shame.

A Note on Play Across Cultures and Neurotypes

Not everyone plays the same way. And that's not a problem to fix.

Some neurodivergent students may engage in play that looks "different" to neurotypical eyes. Lining up objects. Repeating the same game endlessly. Playing "wrong" according to the rules. This IS play. It's just not the play you expected.

Some cultural backgrounds emphasize different types of play. Competition versus cooperation. Physical versus verbal. Group versus individual. Don't assume your play style is the universal play style.

And here's a big one: some kids have never learned to play. Trauma, neglect, or simply not having safe adults who played with them means play feels foreign or even threatening. For these kids, play might need to be explicitly taught, slowly introduced, and never forced.

The goal isn't to make everyone play the same way. It's to find the play that works for each kid and use it as a bridge to connection. Even in high school. Even with "serious" content. Maybe especially then.

~ Amie ~

In my geography class, one of the concepts we teach is biomes. I developed a lesson where kids get a bath mat with a world map on it (it has never been *used* as an actual bath mat, and yes, the kids always ask). They also get a pile of small plastic animals and access to a Nearpod lesson. Students work through the Nearpod, finding information, and then place the plastic animals on the bath mat in their proper locations.

We're blending play with curriculum. Yes, the kids end up playing with the small animals. Yes, I let them. Yes, they're between 12-16 years old. And yes, they seem to genuinely enjoy the lesson.

One year while doing this lesson, a small group brought me a couple of animals that had something... extra... drawn on them with a pen. As we did a little investigating, it turned out that at some point in history, a previous group of students had decorated most of the animals inappropriately. This was just the first group honest enough to tell me. (Of course it's a penis story. I teach middle school.)

Since we couldn't prove who the perpetrators of this plastic-animal-penis-pandemic were, we did the only thing we could do: corrective surgery.

One of my fellow teachers showed up in my room fully committed to the bit. Science apron. Surgical gloves. Face mask. Scalpel in hand. He announced he was there to perform "emergency reconstructive procedures" and got to work. Rubbing alcohol handled most of the artwork, but for the particularly persistent penises, he broke out the scalpel to carefully scrape them away.

I'm proud to report that all the animals survived the operation.

We still laugh about this. The play involved, for both students and teachers, has made it one of my favorite lessons.

We need to play. For them and for us.

Find Your Play Personality

We all play differently, and leaning into our own strengths is what will give kids the courage and ability to lean into theirs.

You can go to the National Institute for Play website at nifplay.org to take a quiz to identify your play personality.

Some teachers are storytellers and directors. They love creating scenarios and guiding experiences. That shows up in how they structure activities.

Other teachers are kinesthetic players. They're constantly moving, acting things out.

Others are competitive. They love games and contests.

Others are explorers. They want to tinker and discover.

Find your play style. Then bring it to your classroom.

Because play isn't unprofessional. Play is building connected relationships. And connected relationships are what makes learning possible.

Practical Ways to Add Play to Any Subject

For elementary teachers:

- Use games to practice math facts (dice games, card games, board games)
- Act out stories during reading
- Make science experiments feel like magic tricks
- Use puppets or stuffed animals to teach social skills
- Create treasure hunts for learning vocabulary

For secondary teachers:

- Use competition strategically (team trivia, review games)
- Build in creative projects with no single right answer
- Let students design their own assessments occasionally
- Use role-play for historical events or literature
- Incorporate movement (gallery walks, stations, acting out processes)
- Allow collaborative problem-solving with low-stakes failure

For all teachers:

- Build humor into your day (laugh with students, even when cringy)
- Allow moments of silliness within structure
- Celebrate mistakes as learning opportunities

- Create classroom rituals that are playful (handshakes, cheers, inside jokes)
- Give students choice in how they demonstrate learning

Connection for Secondary Teachers: The 150-Student Reality

If you teach multiple periods and see 150+ students a day, everything we've said might feel impossible. We get it. Deep individual connection with every student isn't realistic.

But here's what IS realistic:

Try Learning names quickly. Use seating charts, name tents, or whatever system works for you. Nothing says "you matter" like knowing someone's name.

Greeting and presence at the door. Even if it's brief, stand at your door. Make eye contact. Use names. This takes no extra time and sets a completely different tone.

One personal comment per class, per day. You can't connect deeply with everyone, but you can make one personal comment to one student per period. "Nice game yesterday, Kayse." "I like that shirt, Jasmine." "You seemed tired today, everything okay?" Rotate through your roster.

The 2-minute connection challenge with your hardest students. Pick your most challenging 3-5 students across all your periods. Spend 2 minutes connecting with each of them, rotating through the week. These are often the kids who need connection most and get it least. Keep in mind, their behavior is based on them using the skills they have in the best way they know. The behaviors won't change until we teach them the skills.

Consistent warmth with everyone, deep connection with a few. This is the realistic model. You can't be everyone's favorite teacher. But you can be consistently safe, predictable, and warm. And for a handful of students each semester, you can go deeper. Sample reminders of connection strategies can be seen here and in the workbook.

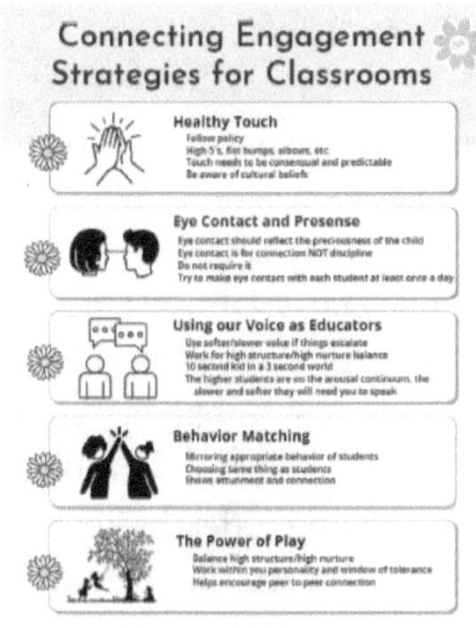

~ Amie ~

Warmth is something you have to cultivate. When I walk into school every day, I sit in my car for a moment and breathe. As I put on my badge, I feel like an actor. I put on my face, put on my smile, and walk into school. I say good morning to every student I see, even if I don't know them. I turn into my Ms. Huggins character. In all honesty, the more I practice this, the more it feels natural. There are days when I don't feel good or was up with kids the night before or we are on the Friday following two days of Parent Teacher Conferences. I try to be honest with kids and say I'm tired today but still try to connect. It is moments like this I know I need to fill my own cup. We will get to that in the self-care chapter.

Practical Applications: Connection Around Curriculum

Here's the beautiful thing: You don't have to choose between connection and curriculum. You can wrap connection activities around your content.

In Spanish class: Walk while practicing dialogues (movement + content).

In math: Use clapping games to practice multiplication tables (play + content).

In history: Act out historical events (embodiment + content).

In science: Do experiments in groups where roles rotate (collaboration + content).

You're not losing instructional time. You're making instructional time more effective by creating the conditions where learning can actually stick.

Classroom culture over individual relationships. Create a classroom environment where connection happens between students, not just between you and students. This multiplies your impact. You do this through structure. You set expectations that all kids are treated fairly. You teach the skills. You model the skills. You create different connective experiences (like pinatas and play-doh and shaving cream) that also incorporate play. Over time, this culture will develop.

A Note from Amie: Why I Finally Bought In

~ Amie ~

I've been the one at the back of professional development making snide comments and getting ready to implement my rebellion through compliance. Let's not even mention the number of times we've heard "build relationships" in some random training but no skills are given and we forget it as soon as it starts.

As a classroom teacher for 30 years, this was not an easy sell for me either. I can honestly tell you, if I hadn't had the kids I did in my personal life, I would have never been open to this. I tried just one skill at a time. I took eye contact and worked on it until it felt comfortable. It helped that I had already started using it at home, so the transition was a bit easier.

I'm also very clear and upfront with students. "We're doing the connection moment each day so that we can all feel safe and seen in the classroom." We can teach this to ourselves and our kids by naming it.

Let's Get Real: When Connection Feels Impossible

Marti: Okay, let's be brutally honest. Some days, connection feels impossible. Some students push every button you have, and you just want to survive the period.

Amie: I hear this from teachers all the time. "I know connection matters, but I don't like this kid. How am I supposed to connect with someone who makes my life miserable?"

Marti: Right? And the honest answer is: some days, you fake it.

Amie: Fake it?

Marti: Fake it. You say the greeting even though you don't feel warm. You make the eye contact even though you're annoyed. You use the calm voice even though you want to scream.

Amie: Because the behavior comes first, and the feelings follow?

Marti: Exactly. I'm not saying to be inauthentic. Remember, these kids have radars for inauthenticity. It signals alarm in their neuroception. I'm saying sometimes you have to act in alignment with your values even when your emotions aren't there yet.

Amie: And here's what's crazy: when you do that, the feelings often shift. When you greet a kid authentically even though you're frustrated, sometimes you remember why you care about them.

Marti: Not always. Sometimes a kid is just hard and you never really like them. But you can still connect. Connection doesn't require liking. It requires consistency.

Amie: What about when you've been trying and trying and the kid still pushes you away?

Marti: Keep showing up. The kids who reject connection the hardest are usually the ones who need it the most. Their pushing away is a test. They're asking, "Will you give up on me like everyone else?"

Amie: So your job is to keep failing the test?

Marti: Your job is to keep showing up. "I see you. I'm still here. I'm not going anywhere." That message, delivered consistently over time, is what eventually breaks through. Maybe not this semester. Maybe not even this year. But you're planting seeds and bringing sunshine.

Amie: Let's also talk about the reality of large class sizes. Because teachers feel like they're failing when they can't deeply connect with all 150 students.

Marti: You can't. You just can't. It's impossible.

Amie: So what do you do?

Marti: You do what you can. You greet everyone at the door. You learn names. You notice when someone's off. But a deep connection? Maybe you get that with 10-15 kids. And that's okay.

Amie: Those 10-15 kids get you as their "one caring adult." The others get a safe, consistent teacher. That's still valuable.

Marti: And you rotate who you're focusing on. Maybe this semester it's these kids. Next semester, it's others.

Amie: You do what you can with what you have. That's all anyone can ask. Connected kids learn better, behave better, and feel better. Connected teachers burn out less. We enjoy our jobs more. We remember why we started.

Takeaways

1. **Connection is how we build the felt safety.** These aren't abstract concepts; they're practical tools. Every skill in this chapter is designed to help students feel safe enough to learn.
2. **You don't need deep therapeutic relationships with every student.** With large class sizes, focus on consistent, predictable warmth with everyone and deeper connection with a few. That's realistic and still makes a difference.
3. **Small moments add up, and persistence matters.** Eye contact, greetings, slow speech, playful interactions,

remembering details. These aren't big gestures, but they build trust over time. And when students reject connection? Keep showing up anyway. Consistency over time is what eventually breaks through.

Reflection Questions

1. Who are the students you naturally connect with easily? What about them makes connection feel natural? Who are the students where connection feels hard? What makes it difficult?
2. How comfortable are you with playfulness in your teaching? What's your play personality? How could you bring more play into your classroom in a way that feels authentic to you?
3. Think about a student who consistently rejects your connection attempts. What might be driving that rejection? What would it look like to keep showing up without taking it personally?

One Thing to Try Tomorrow

The Two-Minute Connection Challenge

Pick one student who's hard for you to connect with. Just one.

Spend two minutes connecting with them every day for two weeks. Two minutes. That's it.

A greeting at the door

A check-in question

A comment about something they care about

A joke

A high-five

Two minutes, consistently, for two weeks.

We promise you: those two minutes will change your relationship with that student. And that changed relationship will change everything else.

CHAPTER 8

Relating Through the Body

Picture this: You're standing at the front of your classroom, arms crossed, eyebrows furrowed, wondering why Liam in the third row looks like he's about to bolt for the door. You haven't said a word yet. The lesson hasn't even started. But your body has already been talking.

Here's the wild thing about being human: we're constantly broadcasting signals we don't even know we're sending. Our posture, our stance, our facial features, and our fingers are all firing off messages faster than any lecture we could deliver. And our students' nervous systems are picking up every single signal like a satellite dish searching for safety.

We talked about building connected relationships through intentional strategies like greetings, eye contact, and playful engagement. Now we're going deeper. This chapter is about the power of the physical: how our bodies communicate care (or threat), how touch can transform tension, and what to do when students push connection away like it's a plate of cold cafeteria peas.

Because sometimes the most powerful thing we do isn't what we say. It's how we show up.

Never Underestimate the Power of…. Body Language

Like a sea witch, our nervous system is lazy and biased towards negativity. It has to be. That's how we stay alive. We are constantly scanning the environment for cues that remind us of things in the past that felt unsafe so that we don't experience them again.

We talked a bit about this in Section One when referencing Dr. Porges and Dr Perry's work about the stress response systems and neuroception. The relevance here is to highlight how body language is subconsciously interpreted as an indication of threat or safety.

History proves time and again that the largest threat to humans is actually other humans. So our brains have developed very specialized and nuanced ways to interpret social cues. A smile can quickly put us at ease while a side-eye can cue us towards distrust.

Tone can indicate respect or defiance when paired with the exact same word, or, "whatever".

How we stand, how we place our arms, even how we cross our legs or arrange our fingers is sending constant social cues to others about our intentions and capacities. Do we look confident? Open? Threatening? Fearful? Ashamed?

When we are familiar with these unconscious messages, we can recognize them in ourselves and in our students. We can choose a purposefully open stance as we welcome our students at the door. We can make a quick glance to see who is feeling connected and who is feeling protective as they sit at their desk.

Here are a few body language decoders that can help build connection:

Cues of Connection	Cues of Protection
Relaxed smile and bright eyes	Hiding head with hands or a hoodie
Shoulders back and chest exposed	Rounded spine and chest covered
Leaning forward toward the person	Leaning away from the person
Hands open and relaxed	Palms hidden or fisted
Shoulders pointed toward a person	Shoulders pointed toward an exit
Hands at sides	Hands in pockets or across chest
Vocal tones with rhythmic patterns	Unpredictable vocal tones of high or low pitch
Mirrored or copied movements	Flinching

When Bodies Speak Different Languages: Neurodivergence and Cultural Considerations

Everything we've said about body language? It comes with a massive asterisk.

Neurodivergent Differences:

People who are neurodivergent often perceive AND express body language differently. This cuts both ways:

They may read body language differently:

- Missing cues of safety you think you're clearly sending
- Perceiving threat where none was intended
- Not noticing facial expressions or tone shifts that seem obvious to you

They may express body language differently:

- Flat affect that looks "shut down" but actually isn't
- Intense eye contact OR complete eye contact avoidance (both normal for different neurotypes)
- Stimming movements that might look like "cues of protection" but are actually self-regulation
- Tone of voice that doesn't match their actual emotional state

Because of this, you can't rely on body language alone. State the obvious clearly. Ask clarifying questions: "It sounds like you're frustrated. Is that right?" or "I'm going to hand you this paper. Is that okay?"

We also need to check our own interpretations. When a neurodivergent student's tone doesn't match our expectation, we may assume they're feeling something they're not.

When you tell them about your new puppy and they reply with "I hate dogs," it doesn't mean they're being rude or dismissing your feelings. Maybe high-pitched barking is sensory overload for them. Maybe they're stating a fact without realizing it sounds harsh. Maybe they're actually trying to connect by sharing their own experience.

It's not personal. It's neurological. Stay curious.

Cultural Differences:

Body language is also deeply cultural. Consider:

Personal space: In some cultures, standing close signals warmth and engagement. In others, it signals aggression or disrespect. That student who keeps "getting in other kids' space" might be using the proximity norms from home.

Gestures: Hand gestures, head movements, and facial expressions carry different meanings across cultures. What looks like a shrug of indifference to you might mean something entirely different to the student.

Emotional expression: Some cultures value expressive communication. Others value restraint. Don't confuse cultural style with emotional state.

Touch norms: What feels like a friendly pat might feel invasive to some students and distant to others, depending on their cultural background.

The practical takeaway: Body language gives us clues, not conclusions. When in doubt, ask. When surprised by a response, get curious. And never assume your reading of body language is the only valid interpretation.

Healthy Touch (What's Appropriate in Schools)

Touch in schools is complicated. For good reasons. Histories of abuse make us rightfully cautious. Boundaries and policies were written out of necessity. We need to respect those boundaries and histories while also recognizing how powerful touch can be.

Healthy touch helps regulate the nervous system and communicates safety and care when it's expected and accepted. Ever notice how you can't tickle yourself? Tickling activates the alarm system, but when the brain knows it's coming, those alarm signals get muted. This is one reason asking permission before touching is more calming than just reaching out. Predictable, mutual touch works best.

In schools, it's always best practice to ask what type of touch (if any) a student wants at that moment. And just like we discussed earlier, teachers need to meet their own sensory needs too.

If you're not a hugger, no need to fake it. There are plenty of ways to build relationships that don't leave you reaching for the hand sanitizer. The key with any sensory connection is consent and curiosity about preferences.

Touch can be incredibly intimate, especially for students who either had abusive touch or lack of touch in their past. Some children have difficulty with being touched at all. Others are eager to touch every part of your body like an octopus trying to climb into your sweater.

Healthy touch in a classroom can look like fist bumps, high fives, a hand on the shoulder, and clapping games. Clapping games are connection gold. They have both proprioceptive input with touch plus rhythm. Powerhouses that calm the downstairs brain. One of our favorite clapping games is "Double This, Double That". Kids love this stuff. It's connective. It's playful. It involves touch and proprioception.

What if we not only allow kids to play clapping games, but add curriculum to it? For early elementary: learning letter sounds while clapping. "T-T" (clap clap) "sound out: /tt/-/tt/" (clap clap). For older kids: vocabulary words, math facts, historical dates can all be instructed to a cadence where clapping can be useful.

When we combine play and healthy touch, we make content more emotive, and build connection between students and between teacher and students. Touch doesn't have to be complicated. It just has to be intentional, appropriate, consensual, and consistent. We can do that.

Eye Contact and Presence

Dr. Purvis used to say that when we look into the eyes of our kids, they need to see their preciousness reflected back to them. That's powerful.

When we look at a student, what do they see reflected back? Annoyance? Judgment? Exhaustion? Or do they see: "I see you. You matter. I'm glad you're here."

Let's dig deeper here, because eye contact is one of the most culturally loaded aspects of connection.

Cultural realities:

- In many Indigenous, Asian, African, and Latino cultures, children are taught that looking down when an adult speaks is a sign of respect and attentiveness.
- What you interpret as "avoidance" or "shame" might actually be a child demonstrating the deepest respect they know how to show.
- Requiring eye contact can put students in an impossible position: disobey their family's cultural values OR disobey their teacher.

Neurodivergent realities:

- For many autistic individuals, eye contact is physically uncomfortable, cognitively draining, or both.
- Making eye contact can actually REDUCE their ability to process what you're saying because it takes so much mental energy.
- Some neurodivergent folks make TOO MUCH eye contact (intense, unblinking) which can be misread as aggression or defiance.

Trauma realities:

- For children who've experienced abuse, direct eye contact can feel threatening.

- Looking into an adult's eyes might have been dangerous in their past. Eye contact can trigger a trauma response that takes them offline.

The shift: Stop using eye contact as a measure of attention, respect, or engagement. Instead, look for other cues: Are they orienting toward you? Did they respond to your question? Are they doing what you asked?

And please, forever and always: never demand "Look at me when I'm talking to you." That's a power move disguised as a connection move, and it backfires spectacularly for neurodivergent kids, trauma-impacted kids, and culturally diverse kids.

Using Our Voice as Educators

We use the "teacher voice" all the time. You know the one.

It's effective because it's rooted in the polyvagal theory. That specific pitch, cadence, and tone are all processed in a way that activates the nervous system. Which is what helps us get from a super relaxed state to a *just right amount of stress for learning* state.

Yes, activation and stress can be good things. Stress that brings us just inside the edges of our window of tolerance is where growth is significant. We need stress to call us to action. However, when that stress pushes us out of that window, we begin to lose access to our learning brains.

Let's link this back to our care gardens. If we have more cares to give, this teacher voice is an excellent tool. It keeps us focused and on-task. However, if we are already stressed due to family dynamics, a relationship drama, fear we don't understand the assignment, or not having the motor skills to complete the requested task, our window closes, our cares are harvested, and the teacher voice can put us out of our window of tolerance into a protective and disconnected learning state of mind.

When we see our students begin to disconnect, we can try *lowering* our voice level and actually *decreasing* our speed. This goes against every natural instinct. When we're scared or upset, we want to talk louder and faster. We want to project authority and control.

But here's what the research shows: when a brain is stressed, it processes information more slowly. Talking louder and faster makes it harder for an overly stressed child to understand you. Remember, high voices also subconsciously signal the nervous system that a threat is coming. If they are already tipped to protection, this is too much for them. Talking slower and softer helps their nervous system not jump to an assumption of danger.

~ Marti ~

Voice can be a little tricky. So let's break it down a bit more from a sensory and nervous system perspective. While holding onto the idea that we all sense things uniquely, let's explore things from a generalized perspective.

Generally, high-pitched tones can signal distress. I once heard that house cats evolved to sound like babies crying to get their needs met. True or not, it's interesting and seems effective. Certain sudden pitch changes, volumes, and rhythms cue us to quick reactions. With this generalization, the "teacher voice" would alert or activate, and the slower, lower voice would calm or deactivate.

However, we have to layer on another nuance. We need to be seen and heard. We need someone to "match our energy." Robyn Gobbel and I talk a lot about this in our shared work. If a student is really loud and arrhythmic, coming in calm and quiet could be interpreted as dismissive.

Imagine a wasp flying into your classroom and you yell for a student to open the window. You don't want them to casually saunter over to do the task. You want that urgency in your voice to be met with urgency in their actions. If that student doesn't act quickly, you would feel like they aren't getting it, and you would get louder. Because that's how nervous systems work when we sense threat. We escalate until we feel matched.

So sometimes, we need to keep that elevated pitch and rhythm to "match" the situation until we can bring it back down together. Once our nervous systems are in co-regulation, we can influence the deactivation.

What does this look like? Imagine a student runs up to your desk and slams a paper down. They are clearly upset with the grade.

If you calmly explain that they needed to study more, I'm guessing it's not going to de-escalate quickly.

Matching their dysregulation would be yelling back at them not to slam things on your desk. That's not what we're going for.

Matching the energy without matching the dysregulation would be saying something validating while holding a boundary. An example could be, "Whoa, Cowboy! Sounds like there's a problem! Let's see if we can figure this out." Then calmly hand the paper back to them as you help them. Maybe you open your laptop right there and help them see where it went wrong. Or maybe you add, "I can't help you right now, but I'll be available during office hours. Shall I save a time for you?"

So yes, most of the time you will be able to lower your voice and influence deactivation. However, sometimes you need to activate a little bit to mirror the person back into co-regulation.

I like to imagine when my puppy runs into the room with a toy. She's sooo excited. But if I ignore her or stay too low energy, it doesn't help her settle. I have to match her energy first. Then we can come down together. Watchdogs are like that. If your student is giving you watchdog energy, you know their window is closing. Our focus moves to felt-safety and getting their needs met in relationship.

Marti once worked with a school that had a student who would resort to violence pretty regularly. Her colleague relayed this story to her. The child had a history of big behaviors in school, and home life appeared to be pretty difficult.

One day in class, the student decided to hold another student in a dangerous way, like a chokehold. Instead of screaming and trying to physically intervene (which could be a very natural first instinct), the teacher had another student go to the office to get help. Then the teacher got below eye level with the student in crisis, spoke calmly and directly, and asked the student to release the other child.

All this was done while the teacher breathed in deep, loud breaths. Very little verbiage. A lot of offerings of relational connection through the mirror neurons and a soft face.

The student released the other child.

Understanding the potential impact of voice quality and volume can be huge in helping us manage and even prevent behaviors. Not only that, but the student and teacher emerged from a very difficult and scary situation with MORE sense of trust and safety. The connection increased, and so the child's need to be in the downstairs brain decreased.

This takes practice and effort. You will forget and yell sometimes. We all do. But every time you remember to go quiet and slow instead of loud and fast, you're building trust and connection.

Behavior Matching - sometimes we need to feel what they feel and mirror it back

This one is going to sound weird. Stay with us.

A teacher we know had a student who was new to the school and came with a long list of behaviors. Many of those behaviors were violent and pretty scary.

One day, this student started escalating. The teacher could hear the student screaming and throwing things from across the hall. Admin and support staff were already involved, trying to deescalate, but the behaviors seemed to be getting worse.

The teacher went into the hall, got below eye level with the student, and slowly asked if the student was in physical pain. A simple, direct, easier to answer question. She didn't ask about feelings. This student didn't have access to verbal information at the time. Again, very few words being used. But the student could nod their head.

The student was able to make fleeting eye contact with the teacher, and the teacher asked if the student was okay to walk across the hall to an empty classroom.

As they started walking across the hall, the student just sat down. Right there. In the middle of the hallway.

Here the teacher was met with a difficult decision: Do they behavior-match and sit down with the student? Do they stand? Do they grab the student and forcefully insist they keep moving?

The real decision was about creating safety. When an adult stands over a student, it can feel scary and intimidating. Grabbing a student forcefully never de-escalates things.

Behavior matching shows connection. It engages mirror neurons in the brain. These are specialized neurons that cue us about social safety. They help us imagine what someone else is feeling.

When someone mirrors us, our own experience feels validated and less alone. We get a sense that they understand how we feel.

The teacher got down on the carpet and sat with the student.

No words were really used. Just sat there.

Eventually, the student rolled around on the ground. And again, the teacher was met with a difficult choice: Behavior-match with the student by rocking back and forth in the same rhythm as she sat, or sit there stationary?

The teacher took a leap of faith and matched the rhythm of the child. Rolling might have triggered a fear of mocking response from the student. But slowly rocking in the same rhythm as the child's rolling sent non-verbal cues to the student's downstairs brain that they were connected.

The student was being seen. Mirrored. Co-regulation. The student's stress response lessened and the teacher was able to gently help the upstairs brain come back online. The teacher's owl was able to soothe the student's watchdog and invite their owl back to their thinking brain.

Eventually, the student stood up. The teacher followed. They walked into the classroom, co-regulated together, and were able to send the student back to class ready to learn.

We tell this story to show the magic of connection that can occur with behavior matching. We also acknowledge that if this was happening in real time in a classroom with one adult and 25 other students, it isn't possible. This is a best-case scenario. It occurred with a teacher who was willing and able to get on the ground. Another teacher could cover her class.

What it does is show the reality of what behavior matching can do. Like everything in this book, we're talking about creating a buffet of ideas we can pull from as we can and are able.

We also need to be sure that we do not expect every teacher to use the same strategies. If teachers are trying to use tactics and skills that are not comfortable, they will be stressed, and that will lead to students who are also stressed.

We have to find our own superpowers and do what we are capable of. Maybe a different choice would be to clear the area and stand within line of sight of the student and mirror from a further distance. Maybe your super power is distraction or humor. Something sudden and playful that shocks the owl back to the situation.

It is the differences in strategies that will make the entire school work. Just like we try to meet individual students where they are, each teacher will bring their own skills to the table. By having a large and diverse skill set in the school, ideally every student eventually gets what they need.

Again, we acknowledge that reality and what works do not always coexist. But we need to move focus from compliance to connection.

Buddies to Buffer: Why Peer Connection Matters

Here's a concept that will show up throughout this book, so let's define it clearly here: buddies to buffer.

The idea is simple: students who have meaningful connections with peers can weather ocean storms that would sink a kid who feels alone. When a student has even one friend, one ally, one person who "gets them," they have a buffer against the hard stuff. Stress doesn't hit as hard. Setbacks feel more survivable. School feels less scary.

This is backed by research on resilience. One of the strongest protective factors for kids facing adversity is having supportive relationships, and those relationships don't have to be only with adults. Peer connections matter enormously. In fact, knowing what we know about adolescents and status, those peer connections are often the most important connections for kids. So our job isn't just to connect with students ourselves. It's to help them connect with each other.

What this looks like in practice:

Intentional pairing and grouping. Think about who you put together. A struggling student paired with a patient, kind peer can be transformative. A lonely student included in a welcoming group can change their whole experience of school.

Teaching connection skills. Don't assume kids know how to make friends, give compliments, or resolve conflicts. Teach these skills explicitly.

Creating structures for peer support. Buddy systems. Peer tutoring. Partner check-ins. Table groups that stay together long enough to build relationships.

Noticing and intervening with isolated students. The kid who always works alone, who sits at the edge, who nobody picks for group work? That kid needs you to help build bridges. The "nice" kid who always gets paired with the more isolated students also needs extra support.

~ Amie ~

I had a class once that was rough. Kids who struggled in the school system. Cliques. Drama. Constant conflict. Attendance and behavior issues.

So I started doing circle time. Every day. Five minutes at the start of class. The first day in my class of 14-16 year olds, we made listening ears and talked about what makes a good listener.

We taught skills: how to give and receive compliments, how to disagree respectfully, how to ask for what you need. We gave kids time to connect, to share, to be human together.

By the end of the year, that class was functioning better than any other period.

Why? Because we didn't just create connection between me and students. We created connection between students and students.

When kids feel connected to each other, they co-regulate each other. They support each other. They hold each other accountable in ways no teacher can.

Buddies to buffer. It works.

Working Kids in Groups Effectively

Group work only works when you teach the skills.

We can't just say, "Okay, work in groups," and expect magic. We have to model collaboration. Teach conflict resolution. Practice active listening.

Some strategies: Assign roles so everyone has a job. Build in individual accountability so no one can just coast. Teach sentence stems for respectful disagreement. Model what good collaboration looks like. Debrief after group work: What went well? What was hard?

~ Amie ~

I know we have all had so much professional development that is supposed to give us all the answers. Especially regarding group work. Here is my own take on group work. I don't necessarily put kids in groups to learn the content. Let's be realistic. They rarely learn deeply from that group project and presentation. One person in the group does the work, and everyone else pretends and adds their name.

I have changed my entire motivation for group work. I now see the purpose of groups as creating connection. Let me give you an example. I teach geography. We have to teach a skill called map distortion. For those of you who don't teach geography, this may sound foreign. This is the first lesson of the school year. The first day of school, the kids make a pinata out of a balloon. The second day of school they paint and color the pinata with continents and oceans on the planet. The third day, we cut the pinata apart and use it to show the issue of distortion.

Along with teaching the content, place-name geography, and distortion, they are also getting to know each other. First day of school they get to sit in groups without making eye contact. They start out not really talking but by the end of the period, they know someone in the class. They get to have a sensory experience. Kids who hate having dirty hands don't help with the pinata. Those kids become the supply runners or scribes. They all get a hands-on object to teach a super difficult concept like map distortion!

I sometimes assign groups. I sometimes do random groups. Sometimes groups are based on level. Or wanting to do the same topic. I try to have the group fit the assignment. Structure vs rigidity. I structure the group work, teach the skills, but am flexible in how we implement it. Connection skills enable group work. Group work reinforces connection skills.

Visual Summary: Connection Skills Quick Reference

Connection Skill	What It Looks Like	Quick Tip
Door Greeting	Stand at door, eye contact, use names, personal comment	30 seconds per student changes the whole class culture
Eye Contact	Intentional, warm, once per student per period	For connection, not discipline. Don't require it when correcting.
Voice Modulation	Lower volume, slower pace when students escalate	Go quiet and slow, not loud and fast. Count to 3 before responding.
10-Second Wait Time	Pause after instructions, count silently	10-second kids deserve a 10-second world
Behavior Matching	Get on their level, mirror posture/rhythm	Shows "I'm with you" without words
Playful Interaction	Games, humor, curriculum through play	Play disarms fear. Find YOUR play style.
Healthy Touch	Fist bumps, high fives, clapping games	Intentional, appropriate, consensual, consistent
2-Minute Connection	Daily intentional time with one challenging student	Pick one kid. Two minutes. Two weeks. Watch what shifts.
Buddies to Buffer	Help students connect with each other	Your job isn't just connecting; it's helping them connect.

Remember: You can't deeply connect with 150 students. Focus on consistent warmth with everyone, deeper connection with a few. That's realistic. That's enough.

When Connection Is Rejected: What to Do When Students Push Back

This is the part most books leave out. What do you do when you try to connect and the student doesn't want it?

Some students will ignore your greeting. Some will respond with hostility. Some will actively push you away. This is especially true for students with attachment difficulties, who may have learned that adults are not safe and that connection leads to pain.

First, understand what's happening.

When a student rejects connection, they're not rejecting you personally. They're protecting themselves. For kids who have been hurt by adults, connection feels dangerous. Your warmth might feel like a setup. Your attention might feel like pressure. Your caring might feel like a trap.

Their rejection is a survival strategy, not a personal insult.

What to do:

Keep showing up anyway. The greeting that gets ignored today might be the greeting that gets a nod in three months. Consistency over time is what eventually breaks through. Don't take the rejection as a sign to stop. Take it as information about how much this student needs safe adults to not give up on them.

Here's what they don't tell you: often, when a child with attachment concerns starts to feel safe, they push the safe adult away more. They get harder. The mentality is "I will push them away before they push me away." You have to hang in there to get over that hump. And for some kids, that takes years.

Lower the pressure. Some students can't handle direct eye contact and warm conversation. It's too intense. Try connection with less pressure: maybe a wave, or a subtle head nod. Seeing a need like needing a pencil and just handing it to them. Keep it small and simple.

Use parallel connection. Instead of face-to-face connection (which can feel confrontational), try side-by-side connection. Walk alongside them in the hallway. Sit next to them while they work, not across from them. Comment on what they're doing without requiring a response. In parenting, this is what we do when we have the hard conversations while driving. No eye contact. They can look away.

Respect their pace. Some students need to observe you being safe with other students before they'll trust you. Let them watch. Don't force it. Connection that feels demanded isn't connection at all. Some kids are genuinely shy. Some just want quiet. Try to respect that.

Notice micro-moments. The student who never responds to your greeting might one day make eye contact for half a second. That's progress. The student who always puts their head down might one day keep it up for five minutes. Celebrate (internally) these tiny shifts. This one is more about you maintaining motivation. Let's be honest, it is really hard to maintain relationships with people who give nothing back.

Don't take it personally (even though it feels personal). Their rejection is about their history, not about you. Keep your own nervous system feeling safe. Keep offering connection without needing a response.

Get support. Students with significant attachment difficulties may need more than classroom connection can provide. Talk to your school counselor, social worker, or psychologist. These students may need therapeutic support alongside your consistent presence. That said, it is not your responsibility to offer these services or try to meet some of their goals. The thing teachers can do is work together. What if you and your friends in the coffee club notice a kid is starting to really withdraw? Every teacher tries to make a micro-connection with that student in the week. We team approach it.

When We Need to be Realistic

Some students have experienced such significant early trauma that their capacity for connection is deeply impaired. These students may:

- Actively sabotage relationships when they start to feel close
- Test you relentlessly to see if you'll give up like everyone else
- Seem to "prefer" isolation even though they desperately need connection
- Respond to warmth with hostility or withdrawal
- Take months or years to show any response to your efforts

These students might need therapeutic work that requires specialized training. Your job is to be a consistent, safe presence who doesn't give up.

This might mean:

- Accepting that progress will be measured in tiny increments over long periods, if at all
- Celebrating when a student tolerates your presence, even if they don't engage
- Maintaining boundaries while staying warm (these students will test both)
- Reporting concerns you have to others in the building. Make sure you follow policy for your school/district/etc.
- Protecting yourself from burnout by having realistic expectations

You may never see the breakthrough with these students. But your consistency might be planting seeds that someone else will harvest years from now. That matters, even when you can't see it.

Let's Get Real: Body Language in the Classroom

Amie: Okay, let's talk about body language. Because I think some teachers hear "watch your body language" and think they need to become some kind of mime artist.

Marti: I think of Ursula when I hear "body language". (Laughing)

It's really not about performing. It's about awareness. Our bodies are already talking. We just need to tune in to what they're saying.

Amie: So what does that look like practically? I have 40 kids staring at me. I can't be hyperaware of my shoulder position at every moment. I'm not an animated cartoon character.

Marti: You don't need to be. Start with the moments that matter most: the door greeting, the redirect, the one-on-one check-in. Those are the times to consciously open up your posture, uncross those arms, relax your face.

Amie: I catch myself crossing my arms all the time. Sometimes I'm just cold!

Marti: And that's fine! Context matters. But if you're crossing your arms while talking to a stressed student, their nervous system might read that as "this adult is closed off, maybe unsafe." It's not about being perfect. It's about being aware when it counts.

Amie: What about reading students' body language?

Marti: Some kids broadcast loud and clear, but we miss it because we're focused on their words or behavior. The kid with their hood up and shoulders hunched? Protection mode. The kid whose shoulders are pointed toward the exit? Part of them is already planning their escape route.

Amie: So instead of getting frustrated they're not paying attention, I should get curious about why their body is telling them to protect or flee.

Marti: Exactly. Their body is giving you information about where their nervous system is at.

Amie: I want to talk about eye contact too. I was trained to say "look at me when I'm talking to you" and now I'm learning that might actually make things worse?

Marti: Think about it: when you're in trouble and someone demands eye contact, what does that feel like?

Amie: Intense. Kind of confrontational.

Marti: For kids with trauma histories, it can feel unbearable. Eye contact during correction can trigger shame responses. And a kid in shame isn't learning anything. They're just surviving the moment.

Amie: So when DO we use eye contact?

Marti: For connection, not correction. The warm glance across the room. The intentional acknowledgment at the door. The moment when you look at them and they see their preciousness reflected back. That's powerful. But "look at me when I'm talking to you" as a discipline move? That's about dominance, not connection.

Amie: Cultural piece too, right? And neurodivergence?

Marti: Absolutely. What feels like connection for one student might feel like confrontation in another. This is where relationship matters. When you know your students, you know what works for them.

Amie: I had a student everyone thought was being defiant. Wouldn't look at anyone, mumbled responses, shoulders always turned away. Turns out she was autistic AND from a culture where girls especially don't make eye contact with adults. Once I stopped interpreting her body language through my own lens, I realized she was actually really engaged. She just showed it differently.

Marti: Same behavior, completely different meaning. We'd never know if we didn't get curious.

Amie: Last question: What about students who flinch? I have a few kids who physically pull away when I get close, even just handing them a paper.

Marti: That flinch is telling you everything. Their body has learned that adults getting close means pain. You didn't cause that, but you have to respect it. Give them more space. Move slowly.

Announce your intentions: "I'm going to hand you this paper." Let their nervous system predict what's coming.

Amie: Bodies keep the score, as they say.

Marti: Bodies keep the score. Our job is to help add points for safety, one safe interaction at a time.

Takeaways

1. **Body language is broadcasting, whether we mean it or not.** Our posture, positioning, and presence send signals to students' nervous systems long before we open our mouths. Learning to read cues of connection (relaxed shoulders, open palms) versus cues of protection (hidden hands, hunched spines) helps us respond with curiosity instead of frustration. And when we consciously choose an open, welcoming stance, we're speaking safety in a language their downstairs brain actually understands.
2. **Touch, voice, and eye contact are powerful tools, but they require consent and cultural awareness.** Healthy touch can regulate nervous systems and communicate care, but only when it's expected, accepted, and appropriate. Eye contact builds connection when offered warmly, but becomes a power move when demanded during discipline. And our voice? Slowing down and softening up when things escalate goes against every instinct we have, yet it's exactly what stressed brains need to process.
3. **When students reject connection, they're protecting themselves, not insulting you.** The kids who push away the hardest often need connection the most. Their rejection is a survival strategy built from past hurt, not a personal verdict on your teaching. Keep showing up. Lower the pressure. Try parallel connection instead of face-to-face intensity. Progress might take months (or years), but your consistency is planting seeds someone else may harvest.

Reflection Questions

1. Think about your typical body language in the classroom. What signals might you be sending without realizing it? When you're stressed, where does tension show up in your body, and how might students be reading those cues?
2. How comfortable are you with touch in the classroom? What kinds of healthy touch feel natural to you, and what boundaries do you need to maintain for your own felt-safety? How could you incorporate more playful, proprioceptive connection (like clapping games or fist bumps) into your daily routine?
3. Consider a student who consistently rejects your connection attempts. What might their history be teaching them about trusting adults? What would it look like to lower the pressure while still showing up consistently?
4. How does your voice change when you're stressed or frustrated? What would it take to practice going "quiet and slow" instead of "loud and fast" when a student is escalating?

One Thing to Try Tomorrow

Posture at Pivotal Points

Pick three moments tomorrow where you consciously check your body language:

1. The door greeting
2. One redirect or correction
3. One individual check-in with a student

Before each moment, do a quick body scan: Are your arms open or crossed? Is your face relaxed or tense? Are you at eye level or towering over them?

Then notice what happens. Does the student seem more receptive when you're physically open? Does lowering yourself to eye level change the tone of the interaction?

You're not trying to be perfect. You're just paying attention to what your body is already saying.

CHAPTER 9

Creating a Safe and Sensory-Friendly Classroom

Environment IS Connection

We talked about how connection creates felt safety. We covered eye contact, voice, play, and touch. Those skills are essential.

Connection doesn't happen in a vacuum. It happens in a space.

When you set up a space that meets a student's sensory needs, you're communicating something powerful without saying a word. You're saying: "I see you. I understand that your body works differently. I've made room for you here."

A student who can chew gum to focus, who has access to a fidget, who can sit on a wobble cushion instead of a hard chair… that student feels seen. That student feels safe. That student feels connected.

So as you read this chapter, don't think of environment as separate from relationship. Think of it as relationship expressed through space. Every accommodation you make is a message: "You belong here. Your needs matter."

Every single human has sensory needs. We all crave certain types of sensory input. Some people need lots of movement (vestibular support). Some need heavy work (proprioceptive support). Some need quiet or background music (auditory support). Some need dim lighting or bright backgrounds (visual support).

The problem is, most classrooms are set up for one type of sensory profile: sit still, be quiet, keep your hands to yourself, eyes on the teacher.

That works for maybe 20% of kids. The other 80%? They're fighting their own bodies all day.

Creating a safe and sensory-friendly classroom is relating through the senses. It means having options available so kids can meet their own unique sensory needs while being offered signals of felt safety.

The Story That Changed How I See Behavior

~ Marti ~

Years ago, I was consulting in an elementary school, observing a third-grade classroom. The teacher had called me in because of Riley, a student he described as "constantly disruptive."

When I observed Riley's classroom, her teacher was right about the behaviors. She was out of her seat constantly. She touched the wall as she walked by. She picked up objects from other kids' desks. She bumped into classmates seemingly on purpose.

But here's what I saw that her teacher didn't: Riley had no idea how her body related to the environment around her. Her brain was having trouble processing signals from her proprioceptive system, the system that tells us how hard we're squeezing things, how far away the wall is, where our body ends and someone else's body begins.

Her nervous system was hungry for deep pressure and heavy work, the kind of input that helps some bodies feel organized and calm. Those "disruptive" behaviors? They were her nervous system's desperate attempt to get what it needed. She was feeling the walls with her fingers because she couldn't *sense* where they were. Her vision and her muscles weren't in sync with her proprioceptors.

She wasn't being disruptive on purpose. She was trying to relate to her environment the only way she knew how.

I suggested a few simple changes:

Heavy lifting jobs: Give Riley a job that involves carrying books to the office or pushing the cart of supplies.

Wiggle cushion: Let her sit on something that provides movement while seated.

Resistance band around chair legs: Give her something to push against with her feet.

Put tennis balls on diagonally opposite legs of her chair: Give her a little rhythmic back and forth bounce without too much movement.

Line leader: Let her go first so she's close to the teacher and he can co-regulate with proximity.

Stress ball or putty: Provide squeezing input during instruction.

More movement breaks: Build them into the schedule for everyone.

Moments of Connection: Riley liked hugs. With written permission from her grandma, her teacher was able to give her hugs when she asked. Knowing about proprioception, her teacher made them a little firmer, consistent in pressure, and longer. Just like her body was craving.

The teacher was skeptical. "Won't that just distract her more?"

I asked him to try it for two weeks.

When I came back, he looked at me like I'd performed a magic trick. "She's a different kid," he said. "She's actually staying in her seat. She's not bothering anyone. She's finishing her work. Those little side hugs helped me, too."

Riley wasn't a different kid. She was the same kid with her sensory needs being met. Her nervous system finally had what it needed to settle, so her brain could show up for learning.

This is what we mean when we talk about creating a safe and sensory-friendly environment. When we meet the nervous system's needs, behavior often takes care of itself.

Sensory Breaks That Don't Disrupt Learning

Five minutes of meeting sensory needs = 25 minutes of effective instruction. Zero minutes of meeting sensory needs = 30 minutes of frustration and chaos. Do the math.

Quick sensory breaks (1-2 minutes):

- Brain breaks: "Stand up. Jump 10 times. Sit down."
- Breathing: "Three deep breaths together."
- Stretching: "Reach high. Reach low. Twist left. Twist right."
- Silly songs: "Head, shoulders, knees, and toes..." (Yes, even for middle schoolers.)
- Cross-laterals: "Touch your right elbow to your left knee."

You're not losing instructional time. You're creating conditions for instruction to actually work.

Classroom Setup and Organization

Creating safe and sensory-friendly environments means setting kids up for success BEFORE problems arise.

It's the opposite of reactive discipline. Instead of waiting for a child to melt down and then responding, we create conditions that make meltdowns less likely.

Your classroom environment is a low-stakes, non-threatening way you communicate care. A fidget basket says "I see your need to feel things." A calm-down corner says "We have space for your feelings here." A visual schedule says " I'm letting you know what's next. I want you to feel safe here."

You're not just arranging furniture. You're inviting connection and felt safety.

Creating safe and sensory-friendly environments has three main components:

Physical environment: Is the space set up to support sensory needs?

Sensory support: Are we meeting the body's needs for movement, input, and individualized sensory stimulation?

Predictability: Can students anticipate what's coming next? This is especially important for times of transition.

When these three things are in place, we prevent the majority of behavioral issues before they ever start.

Physical Environment

Let's talk about our physical spaces. We know we probably don't have control over everything. We can't knock down walls or install new overhead lighting. But there are many questions we can ask to guide us.

As you enter your classroom, what signals of safety or chaos are you sending? Is there predictability of the "flow" of the classroom? What is the path like from the door to the work station or desks? What types of stimulation does the student encounter?

Where is the teacher in relation to the students? Is the teacher's landing spot (desk, chair, podium) accessible and inviting? Or dominating and set above everyone else? What colors, textures, scents, and noises greet the students as they arrive?

Are there a variety of spaces to experience? Or is the student's desk their only square footage for that time period? Who is sitting next to them? Are there friends? Class pets? A window? Something inviting or something distracting?

As we move to the sensory support section, we will break down more specifics about what types of sensations are coded to dial up or dial down the nervous system stress response. But first, let's talk about the calm-down corner.

The Calm-Down Corner: Not a Punishment, a Tool

Let's be very clear. A calm-down space is NOT a time-out corner with a new name.

Time-Out (Old Model):	**Calm-Down Space (New Model):**
Isolation as punishment "Go think about what you did" Shame-based Often escalates dysregulation Breaks connection	Regulation support "Your body needs a break. This space can help." Skill-building Designed to help settle nervous system Maintains connection

Setting Up a Calm-Down Space

Location:

- Quiet corner or alcove
- Some visual privacy (can use a small shelf or fabric)
- Away from high-traffic areas
- Still visible to the teacher (safety)

What to Include:

- Something soft (pillow, stuffed animal, fabric)
- Something to squeeze or manipulate (stress ball, putty)
- Something visual (calm-down jar, pinwheel, I Spy book)
- Visual cards with regulation strategies
- Timer (optional, for students who want structure)
- Noise-canceling headphones
- Calming visuals (nature posters, lava lamps, glitter jars)

What NOT to Include:

- Screens or devices
- Anything that could become a projectile or be broken into a weapon
- Too many options (overwhelming)

Teaching Students to Use It

This is critical: you need to TEACH this tool when students are calm, not introduce it during a crisis.

The Introduction (During a Calm Moment):

- "Sometimes our bodies get really overwhelmed and need help settling down."
- "This is our calm-down corner. It's not a punishment. It's a tool."
- "When you feel your body getting too big, you can ask to take a break here."
- "Let me show you what's in it and how to use each thing."

Practice Together:

- Have ALL students try the space (reduces stigma)
- Practice asking for it: "I need a body break"
- Set expectations: How long? What's allowed? How do you know you're ready to come back?

When a Student Needs It:

- Offer, don't demand: "Would the calm-down corner help right now?"
- Guide, don't punish: "I can see your body needs something. Let's try a break."
- Check in: "How's your body feeling? Ready to try again?"

Some students use the calm-down corner daily. They'll raise their hand and say, "Can I take five minutes in the corner?" Yes. Always yes. They're learning to recognize when they need a break. That's a life skill.

When Students Misuse the Calm-Down Space

Some students will try to use the calm-down corner to avoid work. This is normal. It doesn't mean the system is broken.

Get curious, not furious. A student who's constantly escaping to the calm-down corner IS telling you something. They might be genuinely overwhelmed, struggling with the content, seeking connection, or testing boundaries.

Strategies:

- Set clear expectations upfront
- Use a check-in system
- Limit frequency without eliminating access
- Follow up after
- Address the underlying need

Don't remove access as punishment. If you take away the calm-down corner because a student "abused" it, you've removed a tool from a kid who clearly needs support. Instead, add structure and conversation.

Common Concerns

"Won't kids abuse it to get out of work?" Some might test it at first. That's okay. Track patterns. If a student always needs a break during math, that's data, not manipulation. Maybe they need extra tutoring because the math concepts aren't landing. Maybe they need a movement break, hydration, or a snack prior to math to help them focus. The goal is building self-regulation. Some kids need more practice than others.

"I don't have room for a whole corner." A calm-down KIT (basket with supplies) works too. Students can take it to their desk or a nearby spot. Even a single chair near a window with a stress ball counts.

"What about older students?" Call it something different (reset space, break zone). Focus on regulation language, not "calming down" (can feel babyish). Give ownership: let students design what goes in it.

Sensory Support

In Marti's book, *The Connected Therapist: Relating Through the Senses*, she dedicated larger chapters to sensory support. The goal here is not to re-write that text. Here, we want to give teachers a synopsis along with practical classroom applications. We tried to re-work it a few times and it felt really overwhelming and repetitive. Marti was wishing for an IEP modification on this writing project. Ha! So, for this Sensory Support sub-title, Marti made her own accommodation and uploaded those chapters. She worked with Claude (AI) to give you a few classroom specific ideas. So if this feels like AI, you are correct. Our goal was clarity, not deception. We added a few edits to make it personal. But we really liked what Claude did so we didn't edit it too much.

Proprioceptive Needs (Heavy Work, Pressure, Body Awareness)

Proprioception is your body's sense of where it is in space. This is why kids chew on pencils, lean on their desks, and crash into walls. Remember Riley? This was exactly her challenge.

What we can provide:

- Sugar-free gum or hard candies
- Chewy necklaces or pencil toppers
- Weighted lap pads (2-5 pounds)
- Resistance bands around chair legs
- Squishies, therapy putty, or stress balls
- Heavy books to carry, chairs to stack
- Wall pushes or chair pushes (10 seconds)

Try this: Invite everyone to stand up and push their hands together hard for 10 seconds. Now pull them apart like you're stretching taffy. Takes 30 seconds. Gives organizing input. Kids can refocus.

Vestibular Needs (Movement, Balance, Spatial Awareness)

When students rock in their chairs, spin, or can't sit still, they are dialing up input to the vestibular system to help their brain feel safe.

Ways to incorporate movement:

- Wobble cushions or stability balls
- Rocking chairs
- Movement breaks built into lessons
- Standing or pacing while working
- Balance boards

Try this: Invite students to stand up. Reach high like you're picking apples. Now bend down and touch the ground like you're planting seeds. Up and down, five times. 30 seconds. Huge impact.

Food and Oral Needs

If you are hungry, it's difficult to think. Hunger is a universal cue to the brain to focus on meeting that need NOW. And some students need oral input (chewing, crunching) to stay regulated.

How can we offer food in the classroom?

- Mini drinks in a mini fridge
- Healthy snack options in individual packages
- Chewy offerings like Starburst or gum
- Allow students to access lunch boxes every couple of hours
- If possible, offer ice. Cold can stimulate the nervous system to redirect big emotions.

Lighting

Fluorescent lights are the enemy of most nervous systems. They flicker (even when you can't consciously see it), they hum, and they're harsh.

What we can do:

- Cover some lights with fabric or light filters (you can buy these online pretty cheaply). Be aware of district and school policy on this. In some places, they're against policy. Light covers come in different types: fabric, plastic. Know what your policy allows.
- Bring in lamps with softer bulbs. "Warm" light bulbs tend to be more calming, while "cool" lights tend to be more alerting.
- Use natural light when possible. Open those blinds. Make the curtains sheer.
- Have different lighting for different activities (brighter for active work, dimmer for calm-down time).
- Position desks, pods, and cozy corners in relation to light sources that better meet your goals.

- Red or flashing lights signal attention. Maybe you find a fun themed light to signal transition times. We've seen stoplights that can be set to timers that work as good visual cues that an activity is about to change.

Seating Options

Not every kid (or even adult) can sit in a hard plastic chair for six hours. Our bodies need variety. These options are appropriate for pre-K through college.

What we can do:

- Wobble cushions or stability balls for kids who need movement
- Worksheets on the wall to provide a different position for standing
- Taping the assignment to the bottom of the desk so kids lay down to complete it. Amie calls it the "Sistine Chapel experience." 
- Floor seating with clipboards for kids who work better low
- Standing desks or high tables for kids who focus better standing
- Bean bags or floor pillows for reading time
- Let kids move between options throughout the day
- Provide a "pacing lane" where kids can walk back and forth as they think about assignments

Teenagers' bodies need movement just as much as kindergarteners'.

Visual Supports Everywhere

Our brains process visuals faster than words. When you add visual support, you're helping students understand expectations without constantly having to ask.

What we can do:

- Visual schedule showing the day's activities (with pictures, not just words)
- Anchor charts for routines
- Labeled bins and shelves
- Color-coding for different subjects
- Visual timers kids can see
- Decrease visual clutter; linear designs tend to be more calming
- Blue and green nature colors tend to be more calming

Visual supports aren't just for young kids or kids with IEPs. They help EVERYONE.

Fidgets (Tactile Input)

Fidgets aren't toys. They're tools. Your fidget basket doesn't need to be Instagram-worthy. A shoebox labeled "squeezy things" works just fine. The fidgets don't care if they live in Pinterest perfection or a repurposed tissue box.

Making Fidgets Work for Your Classroom:

We use fidgets as part of our teaching routine, not separate from it. During direct instruction, we'll say something like: "Okay, this next part is pretty intense. If you need a fidget, grab one now." We"ve normalized it so completely that kids don't even think twice.

When we first start teaching about fidgets, we ask the kids to be self-aware and identify if it helped. We'll ask: "Did having something in your hands help you focus today, or was it distracting?" What we are doing is giving kids permission to pay attention to their own needs. This is the first step to meeting needs. Having kids identify them. Some realize they focus better with a fidget during lectures but not during writing. Others notice they need more input on Mondays than Fridays.

Noticing is a life skill. We're not just managing behavior. We're teaching kids to understand their own nervous systems.

What we can provide:

- Fidget spinners, tangles, squeeze balls
- Therapy putty, Velcro strips under desks
- Pipe cleaners, textured fabrics

Rules for fidgets: They don't make noise. They stay in your hands or on your desk. They don't distract others. If you throw it, you lose it.

The "Fairness" Question

"But if one kid gets a fidget, won't everyone want one?"

Yes. So give everyone access. Buy in bulk online. Create an Amazon wish list. Ask parents to donate. Use things you already have.

Marti has found great success with simply providing 2-3 types of sensory support for the entire classroom. Enough for the child to have that buffering buddy. The support loses its shame tendency when the child isn't the only one using it. It also allows students you may not have initially identified as needing the support the opportunity to benefit. The students rotate through the use. It might be a bit hectic the first week or so. But what we find is that the students who actually need the support will continue to use them while the novelty wears out for the students who have other needs.

Interoception: Why "Use Your Words" Fails

There's one more sensory system we briefly mentioned earlier that we need to talk more about, and it might be the most important one for understanding behavior.

Interoception is your body's ability to sense what's happening inside: hunger, thirst, temperature, heart rate, muscle tension, and yes, emotions.

Think of it as your internal GPS telling you where you are in your window of tolerance. When interoception is working well, you notice early warning signs. You catch yourself before your window closes. You can name what you're feeling because you can actually FEEL it.

But here's the problem: for many students, especially those who've experienced trauma or chronic stress, these internal signals are hard to read. Their body might be screaming "DANGER!" but they have no idea why they just punched someone. Honestly, they're as surprised as you are.

This is why "use your words" fails.

When we ask a dysregulated child to tell us what's wrong, we're asking them to access information they can't reach. It's like asking them to read a book written in invisible ink. They're not being defiant. They're not being difficult. They literally don't have access to the data we're requesting.

Interoception Across Neurotypes and Cultures

Interoceptive awareness, the ability to notice and interpret signals from inside your body, varies dramatically across individuals.

Neurodivergent considerations:

Many neurodivergent individuals have significant differences in interoception:

- Some may not notice hunger until they're shaky and irritable

- Some may not recognize the need to use the bathroom until it's urgent
- Some may not connect physical sensations to emotions ("I don't know WHY I'm upset, I just am")
- Some may be hyper-aware of internal sensations in ways that feel overwhelming

This isn't a failure of self-awareness. It's a difference in how the nervous system processes information. These kids need extra support building the bridge between sensation and understanding.

Cultural considerations:

Different cultures have different relationships with internal body awareness:

- Some cultures actively teach body awareness through practices like meditation, yoga, or martial arts. Kids from these backgrounds may have more developed interoceptive vocabulary.
- Other cultures don't emphasize or discuss internal body states. Kids may not have words for what they're feeling because they've never been taught to notice or name it.
- "Emotional vocabulary" itself is cultural. The words available to describe internal states vary across languages and cultures.

Practical implications:

When teaching interoception, stay curious about where each student is starting. Some will pick up body awareness quickly. Others will need extensive support. Neither is "better" or "worse." Both are normal.

Offer multiple ways to communicate internal states: verbal descriptions, pointing to body maps, selecting emoji faces, using color systems. Meet kids where they are, not where you expect them to be.

Building Interoceptive Awareness

The good news: interoception can be taught. *Powerfully You* is an excellent classroom resource for teachers. We must be cautious not to tell others how they feel. Because there really is no way we can truly know because we don't live in their bodies. We haven't lived their past experiences. To be helpful, we make offerings and trust they will find themselves eventually. Here's more ideas to help students build body awareness:

Notice Cues Out Loud

- "Your leg is bouncing. I'm wondering if your body is telling you something."
- "I notice you're rocking. Sometimes our bodies do that when we have extra energy."
- "Your jaw looks really tight. What do you think your body might be saying?"

Teach the Vocabulary

- "When I'm stressed, my shoulders get tight. Where do you feel stress in your body?"
- "Some people feel worried in their stomach. Some feel it in their chest. Where do YOU feel it?"
- "Mad can feel hot. Scared can feel cold. Sad can feel heavy. What does your feeling feel like?"

Build in Body Check-Ins

- "Before we start, let's notice: Are we hungry? Tired? Wiggly? What does your body need right now?"
- "On a scale of 1-10, how much energy is in your body? 1 is almost asleep, 10 is bouncing off walls."
- "Let's do a quick scan: shoulders, jaw, stomach. Notice anything?"

Create Physical Reference Points

- When a student IS calm, help them notice: "Your body looks settled to me. Does that sound right to you?"
- Use visuals: body maps where students can color or point to where they feel different emotions
- Create a classroom "feelings thermometer" students can reference throughout the day

The Classroom Payoff

When students can read their own internal signals, they can:

- Ask for breaks BEFORE meltdowns
- Name emotions instead of acting them out
- Recognize when they need sensory input
- Self-advocate for what they need

This isn't a quick fix. Building interoceptive awareness takes time and repetition. But every time you help a student connect a body sensation to an emotion or need, you're strengthening neural pathways that will serve them for life.

You're not just teaching them to behave. You're teaching them to understand themselves.

Sensory-Friendly Strategies for Secondary Teachers

If you see 150+ students a day, creating a sensory-friendly environment looks different. You CAN:

Create a portable sensory toolkit. Fidgets, stress balls, resistance bands. Students grab one as they enter and return it when they leave.

Establish consistent visual structure. Post your agenda in the same spot every day.

Build in micro-movement. Even a 30-second stretch break helps.

Offer seating choice when possible. You don't need 30 stability balls. You need 3-4 options.

Use your door greeting as a sensory check-in. "Need a fidget today?"

Remember: Don't let the impossibility of "doing it all" stop you from doing something.

Visual Summary: Sensory Supports Quick Reference

Physical Environment

Element	Dialing Up Options	Dialing Down Options
Lighting	Covered fluorescents, lamps, warm bulbs, natural light	Bright overhead, cool bulbs
Seating	Bean bags, floor pillows, rocking chairs	Wobble cushions, stability balls, standing desks
Spaces	Calm-down corner with tent/partition, soft items	Movement corners with tape paths, stepping stones

Sensory Supports

Need	Signs You Might See	What to Provide
Proprioceptive	Chewing pencils, crashing into things, leaning hard	Gum, chewy necklaces, weighted lap pads, resistance bands, wall pushes
Vestibular	Rocking, spinning, can't sit still, tipping back	Wobble cushions, movement breaks, standing work, balance boards
Tactile	Touching everything, picking at skin/clothes	Fidgets, putty, textured items, Velcro strips
Oral	Chewing on everything, always hungry	Gum, crunchy snacks, water bottles, ice
Interoception	Can't name feelings, surprised by own reactions	Body check-ins, feelings vocabulary, physical reference points

Remember: You don't need a Pinterest-perfect classroom. A shoebox of fidgets works. Start with ONE thing.

Deactivating (calming) vs. Activating (alerting) Sensations

Organized by the Sensory Systems

Key Principle: Rhythmic & Predictable = Deactivating | Arrhythmic & Unpredictable = Activating

SIGHT	• Dim/soft lighting, warm-toned bulbs • Natural light, muted colors • Uncluttered visual space • Slow-moving visuals (lava lamp, glitter jar) • Nature imagery, minimal stimulation	• Bright overhead/fluorescent lights • Cool-toned bulbs, flashing lights • Bright saturated colors (esp. red) • Busy patterns, visual clutter • Fast-moving visuals, high animation
SOUND	• Low, slow voices; soft music • White noise, nature sounds, fan • Rhythmic, predictable sounds • Classical music, slow tempo • Humming, soft singing • Low verbal input, quiet spaces	• High-pitched, fast voices • Loud, sudden, or unpredictable noise • Fast-paced music, strong beat • Clapping, stomping, bells, whistles • Body percussion (snapping, clapping) • Multiple competing sound sources
SMELL	• Lavender, vanilla, chamomile • Rose, soft familiar scents • Fresh laundry scent • Calming essential oil blends	• Peppermint, eucalyptus • Citrus (lemon, orange, grapefruit) • Cinnamon, coffee • Strong or unfamiliar scents
TASTE	• Warm drinks (tea, cocoa) • Chewy textures (gum, dried fruit) • Sucking thick liquids through straw • Bland/mild flavors, sweet tastes • Pudding, yogurt, warm soup	• Cold drinks, ice, frozen treats • Crunchy textures (pretzels, carrots) • Sour flavors (pickles, lemon) • Spicy foods, minty flavors • Carbonated beverages
TOUCH	• Deep pressure (weighted blanket, firm hugs) • Soft textures (fleece, velvet)	• Light, unexpected touch • Rough or scratchy textures • Cold temperatures, ice on skin

	• Warm temperatures • Consistent, predictable touch • Massage, sustained firm touch • Compression clothing, bear hugs	• Tickling, feathery touch • Vibration (vibrating toys) • Touch from behind (startling)
PROPRIO-CEPTION (Body Awareness)	• Slow, sustained heavy work • Wall pushes (10+ sec), chair pushes • Carrying heavy objects • Weighted lap pads (2-5 lbs) • Resistance bands (slow push) • Play dough/putty squeezing • Joint compressions (slow, firm)	• Quick, light movements • Jumping jacks, bouncing rapidly • Clapping games, rapid arm moves • Crash pads, pillow fights • Trampoline (fast bouncing) • Wheelbarrow/crab/bear walks • Tug of war, animal walks (fast)
VESTIBULAR (Movement/ Balance)	• Slow rocking, gentle swinging • Linear back-and-forth motion • Rhythmic, predictable motion • Swaying, rocking chairs • Hammock (gentle sway) • Slow dancing, glider swing	• Fast spinning, jumping • Rotational movement • Unpredictable movement changes • Hanging upside down • Freeze dance, stop/go games • Log rolling (fast), roller coasters
INTERO-CEPTION (Internal Awareness)	• Body scan visualizations • Deep breathing (belly breathing) • Meditation, yoga • Progressive muscle relaxation • Mindfulness activities • Guided imagery (beach, forest)	• Noticing heart race after exercise • Temperature changes (hot/cold) • Eating spicy foods • Intense physical activity • Cold water on face/wrists • Quick position changes

Additional Classroom Strategies

Environmental Modifications (Deactivating)

- Quiet corner with bean bag, pillows, soft fabric
- Reduce fluorescent lighting (covers, lamps, natural light)
- Minimize visual clutter on walls
- Predictable classroom layout and routines
- White noise machine or fan
- Calm-down corner with sensory tools

Environmental Modifications (Activating)

- Open windows for fresh air and temperature change
- Bright task lighting for work areas
- Movement breaks built into schedule
- Standing desks or varied seating options
- Upbeat transition music
- Visual timers and engaging schedules

"Organizing" Inputs (The Sweet Spot)

These inputs bring the nervous system to "just right" rather than purely activating or deactivating:

- Proprioceptive heavy work (most reliable!) • Sucking thick liquids through a straw *Chewing gum or crunchy foods
- Slow, rhythmic vestibular input • Deep pressure touch • Oral motor activities (blowing bubbles, whistles)

Critical Reminders

1. **Every nervous system is different.** What activates one student may deactivate another. Watch, learn, and adjust.
2. **Context matters.** A student who needs activating input at 8 AM may need deactivating input after lunch.
3. **Intensity matters.** The same sensation at different intensities can have opposite effects (slow rocking = deactivating; fast rocking = activating).
4. **Duration matters.** Short bursts of activating input followed by deactivating input can help regulate.
5. **Student preference matters.** When possible, let students choose. They often know what their body needs.
6. **Predictability feels safe; unpredictability is activating.** This principle applies across ALL senses.
7. **Relationships matter.** Sometimes it's not the sensation but the relational context that determines whether input feels safe or threatening.

What If Sensory Supports Don't Seem to Help?

Sometimes you'll try fidgets, movement breaks, and seating changes, and a particular student still struggles. Consider:

You might have the wrong sensory input. If one type of support isn't working, try another category entirely.

The need might be bigger than sensory. Some students are dealing with anxiety, depression, or trauma that sensory supports alone can't address.

Medical or developmental factors might be at play. Undiagnosed ADHD, autism spectrum differences, or other issues can look like "sensory needs not being met." Ask for help from related service providers.

The relationship piece might be missing. Environment is connection, but it's not a replacement for human connection.

It might be a teaching problem. Were the expectations taught? Or was it assumed that students would figure it out?

If you've tried everything and it's still not working, it's time to call in reinforcements. Reach out to your friendly funcle OT.

Predictability (Handling Transitions)

Transitions are HARD for kids. Way harder than we realize.

Think about what a transition requires: Stop what you're doing. Shift your attention. Predict what comes next. Organize materials. Move your body. Start something new.

They require the prefrontal cortex to be online. But if a child is feeling unsafe, that part of their brain is offline. That owl has gone off-roading and it's a bumpy ride.

Transitions introduce uncertainty. For kids with insecure attachment, anxiety, or sensory challenges, uncertainty feels unsafe. When kids feel unsafe, they resist. Dig in. Melt down. No wonder transitions are when behaviors spike. It's not defiance. It's a neurological stress response.

Skills to Make Transitions Easier

1. **Visual Schedules.** Post the day's schedule where everyone can see it. Review it at the start of the day. Refer back throughout.
2. **Warnings and Countdowns.** Never surprise a child with a transition. "10 more minutes... 5 more minutes... 2 minutes... 1 minute... Time!"
3. **Transition Routines.** Same routine. Every time. Predictable. Their brains can go on autopilot.
4. **Using Music.** Pick a "clean-up song" and play it every time. The music becomes a cue that doesn't require nagging.
5. **Gamifying Transitions.** "I wonder if we can all be lined up before I count to 20..." You're not bribing. You're making it playful. Play disarms fear.

Life Transitions vs. Daily Transitions

Some kids are dealing with BIG transitions outside of school: moving, divorce, new baby, death, foster care.

When a child is navigating a major life transition, daily classroom transitions feel even harder. Give extra support: check in at the start of the day, give more warnings, offer a predictable peer partner or buffer buddy (someone familiar who can help anchor them through the change), lower expectations temporarily.

Transitions

Strategy	How It Helps
Visual schedule	Predictability calms the nervous system
Warnings/countdowns	Brain can prepare instead of being shocked
Consistent routines	Autopilot reduces cognitive load
Music cues	Fun, non-nagging signal, adds predictability
Gamifying	Play disarms fear

Permission to Iterate

Here's what nobody tells you: sensory-friendly classrooms are built through trial and error. The Instagram teacher with the perfect calm corner? She's had fifteen versions that flopped first. She probably has staff and a ring light. Don't compare yourself to that nonsense.

Your first fidget basket will probably be a disaster. Your first attempt at movement breaks might create more chaos than calm. Your wobble cushions will definitely make weird noises at the worst possible moments. This doesn't mean you're doing it wrong.

Keep adjusting. Keep observing. Keep asking "what does this student actually need?" instead of "why is this student ruining my beautiful system?" The sensory supports that stick are the ones you troubleshoot, tweak, and try again. Not the ones you abandon at the first sign of trouble.

We hope you're looking at your classroom with new eyes now. Not with judgment about what you don't have, but with curiosity about what small shifts might help. We hope you're recognizing that sensory needs aren't special needs. They're human needs. Every brain in your classroom, including yours, is trying to find sensory safety. We hope you picked up at least one idea that feels doable. Cover one light. Add a fidget basket. Post a visual schedule. Try a movement break. Just one thing.

When we set kids up to succeed, they usually do. And when we spend less energy managing behavior, we have more energy for the parts of teaching we actually love.

When Administrators Push Back

Not every administrator will support sensory-friendly classrooms. You might hear:

- "You can't cover those lights. Fire hazard."
- "Fidgets are distracting."
- "That calm-down corner looks like a reward for bad behavior."

Strategies for Working With Resistant Administrators

1. **Speak their language.** Administrators care about outcomes. Frame requests in terms of test scores, behavior referrals, suspension rates.
2. **Start small and document.** Pick one change. Track results. Data is harder to argue with than philosophy.
3. **Know your policies.** Often, things teachers think are "against the rules" actually aren't.
4. **Build allies.** Find the OT, school psychologist, or other teachers doing similar things.
5. **Advocate persistently and professionally.** Ask what would need to be true for them to say yes.
6. **Do what you can within your sphere of control.** A fidget basket at your is your supply area. A visual schedule is your instructional choice.

Let's Get Real: When Your Classroom Isn't Pinterest-Perfect

Amie: My fidget basket is literally a drawer. My calm-down corner is a rug and a "couch" I got online somewhere that breaks into smaller pieces.

Marti: Perfect! That works. Creating safe and sensory-friendly environments isn't about aesthetics. It's about function.

Amie: So we're not saying teachers need to recreate occupational therapy clinics in their classrooms.

Marti: Absolutely not. That would be out of their scope of practice. We're saying: think about what students' bodies need to succeed, and provide what you can with what you have.

Amie: But teachers hear "sensory space" and picture some Pinterest paradise with a $3,000 budget.

Marti: Not even close. A sensory space is a corner, a shelf, a basket of options that gives every kid a chance to find what their body needs so their brain can show up for learning. Think of it like a sensory buffet. Teachers get massive bonus points with me if they make it a sensory Buffett. Just add a touch of island vibe and a nod to the late, great Jimmy Buffett.

Amie: I love it! And, not everyone fills their plate with the same thing. Different seating because not everybody thrives in a hard stationary chair. Softer lighting because fluorescent lights are basically buzzing at a frequency that makes everyone's eyes hurt. Background music to mask sudden noises. The diversity matters because what settles one nervous system does nothing for another.

Marti: And here's the piece people miss: every one of those options is a form of connection. When a student finds the wobble cushion that helps them focus, the room is saying, "There is nothing wrong with you. You are welcome here."

Amie: Environment is connection expressed through space. A fidget basket says "You aren't the only one who fidgets." A calm-down corner says "Your nervous system is allowed to relax." Those are relational messages delivered without words.

Marti: I want to say it over and over: a calm-down corner is NOT a punishment corner. Not a time-out zone with a fancier name. The minute a sensory space carries shame, it stops working. This is proactive, not punitive.

Amie: That's why I teach every kid how to use the space at the beginning of the year. We practice together. I say, "This is for all of us, including me, to take care of our bodies so our brains can do their best work." Then we all try the wobble cushion, someone falls off, everyone laughs, and suddenly the support isn't weird. It's just how our room works. Sometimes they even find me in the calm down corner during my prep time.

Marti: Nobody stands out for using it. You've removed the spotlight and the stigma, and that's inclusivity in action.

Amie: What surprised me most was that my "good" kids benefited enormously. Some of them had been spending so much energy just holding it together. When they had permission to chew gum or sit on a wobble cushion, their engagement improved.

Marti: Yes! Remember, the "good" quiet kids could be in a dissociative stress response. They look calm. But their nervous system is sending cues of threat that say being still and avoidant is the safe way to show up.

Amie: So for the teacher with thirty-two kids, three square feet of space, and a principal who side-eyes anything nontraditional: start small. Some scented wax. A comfy second hand chair in the corner. A portable speaker. That's a sensory space. No ribbon-cutting ceremony required.

Marti: Some of these nervous systems are basically showing up to school starving for sensory input, and we're offering them the equivalent of a single saltine and a stern look. Better doesn't have to be big. Maybe just a small sensory Buffett. "Two empty chairs that say more than the people who ever sit there."

Amie: (laughing) Now you're just showing off your Buffett knowledge.

Marti: Parrotheads unite! I'm still salty he never took me for a ride in his sea plane. My sensory system would have enjoyed that very much. While I didn't meet that goal, I can imagine students enjoying their sensory experiences because of this book and that is pretty amazing. And, truly, it's unrealistic that I could meet all of my life goals. Aren't we keeping it real here?

Takeaways

1. **Environment IS connection.** When you set up your classroom with sensory supports and predictable routines, you communicate care without saying a word. A student whose sensory needs are met feels seen, safe, and ready to learn.
2. **Every student has sensory needs, not just kids with IEPs.** Proprioceptive input (heavy work), vestibular input (movement), tactile input (fidgets), and interoception (body awareness) help

ALL brains focus. When we meet nervous system needs, behavior often takes care of itself.

3. **Transitions are cognitively demanding and require support.** Visual schedules, warnings, routines, and buffer time aren't coddling. They're working with how brains actually function. Predictability prevents problems.

Reflection Questions

1. Look at your classroom environment with fresh eyes. What's one change you could make this week that would support sensory needs?
2. Think about the students who struggle most in your class. What sensory needs might they have? What could you provide?
3. When are transitions hardest in your day? What support could you add?
4. What's your budget reality? If you have zero dollars to spend, what could you create or repurpose?
5. If you anticipate administrator pushback, what data could you collect to make your case?

One Thing to Try Tomorrow

Sneak in a Sensory Break

Pick a transition time when energy tends to get chaotic.

Insert two minutes of movement: "Everybody stand up. Stretch high. Touch the ground. Ten jumping jacks. Sit down."

That's it. Two minutes. Watch what happens to focus and behavior in the next activity.

Small change. Big impact. Zero budget required.

Chapter 10

Responding to Behaviors in the Classroom

Relationally-Informed Strategies That Actually Work

You learned how to build the relationships that create felt safety. You learned how to set up environments that prevent behavioral issues before they start.

But let's be honest: prevention doesn't catch everything. Sometimes, despite your best efforts, behaviors still happen. Kids still escalate. Chairs still get thrown. Words still wound. This chapter is about what to do in those moments.

Here's what you already know: felt safety is the prerequisite for learning, and connection is how we build it. You don't need us to re-explain why this matters. What you need is the practical "how" for those moments when a student is struggling and you have 24 other kids watching. That's what this chapter delivers.

The Scissors-in-the-Outlet Story

Picture a middle school science class. The teacher has gotten the class started, they're working, and there's a quiet hum of kids on task.

All of a sudden, from the corner of the room, a child goes flying back from a lab table. This flight is paired with a loud POP and what looks like sparks.

The teacher walks over to investigate and finds a student with scissors in his hand and a smoking outlet. Turns out the student had put scissors into the outlet to see what would happen.

When asked why he would do that (and yes, we all know better than to ask that question), the student looked up and said, "*I don't know. I just needed to.*" And that, friends, is the entire middle school experience summarized in seven words.

In that moment, it's tempting to get angry. To yell about fire potential, safety, consequences.

But here's what happens when we do that: the kid just looks at us like we're crazy. He's processing nothing. And we're making the situation worse.

This is the exact moment we really need our skills in being relationally informed.

If your classroom is anything like this one, then you know how stuff like this happens all the time. We live in a constant state of chaos and at the whims and mercies of these little darlings.

We need concrete strategies to help us better respond to these behaviors. We've discussed the science behind what's happening in their brains. We've talked about what happens when kids are in survival mode versus when they can access their thinking brain.

Let's get into some really useful, in-the-moment skills we can use to handle these types of situations.

What Is Behaviorism (And Why It Often Doesn't Work Long-Term)

Traditional behaviorism says: reward good behavior, punish bad behavior, and behavior will change.

Sticker charts. Clip charts. Treasure boxes. Detentions. Suspensions.

If you do X, you get Y. If you do Z, you lose W.

Simple, right? They seem to work short term. That's true. But it works because of the beginning stage of the stress response that Dr. Perry calls "robotic compliance". Robyn Gobbel calls it the "Trickster Possum". Dr. Porges would call it the beginning of collapse.

We've all been there. It's easier to just go through the motions than truly change the behavior. We do the thing when someone is watching. But we do the opposite when they aren't around.

We can "make peace" in the moment but then our nervous system pays the price later and we fall apart with our people who feel safe. When the pressure stacks up like the straw on the camel's back, we begin to lie and cover up instead of owning it and changing.

When you think about robotic compliance, it's a clear example of lack of trust and relationship. We don't trust that the task is for our own good and we might think the other person wants to harm us. So we do it without emotion or thought.

We use these types of behavior modification on dogs. Trainers will even talk about "breaking the spirit of the dog" or training it to ignore its instincts. So, yes, we can get the watchdog nervous system to comply because it doesn't feel safe. We break the spirit and teach them the world is dangerous and the adults won't keep them safe.

The real truth is, behaviorism is inhumane. It doesn't work long-term. Not for the kids who need it most.

If it did work long term, there would be no need for this book. We believe you are smart enough that you would have already found the secret solution if it existed. If traditional behaviorism worked, you wouldn't be burned out and frustrated. Our youth prisons would be empty and Principal Navy would be teaching macrame classes.

The long term punitive consequences of behaviorism push a child further down the stress response into survival mode.

When a child is in survival mode, they feel stuck in a stress response that is signaling "danger/protect yourself at all costs" (even relational costs). They're not able to be logical. The thinking brain has gone offline.

In that moment when the negative behavior happens, the student can't think, "Hmm, if I do this, I'll get a consequence, so I probably shouldn't." So when we respond with consequences ("You kicked that chair, now you lose recess!"), we're trying to use logic to address a nervous system problem. It doesn't work.

Worse, it often escalates the behavior because now the child feels punished AND fearful. And a punished, fearful child is even more likely to act out. They aren't trying to insult or disrespect you. Their attachment system is remembering all the times in the past when they felt fearful, disconnected, or punished, and they're trying to relieve that pain in this moment. They aren't thinking of the next moment, or you, at all.

It isn't personal. It's protection persuaded by their unique past experiences.

When Behaviorism Is Even More Harmful: Neurodivergent and Culturally Diverse Students

Traditional behaviorism already doesn't work well. But for some populations, it's actively damaging.

For neurodivergent students:

Behaviorist approaches often punish kids for things they genuinely cannot control:

- Punishing a child with ADHD for not sitting still
- Punishing an autistic child for not making eye contact
- Punishing a child with sensory processing differences for covering their ears or seeking movement
- Punishing a child with executive function challenges for "not following directions" they couldn't process

When we punish neurological differences, we teach kids that their brain is wrong. That THEY are wrong. The shame this creates doesn't improve behavior. It creates anxiety, depression, and deeper behavioral challenges.

For culturally diverse students:

Traditional behaviorism is often applied inequitably:

- Research consistently shows that Black and brown students receive harsher consequences for the same behaviors as white students
- Children from cultures with different behavioral norms (louder communication, more physical expressiveness) are often mislabeled as "defiant" or "disruptive"
- Language barriers can make "following directions" harder, leading to punishment for misunderstanding
- Cultural differences in how respect is shown (eye contact, tone, body language) can be misinterpreted as disrespect and punished accordingly

When the behavioral standards themselves reflect dominant-culture norms, and the enforcement reflects bias, behaviorism becomes a tool of inequity.

The alternative: The relational approach we're describing in this chapter works better for ALL kids, and it's especially important for neurodivergent and culturally diverse students. When we focus on connection, co-regulation, and teaching rather than punishing, we create space for different brains and different backgrounds to succeed.

The Scissors Kid (Continued)

Let's go back to that scissors story.

When that kid stuck scissors in the outlet, his neuropathway, built through years of experience, told him: when I'm bored or curious or need stimulation, I engage my surroundings. That's the learned response. That's the pathway his brain defaulted to.

The consequences and sticker charts don't help. Because in that moment, he wasn't thinking about consequences. He was operating from impulse and curiosity.

What is a more relationally-informed approach?

Step 1: Calm yourself. Take a breath. Get your own watchdog out of panic mode. (Instead of escalating.)
Step 2: Ensure safety. "Everyone step back. Are you hurt? Okay, let's make sure this outlet is safe." (Safety and concern instead of blame and shame.)
Step 3: Get relational. Get down to his level. Speak calmly. "That was scary. You okay?" (Instead of yelling.)
Step 4: Connect. "I see you were curious. That makes sense. And outlets are dangerous. Let's talk about safer ways to explore." (Invite curiosity.)
Step 5: Teach. Not in the moment, but later, when he's safe and calm. "When you're curious about something, what could you do instead of just trying it? You could ask me. You could Google it." (Instead of escalating to the office.)

See the difference? One approach punishes. The other teaches. One approach breaks connection. The other maintains it. One approach stops the behavior temporarily. The other builds skills for next time.

Why Your Relationship Building Work Matters Right Now

Everything you learned about connection pays off in these moments. When a child trusts you, when they believe you care about them, when you've built a relationship, responding to behaviors lands completely differently.

Instead of feeling like an attack, your redirect feels like guidance. Instead of triggering shame, it invites growth. Instead of breaking a relationship, it deepens it.

We can say things to students we have a relationship with that would devastate students we don't have a relationship with. "Hey, that was a choice that didn't work out. Let's try again." To a student who trusts us, that's a gentle redirect. To a student who doesn't trust us, that sounds like criticism and shame.

Relationship is the currency that allows you to influence behavior effectively. This is why we spent an entire chapter on connection skills. Because when the hard moments come, and they will, you need that relational bank account to be full.

Co-Regulation: Why Your Calm Is Contagious

Here's something critical that doesn't get talked about enough. So we will say it again: your nervous system talks to their nervous system.

This is called co-regulation, and it's why your calm matters so much. When you're feeling safe and connected, your steady presence sends signals to the child's nervous system that safety is possible. When you're feeling stressed or unsafe, yelling or panicking, their nervous system reads those cues and escalates further.

Ever notice how yelling "CALM DOWN!" never actually calms anyone down? That's because your words say calm, but your nervous system screams panic. Kids read the nervous system, not the vocabulary. **You have to find your calm before you can share it.**

This isn't about being perfect. It's about being aware. When you feel yourself escalating, that's information. You need to regulate yourself before you can help regulate them.

Five Quick Resets You Can Do While 24 Kids Are Watching

1. **Feet on Floor.** Press your feet firmly into the ground. Feel the pressure. This activates grounding and helps your brain remember you're safe.
2. **Slow Exhale.** Breathe in for 4 counts, out for 6-8 counts. The extended exhale activates your parasympathetic nervous system. You can do this while walking toward the student.
3. **Cold Water.** Take a sip of cold water or touch something cold. Temperature shifts interrupt escalation. Keep a water bottle on your desk.
4. **Anchor Phrase.** Have a phrase ready: "I can handle this." "This is not an emergency." "I've done hard things before." Say it silently to yourself.
5. **Unclench.** Release your jaw. Drop your shoulders. Open your hands. We hold stress in our bodies, and releasing it helps our brain get the message that we're okay.

Your brain is more developed. You have more practice at feeling safe and connected. You have more capacity. Use it.

Preemptive Strategies (Catching It Before It Escalates)

The best behavior strategy is the one you don't have to do because you caught the behavior before it became a problem. This is where your "teacher radar" comes in. You know your students. You can see when someone's starting to escalate.

Signs to watch for:

- Body language changing (fidgeting, bouncing, clenching)
- Facial expression shifting (jaw tight, eyes narrowing)
- Tone of voice changing (getting louder, more clipped)
- Engagement dropping (staring off, shutting down)

When you notice these signs, intervene BEFORE the behavior.

Preemptive interventions:

- **Proximity:** Move closer to the student (your calm presence can help them find safety). Be careful of controlling postures, standing above them, exerting control.
- **Nonverbal cue:** Eye contact, a hand on the shoulder (if appropriate), a thumbs-up
- **Redirection:** "Hey, looks like you need a break. Want to get some water? I'm going to get some water for myself. I'm happy to bring you some, too?"
- **Relationship:** "You doing okay? You seem off today."
- **Sensory support:** "Grab a fidget." "Take a walk to the office and back." "The calm couch looks empty if you want to stretch out."

You're not ignoring the early warning signs. You're addressing them before they become big problems.

We do this constantly. A kid starts tapping their pencil aggressively. We walk over, make eye contact, offer them a fidget. Crisis averted. It's not magic. It's noticing and responding early.

The Four Levels of Engagement (TBRI®'s Framework for Responding to Behaviors)

TBRI has a beautiful framework for thinking about how to respond to behavior. It's called the Levels of Engagement, and it goes from least intrusive to most intrusive.

It aligns with Dr. Perry's arousal continuum but states it a little differently. We want to highlight both because we all learn differently. We hope re-framing similar concepts helps you connect with them in a way that feels meaningful to you.

The idea: start with the least intrusive intervention and only move to more intrusive ones if needed.

Level 1: Playful Engagement

Remember how important play is from our earlier chapters? This is your first line of response. Keep it light, keep it connected.

Examples:

- Humor: "Whoa, those erasers are flying today! Let's keep them on the desk, yeah?"
- Playful tone: "I'm seeing a lot of wiggling over here. Wigglers, give me five jumping jacks!"
- Silly voice: (in robot voice) "Attention students. Return to your seats. That is all."

Why this works: It addresses the behavior without shame. It maintains connection. It keeps the mood light.

When to use it: For minor issues when the child is still mostly settled.

Level 2: Structured Engagement

A little more direct, but still warm. The student still has access to at least part of their thinking brain.

Examples:

- Clear direction: "Ellie, I need you sitting in your seat right now."
- Choices: "You can work at your desk or at the back table. Your choice."
- Redirection: "Let's put the phone away and get back to work."

Why this works: It's clear without being harsh. It gives some control (through choices) while maintaining boundaries.

When to use it: When playful isn't enough, but the child is still mostly feeling safe and connected.

Level 3: Calming Engagement

The child is escalating. Your job is to increase relational connection. The student is moving towards survival mode.

Examples:

- Lower your voice: Speak quieter and slower
- Get on their level: Physically lower yourself
- Breathe with them: "Let's take some deep breaths together."
- Remove audience: "Let's step into the hall for a minute."
- Minimal words: "I'm here. Hold my hand?"

Why this works: You're not trying to teach yet. You're just helping their nervous system settle.

When to use it: When the child is clearly becoming stressed but not yet dangerous.

Level 4: Protective Engagement

The child is a danger to themselves or others. Safety is the only priority.

Examples:

- Clear, calm directive: "Stop. Hands down."
- Remove other students: "Everyone line up by the door."
- Call for backup: "I need support in Room 205."
- Use crisis intervention training protocols

Why this works: It doesn't. Not really. This is survival mode for everyone. The goal is just to get through it safely.

When to use it: Only when absolutely necessary for safety.

The key: Start at Level 1 whenever possible. Only escalate through the levels if needed.

Don't jump straight to Level 4 for a minor issue. Don't stay at Level 1 when a child is clearly becoming more stressed and agitated.

Match your response to the child's current state, not the behavior.

Visual Summary: The Four Levels of Engagement

Level	Name	Child's State	Your Response	Example Phrases
1	Playful	Mostly settled	Light, connected, humorous	"Whoa, those pencils are flying!"
2	Structured	Partially thinking	Clear, warm, choices offered	"You can work here or there. Your choice."
3	Calming	In survival mode, escalating	Quiet, slow, minimal words, breathe together	"You're safe. I'm here."
4	Protective	Danger to self/others	Safety only, call backup	"Stop. Everyone line up by the door."

What to Actually Say: Scripts for the Hardest Moments

Teachers always ask us: "But what do I actually SAY?" Here are scripts for common difficult situations.

When a Student Says "I Hate You"

What NOT to say: "That's disrespectful! Go to the office." (This escalates and breaks connection.)

What to say:

- "You seem really upset right now." (Acknowledge the feeling)

- "It's okay to be mad. It's not okay to hurt people with words." (Hold the boundary gently)
- "I'm not going anywhere. When you're ready, we can talk about what's really going on." (Stay in relationship)

Why this works: You're not taking the bait. You're seeing past the words to the distress underneath.

When a Student Refuses to Work

What NOT to say: "You will do this work or you'll fail." (Threat triggers survival mode.)

What to say:

- "I notice you're not starting. What's getting in the way?"
- "This seems hard today. What would help?"
- "You can do the first three problems or pick which three you want to start with. Your call."

Why this works: You're getting curious instead of demanding. You're offering agency.

When a Student Is Crying and Won't Talk

What NOT to say: "You need to tell me what's wrong or I can't help you." (Pressure increases distress.)

What to say:

- "I'm here. You don't have to talk."
- "I'm going to sit with you for a minute. Is that okay?"
- Offer a tissue, a fidget, or just silence.

Why this works: Sometimes presence is enough. Pushing for words when someone is fumbling in that dark downstairs basement doesn't work. The window is shut and no light is getting in. The possum is still holding that hammer.

When a Student Is Disrupting but Won't Go to the Calm Corner

What NOT to say: "Go to the calm corner NOW or I'm calling the office." (Ultimatum escalates.)

What to say:

- "It looks like you're having a hard time. The calm corner is there when you're ready."
- "Would it help if I walked over there with you?"
- "You can take a fidget to your desk if you're not ready for the corner yet."

Why this works: You're keeping the option open without forcing it. Sometimes kids need time.

When a Student Gets Physical (Pushing, Throwing)

What NOT to say: Yelling, grabbing, or physically restraining (unless trained and necessary for safety).

What to say:

- "Stop. Everyone step back." (Clear, calm, simple)
- To the class: "Give us space please."
- To the student: "I need you to be safe. I'm here to help, not punish."
- After safety is established: "That was scary. Let's take a walk, or some breaths. Maybe a drink." (Don't actually offer too many choices. Assess the vibe and make a guess at one. Then another if needed.)

Why this works: Safety first, connection second, teaching later.

When a Student Shuts Down Completely (Head on Desk, Non-Responsive)

What NOT to say: "Sit up. You need to participate." (This often increases shutdown.)

What to say:

- "I see you. Take the time you need."
- "I'm going to check on you in a few minutes."
- Leave a note that says: "I'm here when you're ready."

Why this works: Shutdown is an intense stress response. Pushing harder makes it worse.

The Pattern in All These Scripts

Notice what's consistent:

1. **Find your calm first.** Your nervous system sets the tone.
2. **Assume positive or neutral intent.** They're struggling, not scheming.
3. **Offer choice and agency.** Prediction (control) reduces power struggles.
4. **Separate behavior from worth.** The behavior is the problem, not the kid.
5. **Stay in relationship.** Don't let the behavior push you away.

Try Again: The Magic of Doing It Different the Next Time

One of our favorite relationally-informed strategies is the "try again."

When a child does something poorly, speaks disrespectfully, grabs something rudely, or ignores a direction, instead of punishing, you offer a chance to replay the experience with the outcome you wish you'd had the first time.

"Uh-oh, that didn't sound kind. Let's try that again."

Then you wait. You give them a chance to do it better.

And when they do? You celebrate it.

"That felt much better. Thank you."

Why try again works:

- It models repair
- It teaches the desired behavior (instead of just punishing the wrong one, working on building a neuropathway that is more appropriate)
- It maintains connection (instead of breaking it with consequences)
- It gives students practice (repetition builds neural pathways)
- It ends on success (instead of shame)

We use try again constantly.
"That volume isn't going to work. Try again."
[Kid takes a breath, tries again more calmly]
"Perfect. Thank you. Now let's talk about what you need."

Try again in action:

- **Disrespectful tone:** "Try that again with kindness."
- **Grabbing:** "Hmm, you can have this notebook. Let's practice asking nicely."
- **Ignoring direction:** "I asked you to sit down. Let's try that again."
- **Unkind words:** "That hurt someone's feelings. How could you say that differently?"

Some teachers worry: "Won't students just misbehave if they know they can just try again?"

No. Because trying again isn't "getting away with it." They're practicing the right way. And practice is work. Practice is what builds the new neural pathways we're hoping to teach them.

Plus, you're still holding the boundary. You're just doing it with connection instead of punishment.

Tone of voice will be super important when using this skill. If we pull out our authoritative, you-are-in-trouble teacher voice, it will often push the kid into survival mode faster. Remember that concept of neuroception? When we use the soft, kind "I need you to try again" voice, the child can stay in the thinking brain where logic, reason, and learning can occur.

Choices and Compromises

Choices and compromises are behavior-influencing strategies that maintain relationship and encourage felt-safety.

Choices

When you need to address a behavior, offer two acceptable options.

"You can finish this now or during lunch. Your choice."

"You can work quietly at your desk or take a break in the calm corner. What works better for you?"

"You can use a pencil or a pen. Pick one."

Why this works:

- They still have control (reduces power struggles)
- You're still holding the boundary (both options are acceptable to you)
- They're more likely to comply (because they chose)

What doesn't work:

- Too many choices (overwhelming)
- Choices you can't live with ("You can do the work or not. Your choice." Nope.)
- False choices ("You can do this the easy way or the hard way." That's a threat, not a choice.)

Meeting Sensory Needs and Choice: A very effective method of helping kids stay connected is providing choices. Often, if they are moving toward survival mode, we need more visual cues than verbal. We created an example of a choice board that you could use in your classroom to help kids. When you notice students start to disengage, you can have the kids go to the board and make a choice.

Compromises

Sometimes, you can meet a child halfway.

"I hear you want more time. Here's what I can do: I'll give you five extra minutes, but then we really need to move on. Deal?"

"I know you don't want to work with a partner. How about you work near them but on your own? Would that work?"

"You're frustrated about the assignment. I can't change the whole thing, but I can let you pick which part to do first. Would that help?"

Why this works:

- You're showing you heard them (validation)
- You're teaching negotiation (life skill)
- You're maintaining relationship (even in disagreement)

What doesn't work:

- Compromising on safety or non-negotiables
- Always giving in (boundaries still matter)
- Making it a fight ("I'm the teacher, we're not negotiating!")

The goal isn't to be permissive. It's to be flexible within appropriate boundaries.

When Behaviors Warrant More Than Classroom Strategies

Let's address something we haven't fully covered yet: what about behaviors that are truly dangerous? What about violence? Property destruction? Threats?

Relationally-informed practice doesn't mean tolerating harm.

Safety Is Always the Priority

When a student's behavior endangers themselves or others, your first job is safety. Full stop.

This might mean:

- Removing other students from the room
- Calling for administrative backup
- Using trained crisis intervention protocols
- Clearing the space and waiting for support

You can be relationally-informed AND prioritize safety. In fact, Level 4 of TBRI's engagement framework (Protective) is specifically for these moments.

After a Safety Incident

Once everyone is physically safe:

1. **Care for yourself.** Safety incidents are traumatic for teachers too.
2. **Care for the other students.** They witnessed something scary. Acknowledge it.
3. **Reconnect with the student.** When they've returned to their "true self" (which may be much later), repair the relationship.
4. **Document thoroughly.**
5. **Debrief with your team.** What led to the escalation? What supports might prevent it next time?

Violence and Physical Aggression

When a student is physically aggressive:

- Protect yourself and others first.
- Use trained restraint protocols ONLY if you're trained and only if necessary for safety.
- Call for backup early.
- Document everything.

The student will likely need more support than a classroom teacher can provide alone. This doesn't mean you failed. It means this child's needs exceed what one adult in a classroom of 25 can address.

What Relationally-Informed Practice Looks Like with Serious Behaviors

Being relationally-informed doesn't mean:

- Tolerating violence
- Ignoring dangerous behavior

- Refusing to involve administration
- Skipping consequences entirely

It DOES mean:

- Maintaining dignity even during crisis
- Returning to relationship after safety is established
- Seeking to understand what drove the behavior
- Advocating for support rather than just punishment
- Recognizing that even students who do harmful things are still worthy of care

Documentation: Why It Matters and How to Do It

Documentation isn't just about "covering yourself." Good documentation can:

- Help identify patterns that reveal unmet needs
- Support referrals for additional services
- Provide evidence for IEP or 504 considerations
- Track whether interventions are working

What to Document

- **Antecedents:** What happened before the behavior?
- **Behavior:** What exactly did the student do? Be specific and objective
- **Response:** What did you do? What strategies did you try?
- **Outcome:** What happened next?
- **Patterns:** Note recurring triggers, times, or situations

How to Document Effectively

- Be factual, not interpretive. "Student threw a book" not "Student had a tantrum"
- Include what worked. "Student calmed after 5 minutes in calm corner with fidget"

- Note your interventions. This shows you've tried classroom strategies
- Keep it brief but complete
- Use a consistent system

Documentation transforms "this kid is always a problem" into "this student struggles during transitions after lunch, especially on days following absences. I've tried X, Y, and Z. I'm requesting assessment for possible sensory needs and counseling support."

The first gets a shrug. The second gets action.

A Sidebar on Restorative Justice

Restorative justice has become popular in schools. The intent is instead of just assigning consequences, we ask: What happened? Who was harmed? What needs to happen to make it right?

We want to be clear: restorative justice is valuable. The shift from "what rule was broken?" to "who was harmed?" represents real progress.

And restorative justice has limitations we should name:

Limitation #1: Timing matters enormously. Restorative conversations require reflection, empathy, and perspective-taking. These are all thinking-brain functions. If we try to have a restorative conversation while a child is still in survival mode, it won't work. The fix: Wait. Do the restorative conversation after the child has settled. This might be hours later or even the next day.

Limitation #2: Forced apologies often backfire. "Go apologize to Sarah for what you did." The kid mumbles "Sorry" while making zero eye contact. Nobody wins. The fix: Help the child understand the impact first. Wait until genuine understanding emerges before suggesting an apology.

Limitation #3: Kids often don't understand what they did wrong. You can't apologize meaningfully for something you don't understand. The fix: Teach first, then restore. Help the child understand what happened from multiple perspectives.

Bottom line: Restorative justice works best when combined with meeting sensory and felt-safety needs, relationship, and developmental understanding. It's not a replacement for the relational strategies in this chapter. It can be a complement to them.

Use restorative practices. Just don't use them alone, and don't use them prematurely.

A Note from Amie: When This Feels Counterintuitive

~ Amie ~

At this point, many of you are probably feeling super uncomfortable and finding every reason to disagree with this. Once again, I get it. This feels so counterintuitive to what we are taught in teacher school and what the majority of our culture supports.

Just like in the building relationship chapter, I am going to invite you to just try it. Give it a shot.

I was born in 1974. As I grew up, children were seen, not heard. When a teacher said sit down, you said yes ma'am and did it.

(For the record, my parents can attest that I did NOT subscribe to this idea as a student. There were a few teachers I actively disliked and truly made my goal that year to make them cry. I was not kind. I think part of it was I was hurting and dealing with some significant trauma in my personal life. But also, I think I just knew somehow that the approach of teacher power wasn't going to work.)

Regardless, as we have talked about throughout the book, when we know better, we do better.

What Success Actually Looks Like (Spoiler: It's Not a Hallmark Movie)

You've just absorbed a lot. Co-regulation, quick resets, scripts for the hardest moments, levels of engagement, try-agains, choices and compromises. Your brain might be spinning with "Will this actually work?" and "How will I know if I'm doing it right?"

Fair questions. Let's answer them.

Here's something nobody warns you about: when you start implementing relational strategies, you might not see dramatic results right away. There's no confetti drops. No slow-motion moment where the kid who's been struggling suddenly becomes your star student. But maybe they could land on a fluffy cloud. We can have less stellar goals.

Real progress is quieter than that. Sneakier, even. It shows up in moments so small you might miss them if you're not paying attention.

Here's the hard truth: you're playing the long game. You're building neural pathways, not installing software. You're earning trust that's been broken by every adult who came before you. That takes time. Sometimes lots of it.

So how do you know it's working? How do you keep going when it feels like nothing is changing?

You look for the tiny shifts. The micro-moments. The small signals that something underneath is starting to move.

Signs You're Making Progress

Connection cues are increasing. The student who avoided eye contact glances at you now. The one who always sat in the back drifts a little closer. The kid who flinched when you approached doesn't anymore. These aren't small things. These are seismic.

They're seeking you out. A student asks you for help instead of shutting down. Or lingers after class for no apparent reason. Or tells you something (anything) about their life. When kids start approaching you voluntarily, your relationship account is building a positive balance.

Behavior frequency decreases (even if intensity doesn't yet). Maybe the meltdowns are still big, but they're happening twice a week instead of daily. Maybe the defiance is still loud, but it's not every single transition anymore. Frequency shifts often come before intensity shifts. Count the wins.

They're using the tools. The student takes themselves to the calm-down corner without being told. They ask for a break. They grab a fidget before things escalate. When kids start using regulation strategies independently, that's evidence that the skills are taking root.

Repair gets easier. Early on, those "try again" conversations might feel like pulling teeth. The student won't look at you, won't engage, won't let you back in. Over time, repair gets shorter. Less painful. Sometimes they'll even initiate it themselves. (This is a big one. Celebrate it.)

You get a glimpse of the kid underneath. They laugh at your joke. They show you something they made. They tell you about their hamster. For just a moment, the armor comes down and you see who they are when they're not in survival mode. These glimpses will get longer.

Your own nervous system stays calmer. This one's about you. Remember all that co-regulation work? It goes both ways. When you notice you're not bracing for impact every time that student walks in, or that your jaw isn't clenched by 9 AM, that's data. Your nervous system is telling you something has shifted, even if you can't name it yet.

A Note About Timelines

We wish we could tell you this will all click into place by Labor Day. But the truth is, for some kids, you might be planting seeds you'll never see bloom. You might be the third grade teacher whose patient presence makes it possible for a fifth grade teacher to finally break through.

That's not failure. That's how healing works. It's cumulative. Every positive interaction is a deposit in a bank account that someone else might get to withdraw from.

And sometimes? Sometimes you will be the one who gets to see it. The kid who spent September under a table will be leading group projects by May. It happens. Not always, but often enough to keep us going.

Track the tiny shifts. Write them down if you have to. On the days when it feels like nothing is working, go back and read your list. Progress is happening. Even when you can't see it yet.

Let's Get Real: When Things Go Wrong

Amie: What do you do when you've tried everything and the behavior isn't changing?

Marti: First, check yourself. Are your basic needs met? Do you feel safe and calm? Have you built connection? Are you matching your response to their capacity level?

Amie: And if yes to all of that?

Marti: Then the child might need more support than you can provide. That's not failure. That's reality. Some kids need therapy, medication, IEPs, smaller settings.

Amie: Teachers feel like they're failing when they can't fix every kid.

Marti: You're not a fixer. You're a teacher. You can be a safe adult, use relationally-informed strategies, and create a healthy classroom. And some kids will still struggle.

Amie: That's hard to accept.

Marti: It is. But it's also freeing. You do your best. You use these strategies. And you recognize your limits.

Amie: What about when you mess up? When you yell or shame or handle something wrong?

Marti: Repair. Apologize. Model that adults make mistakes and make them right.

Amie: "Hey, I was really harsh earlier. I'm sorry. I was stressed and hungry. Just like you. Can we please try again?"

Marti: Exactly. That's teaching too. You're showing them that relationships can survive conflict.

Amie: And then you try again tomorrow. And when this work feels too heavy to carry alone?

Marti: You find your people. We'll talk more about building your support network in Section Three.

Takeaways

1. **Connection before responding to behaviors. Always.** When a student is in survival mode, their thinking brain is offline. Logic, consequences, and teaching don't work. Help them meet their needs first, then teach about other behavioral possibilities. And remember: you need to feel safe with your sensory needs met too.
2. **Relationally-informed responses maintain connection while teaching better skills.** Try again, choices, compromises, and the TBRI four levels of engagement allow you to hold boundaries while preserving relationship. Punishment breaks connection; relationally-informed responses build it.
3. **Some behaviors require more than classroom strategies, and that's okay.** Safety always comes first. Document patterns, involve administration appropriately, and advocate for students to get the support they need. Recognizing your limits isn't failure. It's wisdom.

Reflection Questions

1. When you imagine "success" with a difficult student, what does that picture look like? Is it realistic, or are you holding yourself to a Hallmark movie standard?
2. Which level of engagement (playful, structured, calming, protective) do you use most often? Are you matching your response to the child's needs, or defaulting to one level regardless?
3. How comfortable are you with "try again"? What would it look like to offer "let's try that again" instead of immediate consequences?
4. Think about a student whose behavior isn't changing despite your efforts. What additional support might they need that's beyond what you can provide alone?

One Thing to Try Tomorrow

Try the Try-Again

The next time a student does something poorly, speaks rudely, ignores a direction, or acts unkindly, instead of giving a consequence, say:

"Hmm, let's try that again."

Wait. Give them a chance to do it better.

When they do, celebrate: "Much better! Thank you."

That's it. One try-again. See how it feels. See how the student responds.

You're teaching, not punishing. You're maintaining connection, not breaking it. You're building skills, not just stopping behavior.

You are learning to do better.

Section Three Preview

We hope you're seeing that responding to behaviors doesn't have to mean punishment. It can mean teaching. It can mean connection. It can mean helping a child build the neural pathways they'll need to do better next time.

We hope you're feeling permission to try something different. Try the "try again." The choice. The compromise. The moment where you get quiet instead of loud.

We hope you're recognizing that the relationship you've built and the environment you've created are what make all of this possible. Without a safe relationship, responding to behaviors feels like an attack. With a safe relationship, it feels like guidance.

Kids who feel safe and connected learn better, behave better, and grow better. And teachers who respond to behaviors with relationship and connection burn out less and enjoy their work more.

Relationship and safety always come before behaviors will budge. You aren't a zoo keeper. You can't teach possums and watchdogs in survival mode. They need safety first.

You've got the foundation. You've got the strategies. Now comes the part where we make this sustainable. In Section Three, we'll tackle how to wrap all of this around your actual curriculum (without adding "one more thing"), how to navigate a system that wasn't built for this work, and how to keep going when the odds feel stacked against you.

Let's start moving those odds to your favor.

Section Three

Making it Work

"May the odds be ever in your favor."
-Effie Trinket, The Hunger Games (2012)

CHAPTER 11

Wrapping Strategies Around Curriculum

This Isn't "One More Thing": It's a Different Way of Doing What You Already Do

Picture this. It's third term. You've got a student who has spent the entire year trying to outsource every assignment to AI. Every essay reads like ChatGPT wrote it. Every math problem has that telltale polish that screams "this isn't your work." You've had the conversations. You've called home. Nothing has changed.

Then one day, you open their essay on Canvas and something feels different. There are spelling errors. The sentences don't flow with that artificial smoothness. You actually start reading instead of reaching for your usual comment: "This appears to be AI generated. Please resubmit in your own words."

As you read, you realize this kid might have actually written this. The arguments are simple but present. The information is mostly correct. It's a solid C paper. Maybe even a C+.

Now what do you do?

You decide to ask them about it. They look at you, a little surprised by the question, and shrug. "I don't know. I just felt like I knew the answer this time." That's when it hits you: every single relationally-informed strategy you've been using all year (the door greetings, the movement breaks, the try-agains, the fidgets, the connection activities) have been quietly creating an environment where this kid's brain could finally access learning.

You didn't lower standards. You didn't give easier work. You didn't teach less content. You wrapped connection and regulation around the content you were already teaching. And that made all the difference.

We have given you the practical tools: connection skills, sensory-friendly environments, and strategies for responding to big behaviors. But here's the question teachers always ask: "How do I do all of this AND still teach my curriculum?"

This chapter answers that question. Spoiler alert: you don't add these strategies ON TOP of your teaching. You weave them INTO it.

The Reality: Test Scores and Curriculum Matter

Let's be honest about something: we live in a system that measures success through test scores, graduation rates, and curriculum standards. We can wish things were different. We can advocate for change. Most of us have strong opinions about how the current system falls short. We still have to teach standards. We still have to prepare kids for tests. We still have to cover the curriculum.

That's reality.

~ Amie ~

Almost every time I talk to teachers about relationally-informed classrooms, the first thing they say is: "I don't have time for this. I have curriculum to cover." I get it. I really do. I once said those exact words. Here's what I've learned: these strategies don't take time away from curriculum. They make the time you spend on curriculum more effective.

Think about it this way. A disconnected student who feels unsafe, whose brain is stuck in survival mode, sitting through 50 minutes of instruction is learning almost nothing. Their downstairs brain is scanning for threats and craving connection instead of contemplating chemistry. You're trying to teach them about protons and electrons, and they're poking their neighbor, passing notes, or perfecting their pencil-drumming skills on the edge of their desk.

Now imagine what happens when you pause and play with the moment instead of fighting it. Let's say Andrew is tapping out a beat when he should be listening to your riveting explanation of atomic structure. You could shut it down. Or you could say, "Andrew, that's actually a pretty solid rhythm. Can you tap it out while the class counts the beats? Now let's think about protons and electrons having their own rhythm. Protons are steady, hanging out in the nucleus, keeping the beat. Electrons are the wild ones, zipping around in unpredictable patterns. Andrew, give me a steady beat for protons... now someone add the chaotic electron energy on top."

Suddenly you've got a whole-body, whole-class moment of musical molecular modeling. A little silly, absolutely. And they'll remember it far more than slide fourteen of your PowerPoint.

Connection through creative chaos beats compliance through coercion every single time.

You're not choosing between being relationally-informed and covering the curriculum. You're using the relational approach to make the curriculum actually stick. Examples like this have to feel terrifying for some of you. Allowing the lesson to go in a direction that isn't anything you planned can be more than your own nervous system can handle. That's fine! You can still plan activities and elements. As we move through this chapter, please do not feel like you have to use our ideas. Focus on how you can use this as a start point that fits your own personality, nervous system needs but also the needs of students.

Integration, Not Addition

Here's the mindset shift that made everything click for us. Instead of thinking: "How do we add relationally-informed strategies to our already packed schedule?" We started thinking: "How do we deliver what we are already teaching in a way that supports meeting their needs with connection?" Same content. Same standards. Different delivery.

Instead of: Teach vocabulary → worksheet → test

Try: Teach vocabulary through a clapping game → students create vocabulary skits → test

Instead of: Lecture on the Civil War → students take notes → discussion

Try: Students move to different corners representing different perspectives → active debate → collaborative notes

Math: Instead of the usual lesson → practice → homework grind,

Try: lesson with fidgets available → partner practice with movement breaks → choice of homework problems

You're not doing more. You're doing it differently.

A Day in Amie's Classroom

~ Amie ~

I've structured my classroom to follow the same basic order every day. This gives kids the felt safety of knowing what's coming while still allowing flexibility to adjust as needed. Structure without rigidity.

The anchor of my routine is what I call the daily schedule card. Every day when kids come in, we complete this card together. It helps me stay on task. It gives kids a place to listen and write. (This is dual coding. We will explain more soon.). And it gives parents a clear record of what we covered.

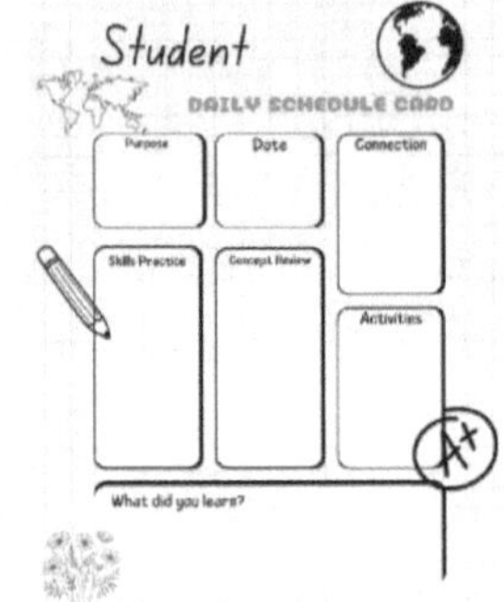

Here's how it flows:

Purpose of the Day: We start by writing and discussing why today's lesson matters. Think of it as an objective, but one the kids can actually relate to. Sometimes I use social media videos. Sometimes humor. Sometimes it's serious. Depends on the day and the content.

The Date and What's Coming: While we write the date, I mention anything important on the horizon. Projects due? Fire drills? Assignments closing? This is where I cover it. No surprises.

Connection Element: Every single day, we do something for connection. Sometimes I teach a skill and we practice it. Sometimes we do a true connection activity, like those we covered in Section Two. It varies, but it never gets skipped.

Skills Practice: This is our time to review previous material or practice skills. I teach social studies, and we realized a few years ago that so much of what we teach could help with skills kids need in math, science, and English. We use this time to practice analyzing charts, reading short paragraphs for main ideas, or interpreting maps. We focus on higher-level thinking skills as well as skills they need across multiple disciplines.

Concept Review: This is my only real direct instruction time each day. We talk about key vocabulary and key ideas. I help them take notes and we work on how to record what we're learning. I use a variety of methods: PowerPoints, infographics, sometimes just good old-fashioned writing on the board.

Activities: I have students write down what we're doing and in what order. They can use full sentences, key words, even pictures. I just want them to have a list. An example might be: first, complete your map assignment on the Louisiana Purchase; second, complete the primary source analysis on Lewis and Clark; third, complete your what did I learn. Then kids are released to work on whatever hands-on, sensory-rich, or play-based assignment I have planned.

What Did I Learn: This is the most important part of my day. In the last 5-10 minutes of class, I give kids time to think about and record what they learned. Sometimes I give specific expectations like an exit ticket. Sometimes they can draw what they learned or write it in paragraphs. I have a lot of student choice here. The research is clear: learning peaks in the first ten minutes and the final ten minutes. This structure lets me maximize those primetime moments with connection at the start and reflection at the end.

I've included a sample of my daily schedule card in Appendix A. Use it as is, adapt it, or let it spark your own ideas. This is what works for me. Your version might look completely different, and that's fine.

One Lesson, Two Ways

Let me show you what this type of integration can look like in practice.

Standard Lesson: The Boston Massacre

The Old Way (Traditional):

- Lecture on massacre (20 min)
- Students read a textbook passage (15 min)
- Students answer questions (10 min)
- Short quiz (15 min)

Total: 60 minutes. Some students may look or actually be engaged but most are zoned out. No connection, no sensory support. And almost certainly someone was sleeping while someone else was seconds from flipping a desk.

The New Way (Relationally-Informed):

0-2 minutes: Starting Class

- Greet students at the door
- "Who has something good from the weekend to share?" (2-3 quick shares)

2-7 minutes: Purpose

- Kids write the purpose that is displayed on the board
- Table discussion about what is a massacre
- Full class discussion about bias and points of view

7-15 minutes: Date and Connection Activity

- We review the date and announce anything coming up
- Connection activity is for kids to have a discussion on which flavor is better: orange or grape. The reason we use something simple is twofold. One, it is silly so kids will laugh and play plus they tend to have strong feelings about it. Two, it creates a simple way to explain people can see the exact same situation from very different points of view and still be friends.

15-25 minutes: Skills Practice

- Show students two different pictures of the Boston Massacre (we use the Boston Massacre lesson from SHEG)
- Make sure one is from the perspective of the British, one from the American perception
- Refer back to the connection activity about how people can have differing beliefs
- Have kids talk to their table mates or partner about what the similarities and differences are between pictures

25-30 minutes: Primary Source

- "Stand up. Let's read a couple of primary sources about the Boston Massacre."
- Students read and analyze the primary sources while standing or sitting, their choice

30-45 minutes: Sensory Input and Application

- Students get some Play-Doh and recreate the soldiers in the Boston Massacre
- While they do this, you are walking around making sure that they are accurate
- Ask students to really focus on the different explanations for the same event

45-50 minutes: Develop Opinion

- Students write a brief explanation of what they think happened
- They are encouraged to choose either side or find middle ground and develop a different opinion than others at their table
- Write a two sentence answer to the question: Who is at fault for the Boston Massacre. (We don't care what the answer is, we care that they developed an opinion and can state why they believe that.)

50-52 minutes: What Did I Learn

- On the daily schedule cards, have students write their answer to the following prompts: What did they learn about the Boston Massacre? Why is it important to look at multiple sources?

Total: 52 minutes. Way more engagement. Better retention. Same standards covered. And nobody threw a chair.

What changed? Amie added movement (stand up/sit down). She built in connection (partner work, sharing). She offered choices (writing format, seating, Play-Doh). She also gave academic freedom and permission to develop an opinion as long as they can provide a factual justification for the opinion. She provided sensory support (fidgets, flexible seating, and Play-Doh). She reduced passive listening and increased active participation. Below you will find sample lesson plans that Amie has used throughout the years. User friendly versions can be found in the workbook.

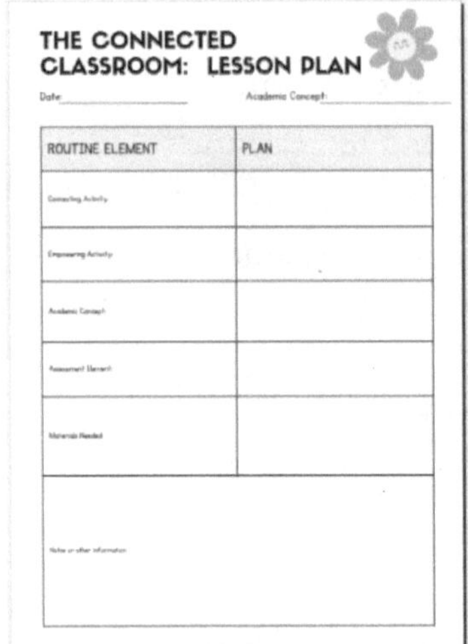

THE CONNECTED CLASSROOM: LESSON PLAN

Date: Academic Concept:

ROUTINE ELEMENT	PLAN
Connecting Activity	
Empowering Activity	
Academic Concept	
Assessment Element	
Materials Needed	

Notes or other information

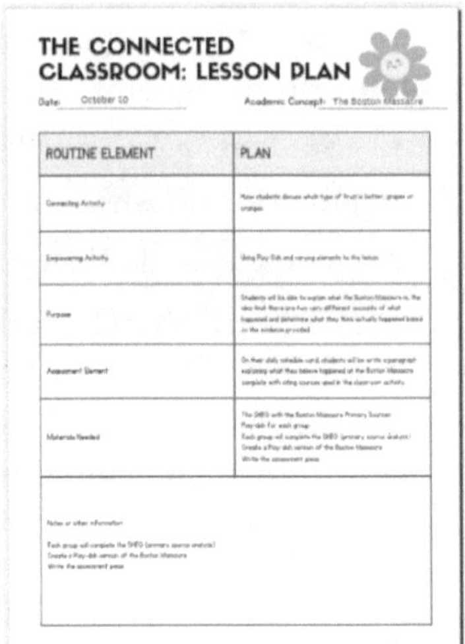

THE CONNECTED CLASSROOM: LESSON PLAN

Date: October 10 Academic Concept: The Boston Massacre

ROUTINE ELEMENT	PLAN
Connecting Activity	[illegible]
Empowering Activity	[illegible]
Purpose	[illegible]
Assessment Element	[illegible]
Materials Needed	[illegible]

Notes or other information

[illegible]

Same content. Different delivery. Better results.

Dual Coding (Why Spoken Word Plus Using Another Sense Works Better)

The brain has different systems for processing different types of sensory input. Words go through one area of the brain. Images go through another. Sounds through another. Movement through another.

When we engage multiple brain systems simultaneously, we increase the likelihood that information will stick. This is called dual coding, and it's one of the most well-researched strategies for improving learning.

Practical examples:

Teach vocabulary words AND have students draw them.
Explain a concept verbally AND show a diagram.
Read a story AND act it out.

Learn a process AND create a flowchart.

Amie teaches junior high school, and she still uses visuals constantly. Graphic organizers. Charts. Diagrams. Icons. Why does she do this, because teenagers' brains benefit from dual coding just as much as younger kids' brains do. For students who struggle with auditory processing or attention, visual supports gives them another way to learn and remember. Not everyone learns by listening to lectures. (In fact, most people don't.) Give students multiple entry points to file the information in their brains. Multiple ways to take in information. Multiple ways to show what they know.

Remember from Section One: when kids feel unsafe, the thinking brain goes offline. During stress, parts of the brain that process auditory input actually dial down before the parts of the brain that process visual input. In other words, this means that as kids increase stress and survival, they can't access the verbal parts of their brain. We have to use other ways to reach them. This is another reason why it's important to use visuals in the classroom as well as focus on body language.

Thinking back to Section One, we can imagine how someone's attachment style might impact their stress level in a given moment that we don't even recognize and they often cannot explain. Providing multiple teaching strategies helps keep students engaged even when we can't see what's happening internally. That's not "dumbing it down." That's honoring how brains actually work.

Sensory Support: Making It Stick

Remember all those sensory strategies? They're not just for calming kids or curbing chaos. They're for learning. When we incorporate sensory experiences into our lessons, we're helping information stick. We're giving kids' bodies something to do so their brains can focus. We're making learning memorable because it's connected to physical experience.

We have more comprehensive sensory charts and plans in our workbook. Let us give you a taste of what this looks like in practice here.

Bodies Have Needs, Too

Kids need to be hydrated, fed, and rested to learn. This can feel impossible to address in a classroom, but small shifts make a difference.

Hydration: Amie allows water breaks pretty much anytime anyone asks. Like the fidgets, she teaches what they're doing, why it matters, and then they practice. Some kids take advantage at first, but it doesn't take long to figure out who those kids are. They are probably the ones needing more connection.

Amie allows water bottles in class. When she has to teach something really difficult, she plays what she's lovingly named the "drinking game" with kids. Every time she says a certain key word (usually vocabulary but doesn't have to be), everyone takes a small sip of water. For example, when teaching about seasons, every time she says "tilt of the Earth," everyone takes a sip. Not only does this increase engagement, but it also keeps them hydrated. Plus, it has an adult-sounding name and kids think it's hilarious.

More water does mean more bathroom breaks. She usually just lets kids go when they ask. Again, some take advantage at first. But as time goes on, most use it only when they need to. When she treats kids with respect and allows them to meet their needs, once they start to trust it, they really don't want to lose that independence.

Snacks: Amie lets kids bring snacks to class with one rule: the first time she has to clean up their mess, snacks are done for them.

She'll never forget the day she was teaching AP Human Geography and suddenly smelled BBQ. She looked around and saw a table of kids eating literal chicken wings. They had ordered them, used the hall pass to pick them up at the front office, and were now eating them in class like it was a totally normal Tuesday. Which, honestly, for this class? It kind of was.

She had two choices: laugh or cry. She laughed. They didn't technically violate the rules, but she has since added the caveat that snacks cannot be distracting to learning. They should probably be in wrappers and not require wet wipes. She tells the wings story every year now. Everyone laughs. Everyone connects. And so far, no one else has tried to eat wings in class.

Connecting Play to the content

Remember: "Play disarms fear." When students feel playful, they're in the optimal brain state for learning. Amie hears frequently that older kids don't want to play. Here is the reality; they really do want to play! The play just looks different.

Games That Teach Content:

For vocabulary, try "Vocabulary Charades." Students act out vocabulary words while teams guess. After a correct guess, the student explains the definition. Movement, connection, play, and content all at once.

For historical figures, try "Historical Figure Speed Dating." Half the class becomes historical figures. The other half rotates, asking questions. Figures answer in character, and the goal is to figure out who they are.

Speed dating can be one of those methods that can be used to teach all sorts of things. Amie has used it to teach the demographic transition model in geography classes. A science teacher friend uses it to "date" parts of the cell. In our 7th grade history classes, we speed date mountain men. It can be as complex or simple as you want. Our science teacher even "sets the mood" with Christmas lights, romantic music in the background then gets every kid a Capri sun and a bag of Goldfish. I mean, who doesn't want snacks while "dating"? We are in no way expecting everyone to take it to this level, but for her, this gave her joy and so the kids enjoyed it more!

Finding Ideas:

We joke about the secret source of ideas for educational activities. Ready for this groundbreaking resource? Pinterest. YouTube. Instagram. Social media of all types. We know. Revolutionary. Search for "classroom games" or "classroom activities" and see what pulls up. Amie has multiple group chats with different teacher groups. When we find a great idea, we send it through in that moment and then we have records of what we were thinking. Then the next time we have a PLC day or department meeting, we can talk about potentially trying these.

What we're really doing here is giving you permission to be creative. Or outsource that creative part. Just play. Have fun. Return to the joy in the classroom. Some of the best ideas start as an elementary school art project we then adapt to fit our curriculum and standards. It takes time, felt safety, and willing participants to do this but once you start, it becomes so much fun and a natural way of getting ideas while you doom scroll.

Connection Activities That Teach Content

Remember the connection skills? Here's ideas to help them do double duty, building relationships while simultaneously teaching content.

Turn and Talk (With Intention):

Instead of: "Does everyone understand?" (silence)

Try: "Turn to your partner. Explain this concept in your own words. You have 2 minutes."

Students connect with each other while reviewing concepts. You'll need to teach kids how to do this effectively. Model what a good turn-and-talk looks like. Always have one member of each partnership share whether they have questions or need clarification. This way you are not forcing kids terrified of public speaking to perform, but giving them the option as they find more safety in class. Often, Amie will have kids do this at tables. They turn and talk to one person then share with the table instead of the class.

Collaborative Note-Taking:

Instead of everyone taking notes silently, try partner note-taking. One person writes while the other adds ideas, then they switch. They're connecting while learning, and they're learning better because they're discussing as they go.

Morning Meeting That Teaches:

Elementary teachers often do morning meetings. Make them content-rich.

- "Share one thing you noticed about weather this week" (science)
- "Show me with your fingers how many tens are in 47" (math)
- "Give a thumbs up if you can name a character from our book who showed courage" (reading)

Amie actually did morning meetings in her middle school and high school classes. She'd start sitting in a circle on the floor and go through the daily schedule card. Some classes or students couldn't/didn't want to sit on the floor but as often as possible she tries to get them to not be in desks. She found that some of her most difficult classes responded really well to just having a couple of minutes to share things from their lives. It usually isn't anything more than "I'm excited for the basketball game" or "I did well on a test." But allowing kids time to socialize and build genuine connection is what creates the felt safety that lets learning happen. Social connection is where their brains are developmentally. Let's honor that.

For Secondary Teachers: Surviving (and Thriving in) Block Schedules

If you teach on a block schedule (80-90 minute periods), integration becomes even more critical. No teenager can passively listen for 90 minutes. We can't sit for that long either. Truly. We are educators that dislike continuing education simply because we're supposed to sit all day when we're used to standing and running around the building.

For block schedules, plan for:

- At least two movement breaks per period
- A shift in activity type every 15-20 minutes

- Partner or group work in the middle of the block (when energy naturally dips)
- A strong end to class that brings everyone back together

If you see students every other day: Start each class with a quick "reconnection" moment. "What's happened since I saw you last?" or "One thing you remember from last class?" This bridges the gap and rebuilds connection after time apart. Amie often does these at tables but you can do it with the whole class as well.

If you teach an elective with rotating students: Focus on consistent routines rather than individual relationship depth. When the structure itself feels safe and predictable, students can settle in faster even when they don't know you well yet. The principles stay the same across all schedules: connection, sensory support, and regulation wrapped around content. The timing just shifts.

Let's Get Real: When You Still Have to Cover Everything

Marti: I can already hear teachers saying, "This sounds great, but I have a pacing guide. I have to cover X chapters in Y weeks. I don't have time to let kids sit in circles singing Kumbaya."

Amie: The reality is most teachers don't have freedom to completely redesign their curriculum. And honestly, that's not what we're asking.

Marti: So what do we actually do?

Amie: We look for the moments we CAN shift. Maybe you can't change the whole lesson, but you can add a 2-minute movement break. Or offer choice in how students show what they learned. Or let kids work with a partner instead of alone. Small shifts, not total overhauls.

Marti: And here's the secret sauce: when students are more regulated and engaged, you actually move faster through content because you're not constantly managing behavior or re-teaching concepts that didn't stick.

Amie: My relationally-informed classes cover more content than my old traditional classes because we spend way less time on behavior issues. The learning sticks better because their brains are actually in a state to encode it.

Marti: What about teachers whose administration requires a specific lesson plan format?

Amie: You can still integrate these principles within required formats. Most templates have sections for instruction, practice, and assessment. You just modify HOW you do each section. Instruction becomes lecture with fidgets available and a movement break halfway through. Practice becomes partner work with choice of location. Assessment becomes multiple ways to show learning. Same template. Relationally-informed delivery.

Marti: What about standardized tests? Students need to be able to sit still and focus for hours.

Amie: And they will be MORE able to do that if they've had opportunities to regulate throughout the year. We're not making them dependent on supports. We're opening their window of tolerance. A kid who has learned to recognize when they need movement, who knows how to use a quick breathing technique? That kid's window has expanded. They have the reserves to handle sitting still in the short term.

Marti: The goal isn't to make everything easy. It's to make learning accessible so students can rise to challenges.

Amie: There's a difference.

Marti: Can we talk about the fear piece? I think a lot of teachers resist this not because they don't believe it works, but because they're scared of looking soft. Scared that administrators will see fidgets and movement and think they've lost control of their classes.

Amie: That's real. I suggest starting with one thing. One small, sustainable shift. Document what happens. If a principal walks in and sees kids doing a movement break, you can explain: "We're doing a brain break to increase focus for the next activity. Research shows movement improves retention."

Marti: Having the language helps.

Amie: It does. "I'm implementing research-based, trauma-informed practices to improve student outcomes" sounds a lot different than "I let kids play sometimes."

Marti: Even though it might be the same thing.

Amie: (grinning) Sometimes, yes. But framing matters. Most administrators want engaged students and good outcomes. If you can show them that, they're usually more supportive.

Marti: And if they're not?

Amie: Then you focus on what you CAN control. Your classroom. Your relationships. Your sensory environment. You can't change the whole system, but you can create a pocket of safety and connection in your room.

Marti: It always comes back to relationship.

Amie: Always.

Takeaways

1. **Relationally-informed strategies and curriculum aren't competing. They're complementary.** When you integrate connection, sensory support, and regulation INTO your lessons, students learn more effectively. A regulated brain in a 40-minute lesson outperforms a stressed brain in a 60-minute lesson every time.
2. **Small shifts spark big changes.** You don't need to redesign every lesson from scratch. Add a movement break. Offer one choice. Include partner work. These small adjustments transform the learning environment without requiring extra hours of planning.
3. **Time spent on connection and regulation isn't wasted. It's invested.** The minutes you "give up" for a brain break or a

morning check-in come back to you in reduced behavior management, better retention, and students who are actually present for learning. The returns are remarkable.

Reflection Questions

1. Look at your lesson plans for next week. Where could you add movement that reinforces content? Where could you build in a moment of connection? Where could you offer even a small choice?
2. Think about a lesson that typically doesn't go well. What's happening in students' bodies and brains during that lesson? What regulation or connection support might help?
3. What's your biggest barrier to integrating these strategies? Time? Pacing guides? Administrative expectations? Worry about how it will look? How might you work within or around that barrier?
4. When have you seen students learn better because they were regulated and connected? What conditions made that possible? How could you recreate those conditions more often?
5. What would your students say if you asked them what makes class more engaging? (Warning: their answers might be more honest than you want.)

One Thing to Try Tomorrow

Movement Meets Content

Pick one lesson tomorrow. Midway through, add 2-3 minutes of movement that reinforces what you're teaching.

Examples:

- **Math:** "Stand up. Show me with your arms: greater than, less than, equal to."
- **Reading:** "Act out what this character is feeling right now."

- **Science:** "Move like a molecule when it's heated. Now when it's cooled."
- **History:** "Walk to the corner that represents the perspective you agree with most."

Movement plus content. Two minutes. Watch how it changes engagement and retention. Content wrapped in connection? That's the sweet spot. That's where real learning lives.

CHAPTER 12

The Reality of Working in a System

Navigating Administration, Policy, and the Messy Reality of Schools

Here's the honest truth: even when you have all these tools, you still have to use them inside a system. A system with policies, pacing guides, and administrators who may or may not understand this work. A system where colleagues look at you sideways when you let kids use Play-Doh in high school, where clip charts are required, zero-tolerance is mandated, and "trauma-informed" gets dismissed as code for "letting kids get away with things."

So what do you do when the system itself feels like the biggest barrier? That's what this chapter is about. How to navigate pushback. How to find your allies. How to follow policy while still honoring children. How to keep going when everything around you seems designed to make it harder.

Having strategies is only part of the puzzle. Knowing how to implement them in the real world of education? That's where it gets interesting.

Let's talk about it.

Amie's Story: Navigating Difficult Leadership

~ Amie ~

As a teacher who has been in the classroom for 30 years, I've lived through countless systemic changes and a parade of principals. Some were great. Some really created a lot of upheaval. Most were just "go about your day" neutral.

In the last decade at my school, we've had five different principals. Five different leadership styles. Five different sets of expectations about what good teaching looks like. During that time we also experienced Covid and all the adventure that brought. (And by adventure, I mean chaos, masks, and learning to unmute ourselves.)

Let me share what I've learned about what makes the difference between leadership that builds trust and leadership that destroys it.

When Leadership Creates Fear

Most teachers can relate to working with administrators who are difficult. Some micromanage everything. Some pit staff and departments against each other, creating division and chaos. Some single out the more vocal teachers and either bring disciplinary action against them or threaten to.

I've watched districts shrug off complaints about harmful administrators, treating teacher pain as acceptable collateral damage while they "work on" developing that leader. I've seen good teachers leave the profession because the system that was supposed to support them became the thing that broke them.

And I've lived it *myself.*

When It Gets Personal

There was a year when an administrator decided I was the problem. Without warning, without conversation, without support, I found my entire career called into question. After decades of effective and highly effective evaluations, I was suddenly labeled ineffective. My professional character was questioned. My job and reputation was on the line.

The details don't matter as much as what it felt like: devastating. Disorienting. Like the ground had disappeared beneath my feet.

When I appealed, a district representative told me to my face that he didn't agree with the evaluation. Then he said the quiet part out loud: the system was designed to make it easy to get rid of teachers. He essentially admitted the system wasn't fair and I had no real recourse.

The Healing Work

Here's where I need to get really vulnerable.

I did not have a secure attachment from my childhood. I have a dismissive adult attachment style. I've done the work to develop earned secure attachment, but it hasn't been easy.

What happened when my entire career and character were called into question triggered all of my non-secure attachment wounds. I did so much therapy during that time. I worked through early childhood trauma. I did the work to understand my own attachment patterns. And most importantly, I did the work to view this administration through a compassionate lens, even after they had destroyed my heart.

During a personal therapy session, I realized I didn't need to hold onto the lies this administrator was telling me about who I was. What I needed was to see the situation through a relationally-informed lens.

Once I had healed enough to see myself with grace, I could extend that same grace to my administration. They truly were doing what they thought was right. Even though they were clearly wrong and had done tremendous damage to me and my emotional health, they taught me something valuable. We are all human. The system isn't human, but it's run by humans. Our job is to see the system clearly and safeguard ourselves while we serve.

When Leadership Creates Safety

Contrast that with a principal who leads in a way that creates felt safety and connection. These principals see us as our true selves. They see our positives and our negatives and they are willing to give us the grace to fail.

The problem is, sometimes after so many difficult experiences, it can be really hard to trust again. I remember meeting with a new principal over the summer before his first year. I had major surgery scheduled for the beginning of the school year, so I wanted to connect early. He asked me how he could help. What did I need?

I wasn't sure what to say, but I tried to be honest. I looked at him and said something along the lines of, "I don't feel safe at work. I don't even know how to answer that question because there is zero trust between me and the system."

He didn't get defensive. He just said, "That's okay. Thanks for telling me. We can work on that."

These types of leaders support teachers and staff. They are patient as we build relationships. They actively work to connect with us like teachers work to connect to kids.

I was out for two months recovering from surgery and complications. When I returned, I felt lost. I'd missed so much of the school year. But slowly, I let my guard down. By the end of his first year, I was finding my footing again. I was experimenting with relationally-informed practices. I was finding joy. I was connecting with kids.

Then, toward the end of his second year, he announced he was leaving. Moving to a district closer to his home. I cried. I felt so lost. I would love to tell you everything turned out great, but that wasn't the case. We had a few more very difficult years before I had leadership that actually helped me find my true self again.

With all that said, here's what that experience taught me: safe leadership is possible. It exists. It's not a fairy tale. And when we find it, even briefly, it reminds us what we're working toward.

What I Want You to Know

If you're reading this and you've been hurt by the system, I want you to know you're not alone. It happens to good teachers. It happened to me.

And if you're still healing from it, that's okay too. The work takes time. But it's worth it. When we do our own healing work, we become better teachers. We become the kind of adults who can offer kids what we needed and didn't always get. The system may not be human. But we are. And that's our greatest strength.

What the System Actually Is (And Why It Won't Change Quickly)

Here's what I've come to understand.

The system exists because things have gone wrong.

It is a reactive response to human failures. It's enormous because humans sometimes make really bad decisions, and education touches every single person. Either you work in it, you're a student in it, your kids are in it, or you work alongside it. Unlike many fields, education affects everything.

The system is not going to change quickly, if it changes at all. We will always have bad administrators. But we will also always have good ones. We'll have districts that listen and districts that don't.

I've only taught in two districts my entire career. Really only two schools. Even within that limited experience, everything has changed over and over. The only things I can keep constant are things within my control.

Here was the hardest truth for me to swallow: the system, with all its faults, is still there primarily to protect kids and teachers. It keeps us safe and functioning. I don't have an answer for how to solve systemic issues. What I do know is that if every level of education used a relationally-informed lens, we would start working through the biggest problems.

Until that happens, we have to protect our own bubble. We have to focus on what's in our control. The way I organize lessons is in my control. Making sure I have connection activities and sensory supports is in my control. Receiving support from my people and my peers is in my control.

I almost burned myself out trying to force the system to change. Now that I know better, I do better. The only way to change the system is connection: connecting with every child I can, supporting my fellow teachers, and staying true to who I am.

For Those of You Drowning Right Now

If you're in a difficult situation, we see you. We are there with you. We have been you. Maybe the chapter on self-care is what you need right now. Maybe you need to take some time off. Maybe you even need to leave the profession for a while. Try to identify your needs so you can find ways to meet them.

Until then, just know that **Marti and I are here.** Sitting in the hard stuff with you. Supporting your efforts to connect with kids and build healthy relationships with a strong sense of safety in our schools. We are raising our voices in support of you and your colleagues.

Structure vs. Rigidity: The Earthquake Building

Think about how engineers earthquake-proof buildings. They don't make them rigid. Rigid buildings crack. Rigid buildings crumble. Rigid buildings fall. Instead, they build structures that can move. The building sways with the earthquake. It bends. It flexes. But the core structure holds. That's what we need in schools.

Structure means clear schedules, consistent expectations, predictable routines, and known consequences. **Rigidity** means zero flexibility, no room for context, one-size-fits-all responses, and inability to adapt.

Structure says: "We start class at 8:15 every day. That's predictable and safe." Rigidity says: "If you're not in your seat at exactly 8:15, you get a tardy. No exceptions. I don't care if the bus was late or your locker jammed."

Structure says: "We expect respectful communication in this classroom. Here's what that looks like." Rigidity says: "If you roll your eyes at me, you automatically get detention. Doesn't matter if you're dysregulated or frustrated."

Structure says: "Assignments are due on Friday. Plan accordingly."
Rigidity says: "Late work gets a zero. Period. Even if your grandma died or you were in the hospital."

See the difference?

Structure with flexibility allows for the human element. You maintain clear expectations while still responding to individual circumstances. The building stands. But it sways. And in the swaying, it survives.

Following Policy While Honoring Children

Here's a hard truth: you have to follow policy. Your district has rules. Your state has mandates. You can't just ignore them because you disagree. But you CAN follow policy while still honoring children.

It's not either/or. It's both/and.

Letter of the Law vs. Spirit of the Law

In education, rebellion often looks like compliance.

We sit in professional development. We nod. We smile. We say, "Great, we'll implement that." Then we close our classroom doors and do whatever we actually think works. (If you're a teacher reading this, you just nodded.) It's compliance as resistance. We aren't saying this coping skill is good or bad. We're just naming what's true.

Here's what we want to suggest: instead of fake compliance, aim for the SPIRIT of the policy while adapting the LETTER as needed.

Example: Zero Tolerance Dress Code

Letter of the law: "Any student not in dress code is immediately sent home." Spirit of the law: "We want students to dress appropriately for learning." How to honor both: Keep backup clothes in your classroom. Pull the student aside privately: "Hey, your shirt's not meeting dress code. I've got an extra one you can borrow today. Sound good?" Problem solved. Kid stays in class. Policy technically followed. Dignity maintained.

Example: Late Work Policy

Letter of the law: "Late work receives a maximum of 50%." Spirit of the law: "We want students to turn work in on time." How to honor both: Accept the late work. Give feedback. Apply the grade penalty. Then have a conversation: "This is solid work. I hate that it's late and gets a lower grade. What can we do differently next time?" Student learns. Policy followed. Relationship maintained.

Example: Consequences for Behavior

Letter of the law: "A student who disrupts class three times goes to the office." Spirit of the law: "Learning environment must be protected." How to honor both: When a student is disruptive, intervene early with connection and regulation strategies. If behavior continues, remove the audience (hallway conversation, calm corner) before it becomes a third strike. If you still need office support, frame it as "getting help" not "punishment." Policy followed. Student not shamed. Learning environment protected. You're not abandoning policy. You're implementing it with humanity.

Transforming Required Tools

Maybe your school requires clip charts, behavior tracking systems, or public accountability boards. You didn't choose them. You can't eliminate them. But you CAN change how you use them.

The Clip Chart Transformation

In an ideal world, we would take that required clip chart and throw it in the trash. Sigh. We know. That's not an option for many of you reading this book. But we want to. If you need a reminder of how horrible they are, go back and read the parts about robotic compliance and how shame can be an effective short term behavior modification tool. But shame really just increases the stress response, closes the window of tolerance, and grows the possum and watchdog while the owl flies off.

Shame doesn't build relationships or make us want to be good community members. It forces our focus inward so we can't even think of others if we wanted to. Not great in the long term for a healthy community.

If we can't trash that chart, we can transform it. Instead of using it as a public shaming device, transform it into a private regulation tool. When a student's clip moves down, don't announce it to the class. Instead, use it as an invitation for connection: "Hey, I noticed you moved to yellow. What do you need right now? Let's figure this out together." Make the chart about information, not judgment. "Yellow means you're struggling. What can we do?" Better yet, if you have any flexibility at all, put the chart on students' desks instead of the wall. Personal regulation tracking instead of public humiliation. Same tool, completely different impact.

The Behavior Tracking Transformation

Use the required behavior tracking system to identify patterns, not just to punish. "I'm noticing Isaiah has incidents right after lunch every day. What's happening at lunch? Is he eating? Is something going on socially? Is the noise overwhelming?" Documentation becomes detective work. You're looking for what's underneath the behavior so you can address the actual need.

The Key Principle

You can't change district policy. But you can control your tone of voice, your facial expression, whether you shame publicly or redirect privately, how you frame your responses, and the relationship you build with students. A teacher using a required clip chart with warmth and without public shaming is doing something very different than a teacher using it punitively. Same tool. Different teacher. Wildly different outcomes for kids.

When You're the Only One Doing This

Let's talk about something uncomfortable: you're going to implement these strategies, and the teacher next door might still be using a clip chart. The veteran down the hall might roll her eyes when you mention "felt safety." Your team might trade war stories in the lounge about who gave the most detentions this week. You exist in an ecosystem. And ecosystems don't change overnight. This is one of the hardest parts of this work. Not the kids. Not the strategies. The loneliness of doing something different when everyone around you is doing something else. So how do you stay the course without becoming insufferable?

Lead With Your Classroom

Here's the truth: nobody changes their practice because a colleague told them they should. (Think about it. Has that ever worked on you?) People change when they see something working and get curious about it. Your job isn't to convert anyone. Your job is to tend your own garden. Water your own plants. Let the results speak. When a colleague notices that your "difficult" student is calmer this year, they might ask what you're doing. That's your opening. Until then? Focus on what you can control, do the work and find your "coffee club".

Resist the Urge to Correct

When you hear a colleague say something that makes you cringe ("That kid just needs more consequences"), you will feel the pull to educate them. To share the research. To explain what's really going on in that child's brain. If you have the relationship with them to have the conversation, go ahead! If you don't have that relationship or the school culture doesn't support difficult conversations, you may need to be a little more self-protective. Nobody likes the person who's always correcting, always explaining, always subtly suggesting that everyone else is doing it wrong. Even if you're right. Especially if you're right. Save your energy for your own classroom. That's where you have actual influence.

When Kids Move Between Classrooms

Here's a reality: your students will spend time in other spaces with other adults who use different approaches. Specialists, substitutes, lunch duty, next year's teacher. You cannot control what happens there. This can feel defeating. (Why bother building felt safety if they're going to get yelled at in PE?) Here's what we know: kids can hold complexity. They learn quickly that different adults operate differently. What matters is that they have at least one place, one person, where they feel safe. One relationship that's different. Here's the other thing we know, different kids respond to different teachers in complex ways! There are kids who thrive in Amie's class but struggle in others. Then there are kids who struggle in Amie's but thrive other places. It is the diversity of our teaching staff that actually meets kids needs.

You can be that person. That's not nothing. That's everything.

What If a Colleague Asks?

Okay, but what if someone actually does ask what you're doing? How do you share without sounding preachy?

Keep it practical, not theoretical. Instead of "I'm using a trauma-informed, polyvagal-based approach," try "I've been doing this thing where I check in with him for two minutes before class starts, and it's actually helping."

Share struggles, not just successes. "I'm trying something new and honestly it's been a mixed bag" is way more approachable than "Let me tell you about the research on attachment."

Invite, don't instruct. "I went to this training that kind of blew my mind. Happy to share the info if you're ever interested." Then drop it. Let them come to you. We don't have to sell this. People who are ready will find us.

Loan, don't lecture. If they seem genuinely curious, offer a resource. "There's this book I've been reading. Want to borrow it?" Much better than a fifteen-minute monologue in the copy room.

A Word About Judgment (Yours and Theirs)

Here's something we need to say gently: as you learn more about this work, you might start feeling judgmental toward colleagues who haven't learned it yet. You'll see a teacher yelling at a kid in the hallway and think, "Don't you know what you're doing to his nervous system?"

That judgment is understandable. It's also not helpful. Judgment creates distance. Distance is the opposite of what we need to actually shift a school culture. Judgement leads to shame. Shame doesn't help kids. It won't help your colleague either. You didn't know this stuff once either. You were doing the best you could with the tools you had. So are they. Stay humble. Stay curious. Stay in your own lane. And when the opportunity arises to genuinely connect with a colleague around this work, take it.

That's how ecosystems change. One conversation, one relationship, one classroom at a time.

Common Objections (And the Fear Behind Them)

When we talk about relationally-informed practices in schools, we hear the same objections over and over. And underneath every objection is fear.

"It's not fair to other students."

The fear: Loss of control. Worry that classroom management will fall apart. Worry that your students will walk all over you.

The truth: Fair doesn't mean same. Fair means everyone gets what they need.

What to say in response: "You're right that students might ask why one kid gets a fidget. Here's what we tell them: 'Some people need crutches to walk. Some people need fidgets to focus. We all have different needs, and that's okay.' Most kids accept that immediately."

You can also just make fidgets available to everyone. Problem solved.

"It costs too much."

The fear: That you're a bad teacher if you can't provide everything. Your resources are already spread thin.

The truth: You can start with almost nothing.

What to say in response: "Stress balls in bulk cost $15. Flexible seating? Let kids sit on the floor. Weighted lap pads? DIY with rice in a pillowcase. Calm corner? Blanket over a desk. Connection? Costs zero dollars. Results? Priceless." You don't need Pinterest-perfect. You need practical and present.

"Administration won't support this."

The fear: Job security. Being seen as not following the program. Worried that admin won't think you are managing your classroom effectively.

The truth: Most administrators care about results. If your students are learning and behavior is improving, they usually don't care how you're achieving it.

What to say in response: "Don't ask permission. Show results. Start small. Document improvements. Then share: 'I tried this strategy and saw a 30% reduction in behavior referrals and a 15% improvement in assignment completion.' Results speak louder than philosophy."

"I'm not trained for this. What's my liability?"

The fear: Doing harm. Legal consequences. Stepping outside your role.

The truth: Relationally-informed strategies reduce liability, not increase it. What gets teachers in trouble is reacting instead of responding. Escalating instead of de-escalating. Isolating and shaming instead of connecting and teaching. Relationally-informed practices give you a framework for responding well. For creating a paper trail of care and intentionality. For being able to say, "Yes, I tried multiple interventions before this consequence. Here's my documentation."

What to say in response: "You're not diagnosing or treating trauma. You're creating a trauma-informed environment. That's best practice, not therapy. Document everything. Keep notes. Show you're trying multiple strategies. That protects you AND the student."

"I'm a teacher, not a therapist."

The fear: Being asked to do one more impossible thing. Fear of failure. Fear of making things worse.

The truth: You're right. You're not a therapist. You're a teacher. And that's exactly what you should say. This book is not asking you to become a therapist. It's not asking you to diagnose, treat, or fix childhood trauma. It's not asking you to ignore your own sensory needs or be inauthentic.

What it's asking you to do is create a classroom environment where learning can happen despite trauma and adversity. Where students feel safe enough to access their upstairs brains. Where YOU feel safe to access your upstairs brain. Where genuine connection comes before instruction. You're not treating trauma. You're teaching in a relationally-informed way. There's a huge difference.

What to say in response: "This isn't therapy. It's teaching in a way that accommodates how stressed brains work. You're still teaching curriculum. You're just doing it in a way that reaches more students. That IS your job."

Here's the thing about all of this: these fears are valid. They're based on real concerns but they're also often based in misunderstandings about what relationally-informed teaching actually is. When someone pushes back, don't argue. Get curious. "It sounds like you're worried about losing control. Tell me more about that." Listen. Validate. Then address the real fear, not just the surface objection.

Implementation Strategies: How to Actually Make This Work

So you're convinced this matters. You want to implement it. But you're teaching in a system that might not support it.

Here's how you start.

Start Small

Do NOT try to overhaul your entire teaching practice overnight. Pick ONE strategy. Just one. Maybe it's door greetings every day. Maybe it's one movement break per class. Maybe it's having fidgets available. Maybe it's re-dos instead of automatic consequences. We have lots of suggestions at the end of each chapter for starting small. We did that intentionally. One thing. Master it. Make it a habit. Then add another.

Small changes compound. You don't need to do everything at once.

Find Your Allies

You cannot do this work alone. You'll burn out. Find the other teachers who get it. The ones who already lead with relationships.

The ones who are frustrated with punitive systems. Build your community.

Remember "coffee club”? Here's something worth remembering: Marzano's educator research shows the number one predictor of teacher retention is having a best friend at work. Not salary. Not class size. A friend.

Find your people. Support each other. You'll need it.

Document Your Wins

Keep track of what's working. When a student who used to melt down daily has a week without incidents, note it. When test scores improve, document it. When a parent emails thanking you for connecting with their child, save it. This isn't about bragging. It's about evidence. When someone questions your methods, you can say, "Here's what I've noticed since implementing these strategies..." and show data.

Anecdotes are great. Data is better.

Work With Administration (When Possible)

If you have supportive administration, loop them in early. "I'm trying some new strategies for student engagement. I'd love your feedback." Ask them to observe when you're using relationally-informed practices well. Show them what it looks like. If you have unsupportive administration, fly under the radar. Don't ask permission. Just do it. Show results later. Follow policy.

Sustainability

This work is hard. You will have days where you want to quit. Where relationally-informed teaching feels impossible. Where you just want to yell and give detentions and maybe also flip a table yourself. That's normal. Set personal boundaries. Leave work at work sometimes. Connect with your allies. Ask for help. You can't run on an empty tank. This work requires a lot of fuel. We will talk more about that soon.

Ideas to Implement

You're not alone. Other schools have successfully implemented relationally-informed practices. Here's some ideas on how you could do this.

Start With One Grade Level: Begin with just the kindergarten team. Train your Kindergarten team, give them a built in coffee club to implement together, support each other. Results will follow and likely be so good that first grade will want to try the next year. Then second. Within three years, the whole elementary will on board. Bottom-up change. Start small. Spread organically.

Find a Champion Administrator: As an administrative team, set the school year goals for professional development as learning how to create a relationally-informed school. Make it a school-wide priority, bring in trainers, create planning time for teacher collaboration, and provide resources. Top-down change, but with genuine buy-in.

Pilot With High-Need Students: Create a small pilot program for your highest-need students. One teacher. Fifteen kids. Full implementation. Track what happens with behavior incidents knowing they will likely drop significantly. Grades will improve. Attendance improves. The next year expand to two classrooms, then four, then school-wide. Prove it works with the hardest cases, and people pay attention.

The Pattern: Start small. Show success. Scale slowly. You don't need your whole district to change. You need YOUR classroom to change. Then maybe your grade level. Then maybe your school.

Change happens one classroom at a time.

A Note From Amie

This book has been primarily about Amie's individual journey as a foster parent, adoptive mom, and teacher working to bring relationally informed practices into the classroom. But this next part felt too important to leave out.

In 2023, after completing her TBRI Practitioner training, Amie was hired by a Utah-based nonprofit specializing in helping kids languishing in foster care find connections and then sustain those connections. One of the areas families struggled with most? Schools. Amie was brought on to help families navigate the school system and translate the relationally informed approach from social work into educational settings.

That work became a turning point. Collaborating with the agency, she created a curriculum to train teachers called Tools for Transformation. It lives separately from this book, but its success felt worth sharing. And "success" is putting it mildly. One program saw behavior incidents drop from multiple per day to zero in a single term. Another saw a child go from requiring two full-time adult aides at all times to needing no dedicated aide at all. Even in Amie's own classroom, the impact on how kids learn and behave has been significant.

At the time of this writing, the data is still anecdotal. Research will be done. Numbers will be validated. But here is what matters: this methodology works. We know it works. People across the country are already implementing these strategies in schools and communities. If you can find the courage to start down this path, you will find your people. You will find your community. We give you full permission to use our methodologies and ideas. We also give you permission to seek out the agencies, groups, and individuals already doing this work and join them.

A Note for Administrators

If you're an administrator reading this, here's what we want you to hear. Use the system for what it's meant to be: a way to create policy that keeps teachers and kids safe, manages finances, and maintains structure. Don't let it become the unbendable, unbreakable building that eventually just... falls down.

For a system to run well, it needs a relationally informed approach at every level. The state school board needs to use this approach with districts. Districts need to use it with administrators.

Administrators need to use it with teachers. So teachers can use it with kids. That's how we survive this. That's how we thrive.

Give your teachers grace to fail. Give them permission to try new things without risking their careers. See them for who they are. Let them be human. Be the principal someone needed and never got.

The day Amie sat in her current principal's office and felt seen, supported, and valued was the moment she'd been waiting her whole career for. It's that relational interaction, combined with her own individual work, that has helped Amie heal to the point where she can actually do this work. Write this book. Exist in this space.

Be that principal for your teachers.

Let's Get Real: When Your Administration is Actively Hostile

Marti: Okay, but what about when your administration isn't just unsupportive but actively hostile to this approach?

Amie: That's hard. I lived it. I won't pretend there's some magic mantra that makes it painless.

Marti: So what do you tell teachers in that situation?

Amie: First, protect yourself. Document everything. Follow visible policies to the letter. Don't give anyone ammunition. Think of it as defensive documentation.

Marti: But you can still do relationally-informed teaching?

Amie: Absolutely. You just don't call it that. When my administrator asked how I was managing behavior, I didn't say, "I'm using trauma-informed practices and co-regulation." I said, "I'm using clear expectations and consistent follow-through." Which was true! I just left out the part about why it was working.

Marti: Strategic truth-telling. Sneaky but sincere.

Amie: (grinning) Exactly. Here is your moment of truth. When they observed my classroom, they saw what they wanted to see and it was not positive. I knew it was working but they still found fault.

Marti: What about the emotional toll? Working under hostile administration isn't just about strategies. That story you told about your evaluation... that was heartbreaking.

Amie: It was. Working under hostile administration is traumatizing. It triggers all your attachment wounds. It makes you question your worth and your calling. What helped me survive? Therapy. My allies at school. My family. And deciding that this one administrator didn't get to erase thirty years of who I was as a teacher. I had to hold onto my own narrative.

Marti: What about teachers in truly toxic situations right now? Soul-crushing, spirit-shredding toxic.

Amie: I tell them it's okay to leave. Life's too short to work somewhere that demands you harm kids or yourself. You can't teach from a shattered spirit. Start looking. Protect your mental health.

Marti: But if you're not ready to leave, or finances won't allow it?

Amie: Then you shrink your focus down to what you can control. Your classroom. Your relationships with kids. Your own regulation. You build your wall around that small space and you protect it fiercely.

Marti: And you find your people. Even if you have to find them outside the building.

Amie: Always. You cannot do this alone. Even if it's just one other teacher who gets it. One person who will text back, "You're not crazy. This is not okay. Want to get coffee?"

Marti: Oh, coffee. My owl brain loves coffee. Coffee is always helpful. Especially coffee for two. Research shows one caring adult matters for kids. But it matters for teachers too. We all need someone who sees us.

Amie: Someone who knows how to bring our owls back from the edge. And brings coffee.

Takeaways

1. **Structure and rigidity are not the same thing.** Like earthquake-proof buildings that sway but don't break, good systems have clear structures that allow for flexibility and humanity. Schedules and expectations can exist alongside responsiveness to individual needs.
2. **Most objections come from fear, not genuine obstacles.** Fear of losing control, fear of doing it wrong, fear of being seen as soft. When you understand the fear beneath the objection, you can address it with compassion and evidence.
3. **You don't need your whole school on board to start.** Find your allies, start small, document your wins, and let your results speak. Change doesn't require permission. It requires patience and persistence.

Reflection Questions

1. Where does your administration fall on the support spectrum? Very supportive? Neutral? Actively hostile? How does that reality shape your strategy?
2. What fears do YOU have about implementing relationally-informed practices? Fear of judgment? Fear of failure? Fear of losing control? Name them honestly.
3. Who are your allies? Who are the teachers in your building who get it? If you don't have community yet, how might you find them?
4. Think about a policy you're required to follow that feels at odds with connection. How could you honor the SPIRIT of that policy while adapting the LETTER?
5. What required tools (behavior charts, tracking systems) could you transform from punitive to supportive? What would that look like in practice?

One Thing to Try Tomorrow

Find Your First Ally

Identify one teacher in your building who seems to lead with relationships. Someone who already does things that align with relationally-informed practices, even if they don't call it that. Reach out. Invite them for coffee. Say something like: "Hey, I've been learning about trauma-informed teaching, and I noticed you already do some of this naturally. Can I pick your brain sometime?"

Start building your support network. You cannot do this work alone. You need your people. Find them. Connect with them. Support each other. Navigating systems with allies? That's how change actually happens. (Also, coffee helps.)

Section Four Preview

In Section Four, we'll talk about building partnerships with parents and families, because consistency between home and school makes everything you've learned work even better. Then, we'll address the one relationship you might be neglecting: the one with yourself. Because the kids need you. But they need you whole. Don't quit now. We are close to the best parts. We even mention ice cream. And coffee. Grab a refill and let's continue.

SECTION FOUR

Sustaining the Work

It turns out community is less about perfection and more about showing up.

You've made it this far. Take a breath. Seriously. Take a micro moment to sniff that lotion or candle that's been sitting on your desk since the last teacher gift giving season. Notice the good in this very moment. We hope you are inspired and full of hope to continue. We are so grateful for you.

Now comes the part nobody talks about enough: How do you keep doing this?

Because here's what we know after decades of this work. The strategies aren't the hard part. The hard part is sustaining them when you're exhausted, when parents push back, when your administrator doesn't get it, when you've given everything to everyone else and there's nothing left for you. This section is about building your village and protecting your sanity.

We'll talk about partnering with parents, because consistency between home and school multiplies everything you're doing. We'll talk about finding your people, because you cannot do this work alone. And we'll talk about self-care, which isn't bubble baths and scented candles (unless those work for you, in which case, enjoy your bubbles, beverage or bath, we won't judge what type).

Self-care is about survival. It's about still being in this profession five years from now. It's about showing up for kids without losing yourself in the process.

The kids need you. But they need you whole. Let's talk about how to make that happen.

Chapter 13

Parent Buy-In and Carryover

Building the Village Together

Imagine you have a student named Tyler in your class.

Tyler is in sixth grade, and his behaviors are... a lot. Outbursts in class. Refusal to work. Arguments with peers. Completely shut down during transitions.

You've tried everything. Connection, empowerment, sensory supports. Some things help, but Tyler is still struggling. And you're exhausted.

At parent-teacher conferences, you brace yourself. These conversations with parents of struggling students rarely go well. Usually, it's either:

- Parents defensive: "He's fine at home. It must be something YOU'RE doing."
- Parents overwhelmed: "I don't know what to do with him either."
- Parents checked out: "Just do whatever you think is best."

And that is if they even show up!

Tyler's mom, Sabrina, walks in, and you launch into your prepared speech about Tyler's struggles.

She stops you. "I know. I see the same things at home. Can we talk about what's actually helping?"

You blink. "What's... helping?"

"Yeah. You're the first teacher who hasn't just called to complain. Tyler actually talks about your class. He says you 'get him.' So what are you doing that's working? Because I want to do it at home too." You almost cry.

You spend the next 30 minutes talking about strategies. You explain the sensory breaks, the re-dos, the choices you're offering. She tells you what she's trying at home, many of which are already relational principles. She just doesn't know the name.

By the end, you have a plan. You'll stay in touch weekly. You'll use similar language and strategies. You'll be consistent across home and school.

Tyler doesn't transform overnight. But he gets better. Steadily. Because he has consistency. Because the adults in his life are working TOGETHER instead of at cross purposes.

Sabrina teaches you something crucial: parents don't have to be the problem. They're potential partners. And when you invite them in as experts on their own child, magic happens.

After everything we've covered about strategies, curriculum, and navigating systems, you might be wondering: who else can help carry this load? The answer is the parents. Yes, even the difficult ones. This chapter is about building that village.

Why Parent Buy-In Matters

Here's a hard truth: What you do at school for six hours a day matters enormously. But so does what happens at home. What happens in both places shapes who they become.

If a student learns at school that adults respond to needs with warmth and support, but at home adults respond with harshness and punishment, the mixed messages create confusion and stress.

Conversely, if home and school are aligned, using similar language, similar strategies, similar expectations, the child experiences consistency. And consistency creates safety.

You can't control what happens at home. But you CAN partner with parents to create as much alignment as possible.

Benefits of parent buy-in:

- **Consistency:** Child experiences similar responses across environments
- **Reinforcement:** Strategies work better when used everywhere
- **Support:** Parents and teachers aren't working against each other
- **Shared problem-solving**: Two perspectives are better than one

- **Reduced shame:** Child isn't "bad at school, fine at home" or vice versa

The goal isn't to make parents do everything you do or for you to do everything they do. The goal is to find common ground and build from there.

How to Communicate These Strategies to Families

Parents are busy. Buried. Often feeling judged and blamed by schools. To be very blunt, they are often experiencing the same overwhelm that we are. When you talk to them about relationally-informed strategies, keep it simple, jargon-free, and action-oriented.

Don't Say This:

"We're implementing trauma-informed practices based on attachment theory and neuroscience research to support co-regulation and executive functioning development."

Parent reaction: "What? Am I supposed to understand that? Is my kid damaged?"

Say This Instead:

"I've noticed [child's name] does better when they have choices and movement breaks. Here are a couple things that are working at school that could maybe work at home. Do you have any strategies that I could try in the classroom?"

Parent reaction: "Oh. That makes sense."

Creating Consistency Between School and Home

The more alignment you can create, the better. It's important to recognize here that it works both ways. If we want parents to work with us, we need to do the same with them! We need to be open and vulnerable and willing to hear them like we want them to hear us.

We acknowledge that as teachers, the current climate has created a lot of hostility between parents and teachers. There's a group of parents who see teachers as a threat. They operate from fear that we will influence their children in ways they don't approve. On our side, we sometimes see parental decisions as damaging. We hear teachers say frequently they want to support kids and keep them safe. Even from parents.

The reality is we cannot control that. Parents have the right to be parents. In social work, we talk about how parents have the right to mess up their kids. (Yes, really.) Just like we're asking parents not to judge us and take us as truly coming from a place of connection and care, we need to do the same with them.

It isn't easy. Sometimes the decisions parents make do hurt their kids. That said, unless it's something that needs to be reported to child protection agencies, we need to find ways to work with them instead of against them. The following ideas are for when you have parents who want to work with you in a partnership. We acknowledge that not all of them are possible. Please do not read this as something you have to do or something that will add to your plate! Read it as suggestions that could help you when you have a difficult student or two you are really trying to help find some level of success. Even if it is just that they stop disrupting the entire classroom on a regular basis!

Share What's Working

Send home regular updates, not just when there's a problem.

"Quick update: [Child's name] had a great week! Here's what I noticed:

- When we had to transition from math to language arts, we pretended to be cats and tip-toed to our desks.
- He was given two choices on how to do his science. He could do it in markers that smelled or pencils. He chose markers and we had no meltdown!
- While we were writing, he chose to use a squishy ball fidget. He didn't bother one other student and got two sentences written!

Thought you might want to know what's clicking!"

Parents LOVE hearing good news. And they love knowing what's actually helping. Keeping it specific can also give them similar language, ideas, and a way to reinforce what is happening in the classroom.

Offer Specific Strategies (Not Vague Advice)

Don't say: "Try to be more consistent at home."

Do say: "If you're working on homework and [child] starts to get frustrated, try offering a 5-minute movement break, jumping jacks, a walk around the block, dancing to a song. Then come back to the work. This is what we do at school and it really helps." Specific. Simple. Proven to work.

Use Similar Language

If at school you say "Let's try that again" for second chances, suggest parents use the same phrase at home. And on the other side, if the parents are telling you something works well at home, try to use their language. Best case scenario is we are a team!

If at school you offer "Choice A or Choice B," suggest that structure for home. If home says "we always say we have two options," can you use that same language? Familiar language creates predictability. Predictability creates safety.

Create a Communication System

Weekly email? Monthly newsletter? Communication notebook that goes home? Find what works and stick with it.

~ Amie ~

I know that this communication system is a big deal for teachers. Some teachers are so comfortable with it. They do it inherently and often. For me, and many in secondary, we just have too many kids. I cannot send an individual weekly email home to every child's parents. (My carpal tunnel would file a grievance.) Here are some examples I have seen work:

- As a school, we have a master list of all students and every teacher tries to write one or two emails a week to a student. We cross it off the list when we do it. Eventually over the course of the school year, all kids will get at least one email home that is positive from a teacher.

- I know many secondary schools have "advisory classes." Could you send one email home to each advisory student at least once a year?
- When I start to notice a theme to parent requests and emails, I send a general email to all kids and parents. For example, I was out sick for a few days so I am behind on grading. I send an email to parents and kids explaining exactly that: I am so sorry, I was out sick, I will grade as quickly as I can, and thank you so much for being patient with me. When I do this, I usually write something like "I never want a kid to suffer because I am behind." It lessens the blow to the parents when we are just honest about wanting to help and be as fair as possible.

I know for many of us, this can feel like one more thing we have to do. I can see that and understand that pressure! Here is my personal experience: when I take the time to write these little things, I often see way less stress between myself and my most difficult students, which eventually decreases my stress level. I have a friend who tells me all the time, "You are going to have to exert the energy to handle the behaviors regardless. If we do it proactively and work in relationships, studies show that over time we will decrease the energy spent on negative behaviors." This ultimately leads to a reduction in actual energy spent, which is something I want to see happen every single day in every element of my life.

When Parents Are Resistant

We cannot tell you the number of times something like this has happened to me. We get a call or a text from a co-teacher: "There is a parent at your door." The teacher gives us their interpretation of the mood of the parent. "They look super pissed off. They are tapping their toes. If looks could kill, I would be dead." You finish your drive to school. Dread the walk in. Prepare yourself to get lambasted with everything you have done wrong.

You slowly walk to your door. You respond either one of two ways: come in hot yourself (watchdog energy), or get a little small and timid (possum energy). The parent says something like, "I have been waiting for you. Yesterday my child got in trouble for doing..."

And from there it is them yelling at you about everything you did wrong and all the ways their child was victimized.

Here is the other elephant in the room we need to address. Not every parent or member of the community is going to love you and sing your praises. That, my friends, is not only OK, but it is actually healthy! (It might feel like Kale healthy but the goodness is great.) It is the diversity of our personalities and methods that make schools work for kids.

In Amie's department at her school, she works with teachers who have very different skills and classrooms. We all teach so differently, and each classroom fits our personality. Amie's classroom does arts and crafts and plays with Play-Doh on the regular. Another teacher in her department loves telling the stories and the details of history. That doesn't interest her in the slightest unless she's teaching the advanced and honors classes.

Here is the beauty of diversity: there are kids who thrive in the storytelling details of Amie's colleague's classroom but drown in the noise and structured chaos of hers. Then there are kids who cannot learn in the storytelling detailed world but thrive in Amie's classroom. We need the teacher diversity in order to provide the best outcomes for all students! When we allow teachers to play to their strengths, it means we won't be every kid's or parent's cup of tea. And that's okay. We have parents in our communities who do not care for us. If we are being completely honest, the feelings are usually pretty reciprocated. The reality is that not all parents will be on board. Some will push back. Here are some ideas on how to handle it.

Resistance #1: "You're Too Soft"

What they say: "My kid needs discipline, not coddling. You're being too easy on them."

What they fear: Their child will become entitled or manipulative. That you're undermining their parenting.

How to respond:

First, thank them for sharing. "I hear you. Discipline is important. Thank you for telling me that." Then, gauge their openness: "I'd be happy to explain what I'm doing, but I don't have to if you'd rather not get into it." If they say no: "That's great. Thank you again. If there's anything I can do to better help your child, I'm always open to a discussion." No justification. No explanation. Energy is finite.

If they say yes: Explain the concept of trying again. "When students have behavior concerns, I let them try again instead of punitive responses. If Sofie yells something out in class, I ask her to please not do that, and then I have her re-ask her question by raising her hand. She's still responsible for changing the behavior." Validate their concern. Show you're not permissive. Point to results.

Resistance #2: "Nothing Works with My Kid"

What they say: "We've tried everything. Nothing helps. This won't work either."

What they fear: More failure. More disappointment. More proof they're bad parents.

How to respond: Amie used to never hear this type of response from parents. If she did, it was super rare. She feels like she hears this more and more. The number of times she has sat and cried with parents at parent-teacher conferences who are in this exact place...

Her first response is always, "Thank you so much for telling me! I can hear how exhausted you are. You've been fighting this for a long time." From there, she says something that will give her an idea of where they are: "I'm not promising miracles. But I am seeing small improvements when we try [specific strategy]. Would you be willing to experiment with me?"

If they say yes, then they talk about strategies and how to implement those at school and at home. If they say "not right now," she says, "That's great. Thank you for being honest with me. If you're OK with it, I am going to continue to work with your child in class, and if you decide you want to talk more, I am always here to support both of you." Either way, she ends with "Let's give it a few weeks and see what happens."

Empathy first. Small commitment. Collaboration, not telling them what to do.

Resistance #3: "I Don't Have Time for This"

What they say: "I'm barely keeping my head above water. I can't add one more thing."

What they fear: Failure. Inadequacy. Being judged.

How to respond: Just like the example above, Amie first thanks them for sharing their concerns. That can be a big moment of vulnerability for them. When we are working from a relational lens, acknowledging the difficulty of sharing things that feel like failure should be acknowledged. Here again, we remind you that y'all are not therapists. Not to the parents either. What teachers are are people who understand to some degree the difficulty of being human. Sharing and validating human emotions and experiences only strengthens our ability to help.

Amie often says something like, "I completely understand. I feel underwater all the time! You're already doing so much. How can I support you? Do you want me to explain what we are doing in class?"

If they say no, she just says, "That's great. Thank you for sharing with me and I will keep checking in with you and your child."

If they say yes, she talks about offering choices or allowing movement. They talk about how they could potentially use these at home, but she's not really problem-solving for them. She is being a sounding board they can use to walk through the solutions. She helps where she can.

Again, Amie ends with "Let's try this and check in in a few weeks." Sometimes she will set an exact day or appointment. Sometimes she just leaves a reminder on her calendar to send home a quick email at a future date. Depends on what she is capable of giving, what they express they need or want, and what is realistic.

One thing. Not ten. One.

Resistance #4: "My Kid is Fine at Home"

What they say: "We don't have these problems at home. It must be school."

What they fear: Being blamed. Their child being labeled.

How to respond: "That's actually really valuable information. Would you be willing to share with me what is working at home? Maybe we can bring some of that to school."

Disclaimer here: Often when we give parents this response, they don't have a lot of answers. They are used to justifying kids' behaviors instead of actually problem-solving. This could be for a myriad of reasons, but if they don't have any ideas, then you really are left with two choices:

1. Respond with "OK. What if I try this? Do you think that would work?"
2. Or: "Do you have suggestions on how we can move forward from here? I would really love to see the same behaviors you do, and I would love to partner with you."

If they shut it down from there, there really isn't much you can do!

Flip the script. They're not the problem. They're the solution. Ask to learn from them.

What About Parents You Can't Reach?

Some parents won't engage. No matter what you try. They don't respond to emails. Don't come to conferences. Don't answer calls. It's frustrating. And heartbreaking. As teachers, we tend to judge this.

Our advice here, as in everything else in this book, is to just be gentle and find grace. Just like we know most teachers are truly trying to do their best, so are parents.

Sometimes we don't know what is going on at home. Sometimes we do. Sometimes they want to be involved but work multiple jobs or have a language barrier. More often than not, the system is just so overwhelming and confusing. We cannot tell you how many parents want to do something but they truly do not know how or what to do. This is especially true for parents of kids with special needs or that are going through something traumatic.

Here's what you can do:

1. Keep trying, but don't take it personally.

Some parents have been burned by schools so many times they've given up. Some are dealing with their own trauma. Some are overwhelmed with survival. Keep sending positive notes. Keep inviting. But don't carry guilt for their lack of response.

2. Focus on what you CAN control.

You can't make parents engage. But you can create a safe, supportive classroom for their child. That child still benefits from relationally-informed strategies at school, even if there's no carryover at home.

3. Connect the child with other supports.

School counselor. Community programs. Mentors. After-school care. Build the village for that child in whatever ways you can.

4. Document your attempts to reach out.

Not in a punitive way. But for your own protection and for the child's benefit. "I've attempted contact via email (dates), phone (dates), and sent home notes (dates)." This shows you tried. And it might matter if the child ever needs additional support. You have heard us say this so many times. As one human, you will not be able to meet all the needs of all the kids. You also will not be able to connect with every parent. It's not realistic. We do what we can. We create safe and connecting classrooms. From there, we set realistic goals.

The other advice we will always give is follow policy. If your situation requires a certain type of documentation, do it. If your school requires a certain type of communication, do it. We talked in the previous chapter about how while the system is nowhere near perfect, its purpose is to provide structure and protections for every stakeholder.

When we follow policy, we protect ourselves, our students, and parents.

The one other element we should discuss is when administration undermines you or makes it difficult to do what you feel is correct. Every teacher I know has a story about something like this with administration. We wish we had magic words for this but the best advice we can give is if you find yourself in this situation, refer back to the previous chapter and try to apply the ideas to this situation. We believe in you!

One More Thing to Consider

We are writing this book in 2025-2026. We feel like it is important to recognize that over the course of our careers, we have experienced so many upheavals. From No Child Left Behind to the banning of books; from phonics as a key pillar to the whole language approach, we seem to be moving back and forth on a pendulum. The good years are the ones we seem to be more in the middle. We would like to tell you that this will change. In all likelihood, it won't every change.

We really feel like education is like this because of who we serve. We serve kids. The most important resource we have. The most important thing in a lot of adults' lives. This invites our protective watchdogs and possums when the conversation really requires our wise and connected owls. Our impact feels bigger than it should be, and everyone involved in this world lives with this reality.

Lawmakers, parents, admin, students, teachers, support staff. We all want what's best.

Like Dr. Greene's skill vs. will. Dr. Becky Kennedy talks about how all kids and adults are doing their best. Everyone is good inside. We just exhibit behaviors for the skill level and set we have. When we view our struggles through the same lens, it gives us compassion with ourselves and the ability to repair relationships. That is the gold. That is where the real connection and real success occurs.

Amie has a little saying she uses when kids make a mistake. It is pulled from multiple sources but is essentially this:

> I made a mistake. I'm still a good kid.
> Next time I will _______. Mistakes are
> how we learn.

This applies to all things relational. It is the backbone of repair. It is the basis of building strong relationships. It's the safety we need to keep our owls around to solve these big conflicts.

We will never have every single parent and student love us! What we can do is our best. Review things through a relationally-informed lens and work on what we can control.

Let's Get Real: When Parents Bring Phones and Politics to School

Amie: Okay, we need to talk about this big, uninvited watchdog. The one holding a smartphone.

Marti: The fear that you're being recorded.

Amie: Teachers are terrified. And honestly? That fear is founded. I know teachers who've had clips taken totally out of context, posted on social media, and suddenly they're trending for all the wrong reasons. It's like being a contestant on the world's worst reality show you never auditioned for.

Marti: Teaching is messy. If you film any human being doing a hard job for eight hours, you're going to find a moment that looks bad without context.

Amie: So what do we do with this fear?

Marti: First, acknowledge it. If you're feeling watched and worried and weary, that's not paranoia. That's the current climate. Your feelings are valid.

Amie: And that hypervigilance is exhausting. How can you focus on connecting with kids when part of your brain is constantly scanning for threats?

Marti: The same nervous system stuff we teach about kids? It applies to us too. Notice when your shoulders climb up. Take a walk. A big exhale.

Amie: Now let's talk about the political piece. Parents who show up with accusations, agendas, and aggressive attitudes. Who've already cast you as the villain before you've said a word.

Marti: When a parent comes in politically charged, I try to find the fear underneath. Fear their child is being influenced in ways they don't approve. Fear their values are being undermined.

Amie: And when we see the fear, it's easier to respond with compassion.

Marti: I might say, "I can see you're really concerned. Can you tell me more about what's worrying you?" Sometimes just being heard takes the edge off. They packed for battle and discovered a peace conference.

Amie: Not always, though.

Marti: No. Some parents won't partner with you no matter what. You could personally cure every disease and they'd complain about your handwriting.

Amie: So what can we control?

Marti: Your classroom. Your responses. The experience students have with you. You cannot control what parents post online or say at the dinner table.

Amie: Document hostile interactions. Loop in administration. Find allies.

Marti: And keep being the teacher you want to be. Not because you're naive about the risks, but because you refuse to let fear steal your purpose.

Amie: The kids still need connected teachers. More than ever.

Marti: If you're reading this and you're scared, that's okay. Courage isn't the absence of fear. It's showing up anyway.

Amie: Especially for the kids with the difficult parents. They need you most of all.

Takeaways

1. **Parents are potential partners, not problems to solve.** Most parents are already doing things that align with relationally-informed practices. They just don't know the terminology. Your job is to validate what's working, offer what might help, and collaborate.
2. **Communication must be simple, jargon-free, and actionable.** Don't send home academic theories. Send home: "This is working. Here's what you could try." One-page handouts, specific examples, and regular positive updates build trust.
3. **When parents resist, address the fear underneath with empathy.** Fear of blame, fear of failure, fear of one more thing. Start small, show results, and make it a partnership, not you telling them what to do.

Reflection Questions

1. Think about the parents you communicate with most easily. What makes those relationships work? How could you replicate that with other families?
2. What's one strategy that's working in your classroom that you haven't shared with parents yet? How could you communicate it in parent-friendly language?
3. When parents resist or don't engage, what's your automatic response? Frustration? Judgment? How could you shift to curiosity about what might be getting in the way?
4. What's one small way you could build community among the parents of your students? Coffee hour? Newsletter? Parent workshop?

*Robyn Gobbel has an on-line community called "The Club" that has excellent resources and community for parents of kids with big, baffling, behaviors. Marti chimes in on occasion (usually when Robyn tags her) as a moderator and has found it to be an amazing place of uplifting support. We encourage you to find a community that works for you. Online. In person. Faith based.

One Thing to Try Tomorrow

Send a Sunshine Note

Pick a student. Write a quick note (or email, or text) to their parent:

"Quick update: [Child's name] did something great today. [Specific example]. Just wanted you to know!"

That's it. Three sentences. One piece of good news.

Watch how it changes your relationship with that family.

And then do it again next week with a different student.

Small connections. Consistent positivity. Partnership building. Can't hurt, might help. And parents as partners? That changes everything for kids.

CHAPTER 14

Self-Care and Survival

Teaching is exhausting. Relationally-informed teaching requires emotional energy you may not always have. Burnout is real. Compassion fatigue is real.

Now imagine it's your 18th year. You've survived clueless new teachers, bitter veterans, bad administrators, budget cuts, and policy changes. You think you're invincible. And then you're not. It starts small. You stop eating breakfast. Stop exercising. Stop calling friends because you have nothing to talk about except how much you hate your job. You wake up at 3am, heart racing, thinking about lesson plans and emails and students you're failing. You catch every cold. Headaches become constant. Your stomach is always upset.

Your family asks if you're okay. Even your dog seems depressed. You snap at your kids for no reason. You cry over nothing. You sit on the couch staring at the TV, not watching, just... numb. You're not just burned out. You're breaking. The only thing that saves you is hitting rock bottom hard enough to finally ask for help. You talk to your doctor. Start therapy. Take a personal day and sleep for 14 hours. Start saying no. Slowly, very slowly, you crawl back from the edge.

Here's what you learn: burnout doesn't happen overnight. It's a thousand small choices to put yourself last. To pour and pour until there's nothing left for anyone. Not your students. Not your family. Not yourself. This chapter? This is the one we wish you'd read before you get to that point. Because self-care isn't selfish. It's survival. We still see you. We're still cheering you on. With coffee.

You Have to Connect to Yourself Before You Can Connect to Others

We've spent this whole book talking about connecting with students. About understanding their needs. About offering them safety and communicating their infinite worth. Here's the truth: You can't help someone else when you are depleted yourself. You can't help students connect to their needs if you don't connect to yours. You can't model healthy boundaries if you have none.

Connection starts with yourself. Before you can truly see your students, you have to see yourself. Before you can ask "What does this child need?" you have to be able to answer "What do I need?" This isn't navel-gazing. It's the foundation. Connecting with yourself enough to know what your body needs to feel safe is the core of self-care.

Check In With Yourself (Actually Check In)

When's the last time you asked yourself: "What do I need right now?" Not "What do my students need?" Not "What does my admin want?" Not "What does my family expect?"

What do YOU need?

Maybe it's:

- Water (when's the last time you drank water?)
- Food (have you eaten today?)
- Bathroom (have you gone in the last 6 hours?)
- Movement (have you stood up today?)
- Quiet (are you overstimulated?)
- Connection (are you lonely?)
- Rest (are you exhausted?)

Basic human needs. Teachers treat them like optional extras. You know how we tell students to check in with their bodies? To notice when they're hungry, tired, overstimulated? Do that for yourself. Set a timer on your phone. Three times a day. Make it a fun ring tone. When it goes off, ask: "What does my body need right now?" When you notice what you need, that's connection. You're paying attention to yourself the way you pay attention to your students. That matters.

Then, and this is the hard part, MEET THAT NEED. Don't push through. Don't tell yourself you'll do it later. Meet the need now. Drink the water. Eat the snack. Take the bathroom break. Step outside for two minutes. Text a friend. Your needs matter. You matter. Just like taking that extra time for our students upfront gives us time back on the other side, the same is true for meeting your needs. Drink the water and your head will stop pounding. Your window will open a little more and your owl can stick around longer.

A Few Somatic Strategies for the Stressed-Out Teacher

Somatic therapy is just a fancy way of saying "body-based healing." Instead of trying to think your way out of stress (spoiler: it rarely works), somatic practices help you release tension through the body itself. The beautiful thing is many of these techniques take seconds, require zero equipment, and can be done while 24 kids are arguing about who gets the good markers.

Feel your feet.

Sounds silly. Works spectacularly. When you feel overwhelmed, press your feet firmly into the floor and notice the sensation. Wiggle your toes. Feel the weight of your body grounded to the earth. This simple act tells your nervous system you're safe and stable.

Shake it off (literally).

Cue up Taylor Swift and Shakira. Shaking is a neurological reset after stress. Animals in the wild shake after a stressful encounter to discharge the stress hormones from their bodies. You can do this too. In the bathroom, in your car at pickup, wherever you can grab 30 seconds of privacy: shake your hands, arms, legs, whole body. It looks ridiculous and feels fantastic. This is a great one to do with the entire classroom after a big stressful event or before a test.

The physiological sigh.

This one's backed by Stanford research and takes about five seconds. Inhale through your nose, then sneak in a second short inhale on top of it (filling your lungs completely), then exhale slowly through your mouth. One or two of these can shift your nervous system faster than any deep breathing exercise. Add a proprioceptive "Ummmmmmm" and you've really re-set your system.

Cold water reset.

Run cold water over your wrists or splash some on your face. The temperature change activates your parasympathetic nervous system (the "rest and digest" side) and can pull you out of a stress spiral surprisingly fast. It's basically a dinner bell chiming into the woods for the owl to return. Drinking something cold through a straw like a smoothie or fizzy water also brings sensations to that same system and sends cues of safety. Better yet, just eat your favorite ice cream. We can officially prescribe it if you need that permission.

Squeeze and release.

Clench your fists as tight as you can for five seconds, then release. Notice the contrast between tension and relaxation. You can do this with your shoulders, your whole body, or just your toes inside your shoes (nobody will ever know). This is an amazing way to "feel your body" and really recognize where you hold your stress. Do you notice that the tension increases more when you squeeze your arms than when you squeeze your shoulders? That's because your arms were relaxed and your shoulders were already tensed up, feeling the weight of what you are carrying. When you activated your shoulders, they were already at 80%.

Orient to the room.

When stress narrows your focus, intentionally look around. Name five things you can see. Notice colors, shapes, movement.

This pulls you out of tunnel vision and reminds your brain that you're here, in this moment, and you're okay.

Identifying YOUR Needs (And How to Meet Them)

Checking in with your body is step one. But self-care goes beyond the basics. What actually restores you? Here's a hard question: What fills your cup? What plants more cares in your garden? Not what you SHOULD enjoy. Not what other people enjoy. What actually restores YOU?

Marti's list:

- Moving her body through tropical or frozen water (snow skiing, sailing, SCUBA, swimming)
- Walking her dog
- Sitting on her porch with iced tea and no agenda
- Quilting
- Laughing with her friends and family
- Dissociating into a good series on TV with her husband
- Laughing at stupid inside jokes with dear friends
- Exercise
- Eating animal crackers or ice cream - mint chocolate chip ice cream
- A hammock near water with a good playlist

Amie's list:

- Trashy romance novels (Hockey players. Don't judge.)
- Spending time with her kids and grandkids. There is nothing more healing than a grandma snuggle!
- Twice-monthly massages. Here's why: Because of childhood trauma, I learned to dissociate from my body. Working with a therapist, I started using massage as a way to reconnect. As the masseuse works through my

body, I pay attention to what I'm feeling and what emotions surface. I used to bring those to therapy. Over time, I've developed the skills to do this processing on my own. The massage is still the tool that gets me there.

- Sensory deprivation floats. Yes, these are real. Yes, they feel weird. No, they're not for everyone. But for me, floating in warm, dark, quiet water resets my nervous system completely. In education we live in sensory overload. This lets me leave that state.
- Taking the pause. In her book Real Self Care, Pooja Lakshmin talks about self-care being about the pause. Giving ourselves permission to stop and think before we accept or act. When asked to take on a new student or teach a new grade, I ask for time to think. I don't always get what I want. But the pause lets me evaluate realistically: Can I do this? What would I need? The pause is the self-care

For you, it might be:

- Exercise
- Creating art
- Playing music
- Gardening
- Gaming
- Baking
- Being alone in complete silence
- Cooking
- Sweet treats (ice cream again!)
- Texting a friend a funny meme
- Shopping
- Time with friends
- Time with pets
- Time with family

Whatever it is, you need to DO IT. Regularly. Not as a reward for getting everything done (you'll never get everything done). As a non-negotiable part of staying human.

Make a "Fill My Cup" List

Write down 10 things that restore you. Include:

- 5-minute things (stretch, listen to a song, step outside)
- 30-minute things (read a chapter, take a walk, call a friend)
- 2-hour things (hobby, exercise class, movie)
- Half-day things (hike, visit a museum, lunch with friends, extended outdoor movement)

Keep this list visible. When you're depleted, pick something from it and DO IT. Don't wait until you have time. You'll never have time. Make time.

Downtime in Personal Life (And Why It Matters for Your Classroom)

What you do outside of school directly impacts what you can do inside school. If you spend every evening and weekend grading, planning, and thinking about work, you have ZERO recovery time.

Your brain needs downtime to:

- Keep your owl online
- Process experiences
- Consolidate learning
- Rest and repair
- Generate creativity
- Feel emotions

Without downtime, you're running on empty. And that shows up in your classroom.

When you're depleted:

- Your owl flies away
- You're more reactive
- You have less patience
- You can't think creatively
- Everything feels harder
- You resent your students

When you're rested:

- You're more resistant to stress
- You have more capacity
- You can problem-solve
- Teaching feels more joyful
- You actually like your students

Rest isn't selfish. It's strategic. Rest restores resilience. Here's what we don't talk about enough: downtime is when connection happens. You can't have a real conversation with your partner while grading papers. You can't be present with your kids while mentally writing lesson plans. Downtime creates space for the relationships that sustain you.

Downtime IN the Classroom (Building in Recovery)

It's not just YOUR downtime that matters. It's also building downtime into your classroom. Bell-to-bell curriculum sounds great in theory. In practice, it's exhausting for everyone. When kids have assignments complete, why can't we use that time to practice social skills? To build connection? To just BE?

Create Space for Connection and Play

Have games in your classroom. Art supplies. Perler beads. Jewelry-making kits. Puzzles. When students finish work early (or when we all need a break), they can choose what to do. They're creating connection with each other. They're practicing meeting their own sensory needs because they get to choose. They're learning social skills. Is this curriculum? Not in the traditional sense but it IS part of what we are teaching them: How to be human. How to connect. How to form healthy relationships. How to exist in a community.

And honestly? We need those moments too. Watching students choose connection over isolation, play over performance, reminds me why we do this work. Bell-to-bell curriculum is important. But allowing space to meet sensory needs and build connection IS part of our curriculum. Give yourself, and your students, permission to breathe.

Maintaining Your Own Boundaries

Boundaries are hard. Especially for teachers who want to help everyone. But boundaries aren't mean. They're necessary. They protect your capacity for connection.

Boundaries You Might Need to Set

With students:

- "I'm available for extra help Tuesday and Thursday after school. Other days I have commitments."
- "I respond to emails within 24 hours on school days. I don't check email on weekends."
- "I care about you, but I'm not your therapist. Let me connect you with the counselor."

With parents:

- "I'm happy to communicate via email or scheduled phone calls. I'm not available for drop-in conversations before school starts."
- "I understand this is urgent to you. School policy is that I have 48 hours to respond to emails."

With admin:

- "I'm committed to being a great teacher. I'm not able to take on additional committees this year."
- "I need to leave by 4pm on Tuesdays for a personal commitment."

With yourself:

- "I'm doing my best. That's enough."
- "I can't save every student. I can show up and try."
- "It's okay to not be perfect."

Here's what boundaries actually look like in practice: Last semester, a parent emailed me at 10pm expecting an immediate response about her child's grade. Old me would have answered at 10:15pm, anxious and resentful. New me responded the next morning during planning: "Thank you for reaching out. I'm happy to discuss this. My response window is within 24 hours on school days." She wasn't thrilled. But I slept that night. That's the trade. Whatever boundaries you set, KEEP THEM. Boundaries bring breathing room.

Will there be exceptions? Yes. Will admin push back? Maybe. Will you feel guilty? Probably. Do it anyway. Your mental health is worth it. Boundaries often feel terrible in the moment. They feel like freedom six weeks later.

When to Ask for Help

Boundaries protect your energy. But sometimes, even with perfect boundaries, you need more than you can give yourself. That's when you ask for help. You don't have to do this alone. You CAN'T do this alone.

Here's when to ask for help:

When you're overwhelmed: Don't wait until you're at rock bottom. When you start feeling consistently stressed, reach out.

When a student needs more than you can provide: "This child needs support I'm not trained to give. Can we get them connected with the counselor, specialist, or therapist?"

When you're making mistakes you don't usually make: Forgetting things. Snapping at students. Crying in your car. These aren't character flaws. They're signals. Your system is telling you something.

When your physical health is suffering: Constant illness. Insomnia. Stomach issues. Headaches. Your body is telling you something.

When you've lost joy: If teaching feels joyless week after week, something's wrong. Ask for help.

Who to Ask for Help

- School counselor
- Trusted colleague
- Administration (if safe)
- Your own therapist
- Your doctor
- Friends outside of education
- Family
- Online teacher support groups

There's no shame in asking for help. The shame is in suffering in silence when support is available.

Finding Your People (You Can't Do This Alone)

Remember our coffee club from earlier? That group of teachers who meet every morning to vent, celebrate, and support each other? That's not optional. That's survival. You may have noticed that throughout this book, coffee club has been referred to in various ways. Toxic negativity, self care, connection. The thing about finding your people, depending on what is going on with your world, your people will serve all of these needs.

There are days we need to just vent. Coffee club can be very toxic in these moments but, as a human, sometimes that is what we need. Someone to sit in the mess with us. Toxicity and all. Sometimes they problem solve with us, help us get creative, help us better understand a situation. My coffee club is also where we discuss our wins and our losses. Our ups and our downs.

You have heard the phrase, two things can be true. That is the thing about finding our people. Multiple purposes can be found. We can be toxic together but also positive. It is in this exact humanness that we find the true connection. Find our support. We encourage you to allow your walls down enough to experience all of these elements with your people!

We talked about finding allies at work, the teachers who get it. That matters. But you also need people OUTSIDE of school. People who don't want to talk about lesson plans. People who remind you that you existed before you became a teacher. You need your people. The ones who GET IT. Who understand that you love your job and also sometimes want to quit. Who will listen to you complain without trying to fix you.

How to Find Your People

At your school:

Look for teachers who:

- Talk about students with compassion, not contempt
- Try new things
- Admit when they're struggling
- Have a sense of humor about the chaos

Invite them for coffee. Or lunch. Or just show up at their classroom during planning.

Outside your school:

- Join online teacher communities (Robyn even has a Club for professionals)
- Attend education conferences
- Connect with teachers from training programs
- Join a hobby group (connection outside of teaching is good too)

Create your own group:

- Invite 3-4 teachers for monthly happy hour
- Start a book club (Use this book! We even created the questions for you)
- Create a group text for daily check-ins
- Organize a potluck

Community isn't automatic. You have to build it intentionally, but once you have your people, hold onto them. They'll save you. We hope you know you're not alone in this work. We hope you find your people and protect your peace. Remember, taking care of yourself isn't abandoning your students. It's ensuring you'll still be there for them tomorrow.

The Permission You Might Be Waiting For

Let us remind you of some permissions.

You don't have to be perfect. You're going to mess up. You're going to have bad days. You're going to lose your patience with a student who didn't deserve it. Repair and move forward. The repair is what matters.

Your needs aren't optional. Taking care of yourself isn't an indulgence. It's the thing that makes everything else possible. Work can wait. You don't have to grade every night. You don't have to answer every email within the hour. Being "off duty" doesn't make you a bad teacher. It makes you a sustainable one.

You can't save everyone. Some students won't thrive in your class. Some needs are beyond what you can meet. That's not failure. That's reality.

Leaving is allowed. Teaching isn't martyrdom. If it's destroying your health and happiness, finding something else isn't quitting. It's wisdom.

Contradiction is normal. You can love your job and want to quit on the same Tuesday. You can be grateful and frustrated. Both are true.

Being human is enough. You don't have to be superhuman. Just human. Showing up, trying, repairing when you fail. That's enough.

Finding Joy in Humor

~ Amie ~

While we were writing this book, there was a lot of discussion amongst my teacher peers about what would actually be helpful and meaningful. I have a friend who started at my current school the same year I did. We grew up together as teachers.

We have done all the hard stuff together but when I was talking to her, I realized we had also done all the fun stuff. While we may not see each other as often as we used to, the stories hold.

One time, we decided that it would be hysterical to put 118 cans of creamed corn in another teacher's room. We hid them everywhere. For the record, it was funny! This teacher was finding creamed corn for the entire year in random places.

Another time, we decided to put sticky notes all over the office of an assistant principal. We covered the walls, the desk, the cabinets in random colors so when they came in the next day they were met with more sticky notes than any human needs in a lifetime.

Another time, I was teaching World War I and we decided to "surprise attack" a teacher down the hall from me. My class made a million snowballs with paper and secretly snuck down the hall and threw these paper snowballs at his class. Do not fear, he returned the favor by turning every desk in my room upside down one day after school so when I came in, I was not ready for a day of education.

I share these stories, not to give you ideas or encourage bad behaviors, but to show you just how we build these connections over time. Often it is the humor that goes with this job that makes it as wonderful as it is. When I am in my good head space, I can find joy and humor in everyday experiences. There have been times in my career where that has not been the case. These stories and experiences are what hold me together when I feel like I may not have the stamina to continue.

Ultimately, this job is mentally exhausting BECAUSE of the relationships. When we do it right, we will expend energy on the relationships. We also fill our cup from these same relationships. It's the beauty and the difficulty of what we do. The more cares we plant, the bigger our garden grows. It sustains us for the larger harvests.

The Week That Tried to Take Me Out

I want to share a story that happened recently. Because nothing says "self-care expert" like writing about self-care while your own window of tolerance slams shut like a screen door in a tornado.

Here's the truth: I am a mom, a grandma, a teacher. I work full time in the classroom and part time for a nonprofit. I'm active in my community and find myself adding to my plate like it's an all-you-can-eat buffet and I'm determined to get my money's worth. When I reached out to Marti about writing this book, I pictured us working slowly over a year or so. Like all things in my life, reality had other plans.

Last week, I had nothing left to give.

In the span of five days, I had spoken at the state legislature, juggled a million appointments, dealt with a serious medical situation, been asked to join a time-intensive committee at school, accepted a change in my position that would pull me partially out of the classroom, AND had midterms due. This was on top of the usual emotional chaos that constitutes my existence.

And through all of this, I was living in this book. All I wanted was to write and work here. Writing about nervous system regulation while my own nervous system was staging a full-scale revolt.

Friday hit hard. I was finishing midterms when someone came in to talk. This individual was visibly upset and needed someone to listen. Without getting into details, their story triggered me in multiple ways. And as I listened, my ability to stay out of my downstairs brain was diminishing by the second. I could feel my owl packing for a trip far away without me.

I finished the conversation. I connected the person with the appropriate people and resources. Then I found myself in the hallway, talking to a fellow teacher, unable to stop crying. Now, I'm all for honesty and vulnerability with emotions. But this particular individual didn't need the added stress of watching me fall apart. The teacher I was crying with was young and new to the profession. They didn't need that weight either.

Here's what I've learned to do: I have built a small network of people who exist for exactly these situations. People with the skills to cope with what I share. People who won't try to fix me. I work to not dump difficult emotions on people who don't yet have the tools to process them. (This is growth, people. This is the work paying off.)

I left school early that day to make an appointment at another school. It was at this school that I found a beautiful juxtaposition. The program I left to visit has been implementing the relationally-informed approach for almost three years now, and they're not just embracing it. They're living it. I walked into that building and was immediately reminded why we do this work.

The first time I visited this program earlier in the year, I met a student who is autistic and struggling with friendships. That first visit, he rolled around on the floor, refused eye contact, and cried. I'm still working with his teacher to embrace this new way of teaching. I could see this little one was drowning, and I desperately wanted his teacher on board with me to help him.

When I walked in last week, this same student was one of the first kids I saw. He remembered me and said hello. Here's why I'm telling you this. This student was working with a group of peers on a project. They were coloring hearts and listing their "inside hurts." His included things like "when a student pushes me down" and "when a teacher is mean to me."

The second part of the activity had them write on paper Band-Aids something they would want to hear from a friend when they had inside hurts. They were using Band-Aids and crafts like our care garden metaphor. I watched a little girl sitting next to him. She used zero words. She wrote on her Band-Aid, and it took me a minute to decode her child-like spelling: "I love your smile."

She gave it to him. He asked me to read it.

As I read that she loved his smile, this precious child made eye contact with me. His face lit up with the biggest smile and the most joy I'd seen all week. Then he turned to this little girl, said thank you, and they hugged each other. Below is an actual picture of his heart. Used with permission.

This. This moment. In six hours, I went from the lowest of lows to the highest of highs. From heartbreak and helplessness to watching the most beautiful example of how simple relationship building and connection can change a child's entire demeanor, maybe even trajectory.

On my way home, I called a dear friend and co-worker from my trusted network. As I told her this story, I started crying again. I talked about how my heart had literally broken and then started to heal. All of it relational. The highs. The lows. The healing. The support. I decided to take the night off and tend to my own care garden. I read a trashy romance novel. I snuggled my grandbabies. I ordered takeout for dinner.

Saturday morning, I did my Zoom call with Marti, who allowed me to be vulnerable and share enough to process my emotions. She didn't problem-solve. She simply related to my experience. None of my people could fix the emotional stress. Nobody can. I didn't need them to. I just needed to not be alone in it. My owl just needed another owl to reflect my preciousness. What they did was sit in the mess with me. Listen. Validate.

Notice what my Saturday wasn't about: doing. It was about being. Being present with my grandbabies. Being honest with Marti. Being still enough to hear what I needed. I spent the rest of Saturday with my grandbabies, watching them perform in their various activities. My plan was to come home and work on the book. But after a self-check-in, I realized I wasn't quite ready to re-engage that part of my brain. I read a little more. I slept.

Here's Why I'm Sharing This

Even two years ago, this same day would have resulted in me shutting down for the entire weekend. I would have felt super anxious. I would not have called my support people to debrief. I would not have rested. I would have hibernated. My possum would have boarded my window shut. I would have let my house fall apart while kids roamed feral. I would have either eaten nothing or eaten everything. I would have slept or maybe just read or watched TV or dissociated. Going to my grandkids' events would have annoyed me, or I would have been physically present but mentally checked out.

Sunday would have come, and I would have worked on this book because I was supposed to, but I would not have been authentic or vulnerable. I would have just been going through the motions. This relationally-informed journey has brought me to a different place.

A place where I'm learning the value of structure without rigidity. Where I'm learning to find my people and actually use them to process and cope. Where I understand the value of rest. Where I've accepted that I can't handle everything on my own. You see, I'm learning to use the same skills and abilities with myself that I try to use with my students. I'm internalizing this approach across all elements of my life.

That is what self-care really is. It's not a bubble bath, though bubbles are still allowed. It's not a quick fix. It's the accumulated result of doing the work. Building your network. Learning your limits. Practicing the same tools we teach. And sometimes, self-care looks like reading a trashy hockey romance and eating coconut caramel cookies while your grandbabies sleep in the next room. That works too.

Let's Get Real: When Self-Care Feels Impossible

We've given you permission. Now let's talk about what happens when permission isn't enough, when you're so depleted that self-care feels like one more impossible demand.

Marti: I can hear teachers reading this and thinking, "This all sounds great, but I literally don't have time for self-care."

Amie: Right. When you're drowning, "take a bubble bath" feels insulting. I don't need MORE water.

Marti: Exactly. So let's be honest. Sometimes self-care isn't a yoga class. Sometimes it's just surviving.

Amie: What does that look like?

Marti: Sometimes self-care is eating something. Anything. Even if it's gas station food.

Amie: Drinking water instead of your fifth cup of coffee.

Marti: Taking your sick day when you're actually sick instead of pushing through.

Amie: Saying no to one thing.

Marti: Crying in your car between classes and then going back in.

Amie: That's self-care?

Marti: When the alternative is having a breakdown in front of students? Yes. That's survival self-care.

Amie: I think we need to normalize that. Self-care isn't always luxurious. Sometimes it's just basic functioning.

Marti: And that's okay. We don't need to feel guilty that we're not doing yoga and meditation and eating organic kale. If you can't do the fancy stuff, just do the basics. Eat. Sleep. Hydrate. Ask for help.

Amie: Start there. Build up when you can.

Marti: Better. Not perfect.

Takeaways

1. **Pause, Pay attention, Pour into yourself.** You cannot pour from an empty cup. (We know, we know. You've heard that one before. But have you actually tried drinking from the cup?) Self-care starts with the radical act of checking in with your own body three times a day and actually meeting the need you find there. Drink the water. Take the bathroom break. Your students need a regulated teacher, not a dehydrated martyr.
2. **Boundaries bring breathing room.** Setting limits with students, parents, and administration isn't selfish or mean. It's the thing that keeps you in the classroom long enough to actually make a difference. Boundaries feel terrible on a Tuesday and feel like freedom six weeks later. Keep them.
3. **Find your flock and hold on tight.** You were never meant to do this work alone. The colleagues who show up for coffee, the friends outside school who remind you that you existed before you became a teacher, the trusted network you call on your worst days: these people are not optional extras. They are survival. Community doesn't happen by accident. Build it intentionally. Then protect it fiercely.

Reflection Questions

1. When's the last time you asked yourself, "What do I need right now?" and actually met that need? What gets in the way of doing this regularly?
2. Look at your "Fill My Cup" list (or create one now). When was the last time you did something from that list? What would it take to do one thing this week?

3. What boundaries do you need to set: with students, parents, admin, or yourself? What's one boundary you could implement this month?
4. Who are your people? The ones who get it? If you don't have them yet, where could you find them?

One Thing to Try Tomorrow

The Self-Care Audit

Take 5 minutes to honestly rate yourself on the basic needs checklist in this chapter.

Look at your lowest-scoring area.

Pick ONE thing to address this week. Maybe it's:

- Drinking more water
- Taking a real lunch break
- Leaving work by 5pm one day
- Texting a friend
- Going to bed 30 minutes earlier

Small step. That's it. Next week, pick another one.

Small changes. Consistent care. Over time, it adds up.

You matter. Your wellbeing matters. Not just for your students. For YOU. Take care of yourself. Please.

A Final Word

We've reached the last page, but not the finish line. That's wherever you decide to take this. You've got the science. You've got the strategies. You've got a toolkit for connection, sensory support, behavior response, curriculum, systems, parents, and your own sanity.

Now comes the part we can't do for you: actually using it. Information isn't transformation. This book changes nothing until you do something with it. Start small. One greeting at the door. One deep breath before responding. One fidget basket. One "let's try that again." Small shifts compound. They become habits. Habits reshape classrooms. Classrooms reshape kids. And somewhere along the way, they reshape you too.

You won't get this perfect. You'll have days where you respond beautifully and days where you snap at a kid before your coffee kicks in. That's not failure. That's being human. What matters is that you keep showing up.

If all you get from this book is knowing that one caring adult can change a child's trajectory, we will consider that a win. You might be that adult for someone right now, even if you never see the impact. Especially if you never see the impact.

You are enough, just as you are.

The kids need you. Your people need you.

When we know better, we do better.

You know better now.

Keep going.

With love and hope,
Marti and Amie

About the Authors

Amie Huggins, M.Ed. ARH, LLC

Amie has been a classroom educator for over 30 years. She has taught social studies, science, served as department chair and as an instructional coach. In 2023 she became a TBRI Practitioner which allowed her the chance to co-write the Tools for Transformation curriculum for teachers and schools. This curriculum uses TBRI as the foundation for classroom change but also incorporates learning theory. When she isn't in the classroom you can find her working with the non-profit, Raise the Future. She co-wrote the book Creating the Connected Classroom with Marti Smith, fulfilling her life long dream of publishing a book! Amie loves speaking and working with teachers in all capacities. She feels at home on the stage and sharing her story.

Amie was raised in Utah. She has the most amazing parents and is the oldest of 8 children. She graduated from Weber State University in 1997 with a Bachelors of Arts degree and in 2007 with a Masters of Education in Curriculum Design and Assessment. In 2010 she decided to fulfill another dream of hers and became a foster mom. She ended up creating a family with 4 of the 5 girls she fostered and is now grandma to 5 beautiful grand babies! Her unique life experiences has allowed her to merge the worlds of foster care, using trauma and relationally informed behaviors and schools. She is deeply committed to helping children with the most challenging behaviors through advocacy work, speaking, training and writing curriculum. When she isn't with her family, you will find her working with people in the foster care community and schools. She loves to read (especially those trashy romances) and travel.

Marti Smith, OTR/L

Marti specializes in sensory healing for individuals recovering from developmental trauma. As the author of two best-selling books on trauma intervention from an occupational therapy perspective, her work draws from TCU's Trust-Based Relational Intervention® (TBRI®), Dr. Bruce Perry's Neurosequential Model (NM), and Robyn Gobbel's Baffling Behaviors Training Institute framework, alongside her 30+ years of clinical experience.

Throughout her career, Marti has made significant contributions to the field. She has served as a Child Trauma Academy Fellow, a small group coach within the Baffling Behaviors Training program, and a participant as a TBRI Practitioner in the Travis County Collaborative. She has delivered training worldwide and contributed to the development of the sensory components of CTA's NMT and TBRI.

Her therapeutic services include zoom consultations for clients across the globe and in-person at the care farm that she co-founded in 2017. Marti's approach focuses on guiding and empowering the family in ways that stretch beyond the treatment session.

Marti's extensive training includes certifications in Interactive Metronome, STEPPSI-2, SpIRiT, Therapeutic Listening, Wilbarger Deep Pressure Protocol, therapeutic massage, Floor Time, vestibular dysfunction, reflex integration, picky eating, athletic training, CISM, Astronaut Training, and even Rescue Scuba Diving. She has a passion for traveling the world to provide quality keynotes and working alongside the care farm animals to help children in creative, fun, affordable, and simple therapeutic ways.

www.ingramcontent.com/pod-product-compliance
Lightning Source LLC
LaVergne TN
LVHW041110080826
845145LV00007B/1754